The Future of Training in Psychotherapy and Counselling

Instrumental, Relational and Transpersonal Perspectives

John Rowan

Routledge
Taylor & Francis Group
LONDON AND NEW YORK

First published 2005 by Routledge
27 Church Road, Hove, East Sussex, BN3 2FA

Simultaneously published in the USA and Canada
by Routledge
270 Madison Avenue, New York, NY 10016

Routledge is an imprint of the Taylor & Francis Group

Typeset in Times by RefineCatch Ltd, Bungay, Suffolk
Printed and bound in Great Britain by TJ International Ltd, Padstow,
Cornwall

British Library Cataloguing in Publication Data
A catalogue record for this book is available
from the British Library

Library of Congress Cataloging-in-Publication Data
Rowan, John
  The future of training in psychotherapy and counselling:
instrumental, relational and transpersonal perspectives / John
Rowan.
    p. cm.
  Includes bibliographical references and index.
  ISBN 1–58391–235–5 (hbk) – ISBN 1–58391–236–3 (pbk)
  1. Psychotherapist–Training of.   2. Psychotherapy–Study and
teaching.   3. Psychotherapist and patient.   I. Title.
  RC459.R69   2005
  616.89′14′0711 – dc22   2004018536

ISBN 1-58391-235-5 (hbk)
ISBN 1-58391-236-3 (pbk)

Contents

Preface ix

Introduction 1

Recent history 1
This is really three books in one 3
Evidence 8
DIALECTICAL INTERPOLATION 0: THERE IS AND IS NOT A
    DIFFERENCE BETWEEN COUNSELLING AND
    PSYCHOTHERAPY *20*

1   Do we need training? 25

Research findings 25
The threefold division 29
DIALECTICAL INTERPOLATION 1: WE ARE AND ARE NOT DEALING
    WITH A DISTINCT AND SEPARATE INDIVIDUAL *37*

2   Theory 41

A map of the realm 41
The mental ego 42
The centaur level 43
The subtle level 46
The causal levels 48
Psychotherapy integration 49
Implications 50
DIALECTICAL INTERPOLATION 2: WE KNOW AND DO NOT KNOW
    HOW CHILDREN DEVELOP *52*

3 Skills   **57**

Instrumental 57
Authentic 71
Transpersonal 73
Listening 74
The transcultural 78
Sexual politics 78
DIALECTICAL INTERPOLATION 3: WE MUST AND MUST NOT
     HOLD ONTO OUR MODEL OF THE PERSON AS BEING THE
     CORRECT MODEL *79*

4 Supervision   **82**

Instrumental 82
Authentic 85
Transpersonal 87
DIALECTICAL INTERPOLATION 4: WE ARE AND ARE NOT LOOKING
     FOR THE ORIGINS OF DISTURBANCE IN OUR CLIENTS – WE ARE
     AND ARE NOT LOOKING TO SEE HOW THE PROBLEMS ARE BEING
     MAINTAINED IN THE PRESENT *94*

5 Own therapy and groupwork   **98**

Own therapy 98
Groupwork 114
DIALECTICAL INTERPOLATION 5: WE ARE AND ARE NOT
     CONCERNED WITH CURE *131*

6 Written work   **134**

The academic and the experiential 134
Instrumental 135
Authentic 135
Transpersonal 136
DIALECTICAL INTERPOLATION 6: WE CAN AND CANNOT TAKE OUR
     OWN CULTURE FOR GRANTED *137*

7   Ethics   **140**

Instrumental 140
Authentic 143
Transpersonal 147
Suicide threats 149
DIALECTICAL INTERPOLATION 7: EMPATHY IS AND IS NOT
    A SKILL *150*

8   Research   **158**

Research awareness 158
Social effects 158
Research methods 158
Philosophy 159
Reification 159
Research is complicated 160
Research is simple 164
Reflexivity 169
Maslow and authenticity 170
The transpersonal angle 174
Conclusion 183
DIALECTICAL INTERPOLATION 8: WE MUST BELIEVE AND
    DISBELIEVE THE CLIENT *184*

9   Dangerous omissions   **186**

Therapist resistance: a common problem? 186
Psychosis 197
Pre- and perinatal experience 197
Transpersonal psychology 199
DIALECTICAL INTERPOLATION 9: INTEGRATIVE PSYCHOTHERAPY
    IS AND IS NOT INTEGRATIVE *200*

10   The body in therapy   **202**

Level 1 202
Level 2 203
Level 3 210
Implications for training 214

Appendix: The spectrum of interventions   **216**

References   218
Subject index   241
Author index   243

Preface

This is an unusual book, and the title only gives a hint of the story. It is not designed to be a forecast of what is going to happen; it is not a trawl through the existing trainings to look at trends; it is not a blueprint for what should happen; it is not much of a help to someone who wants to design new and better training. So what is it?

It is an attempt to look afresh at the whole question of training, using a very simple but deep framework which I have found valuable. It basically says that there are three ways of doing therapy, and that any examination of training has to look at all three of them. They are: the instrumental way, where the main emphasis is on treating the client or patient; the authentic way, where the main emphasis is on meeting the client or patient; and the transpersonal, where the main emphasis is on linking with the client in a rather intimate way.

This means that the book has become rather complex, having all the time to look at the question of how each of these approaches handles the topic in question. If we look at skills, for example, we find very different emphases as we move from one of the three approaches to another. At the instrumental level, this is the main thing we are interested in; at the authentic level, we may be very creative in calling up new ideas to try out; and at the transpersonal level, we have a problem in limiting the cornucopia of skills which come forward of their own accord.

There are also some perhaps surprising things to be found here. There is the fullest account I have seen of what actually happens in a complete therapy career; there is the fullest account I have seen of the possible interventions open to a therapist; there is the fullest account I have seen of the persons and schools to be found in the therapy field. There is a whole set of dialectical interpolations, which bear only the sketchiest relation to the chapters before and after them, and are really there to challenge expectations in unexpected ways.

So here is a book which challenges the reader to come out of their customary groove, whatever it may be, and to look at a range of possibilities which they many not have considered before. To the extent that this can happen, this book can perhaps act as a sort of yeast, enabling consciousness in this field to rise into new shapes.

Introduction

Training has not been much of an issue until recently. Training institutes just went on doing what they had been doing since their inception. Traditions formed rapidly and seamlessly – and exclusively. Each one tended to think theirs was the best, or even the only way of going on. There was a kind of sleepy sense of normality.

Recent history

But three things have woken people up to a new alertness in these matters. The United Kingdom Council for Psychotherapy (UKCP) put training institutes much closer to each other. I mean by this that the formation of an umbrella organization for all forms of psychotherapy in the UK, even though divided into sections, forced organizations to look at their bedfellows with new eyes. This cheek-by-jowl existence forced them to look at what they were doing in a much more critical way. The Training Standards Committee actually did very little to make this happen – it was much more the inspection of one institute by two others that brought to the surface all the imperfections and strangenesses which had been taken for granted up to that time. And some of them were quite strange, as we shall see. The implication also emerged that students of one form of therapy would do well to be aware of other forms of therapy, rather than remaining in blissful ignorance of them. This was actually one of the few requirements which the Training Standards Committee insisted on. This had a great effect in making courses more aware of the range of possibilities inherent in the therapeutic endeavour. Unfortunately the same thing has not happened in the field of counselling, and some of the counselling courses now on offer are much too narrow, often just offering Carl Rogers or Gerald Egan as the answer to everything. If counselling wants to be seen as equivalent to psychotherapy, it will have to do better on this front. Perhaps this book may act as one element in such a reform.

The second thing was the upgrading of many of the courses to MA or MSc standard through linking with a university. The universities themselves have been going through a revolution of stricter standards through Quality Assurance programmes of one kind or another, and institutes suddenly had to conform to standards laid down elsewhere. They had to clarify their aims, specify their outcomes, polish up their booklists, pay more attention to the needs of students and so on. The strength of the microscope was sometimes a bit strong and at times inappropriate, because therapy is only partly an academic subject. Academia has a hard time accepting the idea that a disciplined subjectivity is just as important as any kind of objectivity – and much harder to specify, weigh and measure.

The third thing was the invasion of the therapy field by accountants. In the USA the truly hideous influence of the Managed Care programme, which puts the funding of therapy into the hands of insurance companies and the like, gradually started spreading to the UK. It mostly took the form of an insistence by funding bodies in the National Health Service (NHS) and elsewhere that there be some kind of empirical validation of what they called 'treatments'. The gold standard, so to speak, of such validation, was considered to be randomized trials of these treatments, of the type used in medicine. Unfortunately, this only suits certain types of therapy – those with specific short-term aims. But even these were done a disservice by the medical assumptions of this form of financial control. In the USA, and again spreading to other countries, funding was refused unless a psychiatric classification (from the manuals such as *DSM-IV* and *IC-10*) could be applied to the 'patient'. Psychiatry is, of course, not the same thing as psychotherapy or counselling, but accountants find psychiatric classifications much easier to measure and deal with, and much prefer the medical approach.

As we shall be seeing in some detail, there are indeed forms of psychological therapy which fit well with the medical model, but the more sophisticated forms of therapy do not. Medicine most often assumes that the disease or disorder is what is in front of them, and it is this that needs to be treated, although within medicine itself there are holistic approaches which do not make this assumption.

As a result of all these changes, everyone has had to become much more aware of the training in this field. It is only recently that the first general manual of training appeared (Bor & Watts 1999), and it has been much welcomed by students, who for the first time were given advice on how to look at and deal with some of the basic features of any training course. Like any pioneering work it has its limitations: for example, the chapter on essay writing has nothing on how to quote from the internet.

The present work has a different aim. It is a much more speculative attempt to peer into the future and to see what is likely to happen in training if it is to meet the needs and challenges of the next 20 years or so. It is designed to open up crucial areas which will have to be considered and dealt with if therapy is to answer the myriad attacks on it which have come and will come from outside.

This is really three books in one

This book takes the view that there is not just one thing called therapy, but three. Each of the three makes different assumptions about the self, about the relationship and about the level of consciousness involved in doing therapy. They are the instrumental, the authentic and the transpersonal.

In the *instrumental* way, the client is regarded as something like a machine, and so is the therapist. Technical wizardry is regarded as something both possible and desirable. In rational emotive behaviour therapy, in neurolinguistic programming, in many cognitive-behavioural approaches, and even in some psychodynamic circles, this is the preferred mode. An emphasis on success is very characteristic of the instrumental approach. All the treatment approaches in vogue under managed care and employee assistance programmes, and all the manual systems we have just mentioned, take this view. The client or patient is there to be cured, and application of the correct techniques will achieve this in a high percentage of cases. More and better techniques are the way forward, and to test these objectively is the main goal of research. Working with the unconscious can be just as much part of this approach as not working with the unconscious. Freudians and Jungians and Kleinians do at times speak and work in an instrumental way. Every form of therapy resorts to this level of working at times, and the famed 'working alliance' is firmly based on it, but it is basically an I-it relationship rather than an I-thou relationship. Key words here are 'contract', 'questionnaires', 'formal assessment', 'treatment goals', 'empirically validated treatments', 'technical boundaries', 'homework' and so forth. It needs to be said that most therapists, most of the time, find themselves working in this way, simply because that is what most clients want, most of the time. There is nothing wrong with it. Any therapist who does not pay attention to the working alliance, and to the questions associated with boundaries and so forth, is just not being professional. But it is limited and narrow on its own, more suited to short-term and highly-focused work. And it is very prone to falling into the fallacy of the clockwork client – the erroneous belief that the client is single-minded and has no internal conflicts. Even a computer is more complex than that, in spite of the efforts of clever and efficient programmers.

In the *authentic* way, the therapist stays separate from the client, but is much more sceptical of the idea of cure. Personal involvement is much more acceptable, and the therapist admits that he or she is much like the client. The idea of the wounded healer is often mentioned, and so is the idea of personal growth. The schools who favour this approach most are the humanistic ones: person-centred, Gestalt, psychodrama, bodywork, focusing, experiential, existential and so on. It is these schools which prefer the term authentic; other schools prefer terms like relational, because of their history, but the term authentic is more precise and more accurate, I believe. Some psychoanalysts (such as Casement, Winnicott, Searles, Lomas and the later Bion) and many Jungians adopt this attitude too. Clarkson (2003) calls it the person-to-person relationship. And again it is possible to work in this way whether one believes in the unconscious or not. Those who do believe in the unconscious often speak about this way of working as a positive use of the countertransference. Obviously, to be in touch with one's unconscious is to be self-aware in the same way as to be in touch with one's organismic self. Both are attempts to be authentic through being in touch with one's whole self rather than just the surface persona. But to adopt this way of working, it is essential to have had some experience of what Ken Wilber (2000a) calls the 'centaur level of psychospiritual development', or what Jenny Wade (1996) calls 'authentic consciousness'. They both explain that self-awareness is highly valued at this level. Key words here are 'authenticity', 'personhood', 'healing through meeting', 'being in the world', 'intimacy', 'openness', 'presence' and so forth. What they do not emphasize enough, in my view, is the importance of body-mind unity at this level. Instead of the instrumental view, that the body is to be disciplined by the mind, much in the manner of a rider on a horse, the sense is that body and mind are a unity. Philippa Vick (2002) speaks of mind/body holism. This is of course a much more demanding way of working, and the therapist has to have a good deal of self-knowledge to engage in it.

In the *transpersonal* way, the boundaries between therapist and client may fall away. Both may occupy the same space at the same time, at the level of soul. Some speak of heart rather than soul, but what they have in common is a willingness to let go of the usual aims and all assumptions. Clarkson (2003) is clear that this is one of the five important relationships which have to be acknowledged in therapy. What she does not make clear, however, is that to adopt this way of working it is essential to have had some experience of what Wilber (2000a) calls the 'subtle level of psychospiritual development', or what Buddhists call the *Sambhogakaya*. Rosemary Budgell (1995) in her own research, has described the relationship here as *linking*, meaning that the two circles (the circle of the therapist and the circle of the client) may overlap. Key words here are 'interbeing', 'linking', 'transcendental empathy', 'resonance', 'dual unity', 'communion', 'the four-dimensional state' and so forth. This the least well-known of the three, and it will be necessary to explain its features in some depth, because it is growing in popularity at present. We shall also see that there is a further step into the transpersonal, which I have called transpersonal 2.

In Table 1, this approach is summarized in a tabular way, so that the main outlines can be seen clearly. The horizontal dimension is taken from the work of developmental researchers and theorists such as Ken Wilber (2000a) and Jenny Wade (1996).

In Column 1 we find the exponents of the instrumental way of doing therapy. In Column 2 we find those who favour the authentic way. And in Column 3 we find the first level of the transpersonal way in some detail. In Column 4 we find the second level of the transpersonal way, which is less used in therapy, and more often used to deepen the experience of the therapist. We shall see, however, that it can in fact be used in therapy. Column 3 is not the end of the road developmentally: I used to say that in Column 4 therapy is less relevant, because it is more likely that a spiritual path of some kind is the way to enter such a realm, but now I believe that psychotherapy itself can be a spiritual path, a spiritual discipline.

Table 1 A comparison of four positions in personal development

	1 Mental ego	2 Centaur	3 Subtle	4 Causal
Wilber level	*1 Mental ego*	*2 Centaur*	*3 Subtle*	*4 Causal*
Rowan position	*Instrumental self*	*Authentic self*	*Transpersonal self (1)*	*Transpersonal self (2)*
Wade level	*Egocentric* *Conformist* *Achievement* *Affiliative*	*Authentic*	*Transcendent*	*Unity*
Definition	I am defined by others	I define who I am	I am defined by the Other(s)	I am not defined
Motivation	Need	Choice	Allowing	Surrender
Personal goal	Adjustment	Self-actualization	Contacting	Union
Social goal	Socialization	Liberation	Extending	Salvation
Process	Healing – ego-building	Development – ego-extending	Opening – ego-reduction	Enlightenment
Buddhism	*Nirmanakaya*	*Nirmanakaya*	*Sambhogakaya*	*Dharmakaya*
Great exemplar	Albert Ellis	James Bugental	Roberto Assagioli	Shankara
Ego	Dominant	Transformed	Light	Open
Story example	Erickson	May or Wheelis	Naropa	George Fox
Traditional role of helper	Physician, analyst	Growth facilitator	Advanced guide	Priest(ess), sage
Representative approaches	Hospital treatment Chemotherapy Some psy-ana Directive Behaviour mod Cognitive-behavioural Some TA Crisis work REBT	Primal Integration Gestalt therapy Some psy-ana Psychodrama Open encounter Bodywork therapies Some TA Person-centred Co-counselling	Psychosynthesis Some Jungians Some pagans Transpersonal Voice dialogue Some wicca or magic Some astrology Some tantra	Mystical Buddhism Raja yoga Taoism Monasticism Da Avabhasa Christian mysticism Sufi Goddess mystics Some Judaism

Focus	Brief therapy Solution based	Regression Experiential	Shamanism Core process	Advaita Impersonal
Representative names	Individual and group Freud Ellis Meichenbaum Beck Eysenck Skinner Lazarus Watzlawick Wessler Haley Erickson Linehan Ivey Egan Chancy	Group and individual Maslow Rogers Mahrer Perls Searles Laing Moreno Winnicott Lomas Bugental Hycner Bohart Satir Bozarth	Supportive community Jung Hillman Starhawk Assagioli Gordon-Brown Watkins Houston Bolen Grof Boorstein Whitmore Field Fukuyama Maguire	Ideal community Eckhart Shankara Dante Epstein Rosenbaum Ram Dass Almaas Lao Tzu Fox Brazier Sheng-Yen Mindell al-Ghazali Maharshi
Intuition	Subject to fatigue	Reliable	Main way of thinking	Not needed
Compassion	Hard to hold	Reliable	Juicy	Constant, steady
Core conditions		Reliable	Deeper styles	Not needed
Research methods	Qualitative, quantitative	Collaborative, action research	Transformative, mindful	None
Questions	What is the best method?	What is the best relationship?	How far can we go together?	Dare you face the loss of all your words?
	Dare you face the challenge of the unconscious?	Dare you face the challenge of freedom?	Dare you face the loss of your boundaries?	Dare you face the loss of all your symbols?
Key issues	Acceptability Respect	Autonomy Authenticity	Openness Vision	Devotion Commitment

Evidence

There is a great deal of evidence to back up the general case being made here. The *instrumental position* in Column 1 is described by Abraham Maslow (1987) as the motivational position where people need the esteem of other people. People at this level think it very important to find a role in society, to play one's roles well and only to value praise from people who they respect. They are interested in social status and recognition. It was Maslow who did the basic research on self-actualizing people, and in fact put the term 'self-actualization' on the map, although it was first described by Kurt Goldstein ([1934] 1995).

The same outlook is described by Laurence Kohlberg (1981) and his co-worker Carol Gilligan (1982) as the conventional moral level, adopted by most people in our culture most of the time. The central concern is law and order and the maintenance of authority. Kohlberg's research was on moral development, and was conducted on a worldwide basis. Most of it was carried out on men and boys, and Carol Gilligan argued that the scoring was unfair to women and girls. However, she did not argue with the concept of levels, nor with the basic finding that this was a level characterized by conformity.

The work of Jane Loevinger (1976) on ego development, this time mainly carried out on women and girls, confirmed that this was the conformist level of ego development. People at this level seek general rules of social conformity as justification. Her work is considered as methodologically superior to many of the other researches in this field, and it is therefore all the more impressive that she comes up with the same kind of description.

Jenny Wade (1996) sees it as the (mainly masculine) achievement level and as the (mainly feminine) affiliative level of personal development. This comes from the important work of Mary Belenky and her co-workers (1986), who carried out research on college women and found that they preferred the 'believing game' to the 'doubting game' favoured by men. They call this the level of 'procedural knowing', where the emphasis is on getting things right in accordance with the rules. Again it is quite conformist.

Ken Wilber (2000a) describes it as the 'mental ego level of psycho-spiritual development'. His research was the painstaking reconciliation of a large number of models of development from many different cultures and many historical periods.

All these investigators are, of course, using a stage model of development, as do other well-known names such as Jean Piaget (1977) and Eric Erikson (1965). Such well-researched models have been found very useful in education, management training and social science generally.

Moving on now to the *authentic position* in Column 2, the same authors describe this in their own terms as follows.

Self-actualization is the state of consciousness characterized by Maslow (1987) as exemplifying the following 19 points:

1   *Perception of reality*: an unusual ability to detect the spurious, the fake and the dishonest in personality and in art.
2   *Acceptance*: a relative lack of overriding guilt, of crippling shame and of extreme or crippling anxiety; lack of defensiveness.
3   *Spontaneity*: simplicity and naturalness, lack of artificiality or straining for effect; a superior awareness of their own desires, opinions and subjective reactions in general.
4   *Problem-centring*: not ego-centred; they usually have some mission in life, some task to fulfil, some problem outside themselves which enlists much of their energies.
5   *Solitude*: they like solitude and privacy to a definitely greater degree than the average; self-actualizing people do not need others in the ordinary sense.
6   *Autonomy*: these people can maintain a relative serenity in the midst of circumstances that would drive other people to suicide; they are self-contained.
7   *Fresh appreciation*: they have the capacity to appreciate again and again, freshly and naively, the basic goods of life, with awe, pleasure, wonder and even ecstasy.
8   *Peak experiences*: spontaneous mystical experiences are common; those who have them may be called 'peakers', and contrasted with 'non-peakers'.
9   *Human kinship*: they have a deep feeling of identification, sympathy and affection; they feel kinship and connection, as if all people were members of a single family.
10 *Humility and respect*: they have a democratic character structure in the deepest sense; they are able to learn from anybody who has something to teach them.
11 *Interpersonal relationships*: they can have deep and profound interpersonal relations; the other person in the relationship is often also close to self-actualization.
12 *Ethics*: these individuals are strongly ethical, they have definite

moral standards, they do right and do not do wrong; needless to say, their notions of right and wrong and of good and evil are often not the conventional ones.

13 *Means and ends*: they often regard as ends in themselves many experiences and activities that are, for other people, only means; they appreciate the doing itself.

14 *Humour*: they laugh at the ridiculous, but there is no hostilify in their humour, and no rebellion; they don't make jokes that hurt someone else.

15 *Creativity*: they are creative in a special way; their creativity touches whatever activity they are engaged in; they even see creatively.

16 *Resistance to enculturation*: they maintain a certain detachment from the culture in which they are immersed.

17 *Imperfections*: they can be ruthless; they may be absent-minded; they may shock by lack of politeness; they may be too involved with sick people; they may have internal strife and conflicts; they can be stubborn and irritating – there are no perfect people.

18 *Values*: the topmost portion of the value system of the self-actualizing person is entirely unique – this must be true by definition, for self-actualization is actualization of a self, and no two selves are alike.

19 *Resolution of dichotomies*: the age-old opposition between head and heart, reason and instinct, thought and will disappears in healthy people; they become synergistic rather than antagonistic; desires are in excellent accord with reason; be healthy and then you may trust your impulses (summary of pp. 128–49).

Since this was written, much has been published on this level of consciousness, and I have tried to summarize these further findings in my own way, as follows:

20 *Authenticity*: combination of self-respect and self-enactment; 'walks the talk'; no gap between intentions and actions; can relate to people directly and uniquely; 'I and you' rather than 'I and it'; coming from the centre, not from a role.

21 *Integration*: there is no split between thinking and feeling, mind and body, left brain and right brain, masculine and feminine, persona and shadow, operating potentials and deeper potentials, conscious and unconscious, and so on; if new conflicts are discovered, there is no resistance to working through them.

22 *Non-defensiveness*: more inclined to find the truth within what the other person is saying than to defend against it or try to prove it wrong; may defend own right to be different, but still not in terms of right and wrong; it is possible to go even further in terms of non-defensiveness, as we shall see later.

23 *Vision-logic*: not constrained by the rules of formal logic; may be interested in alternative logics, such as fuzzy logic, many-valued logic or dialectical logic; 'Never let yourself be bullied by an either-or' (this is Wilber's 2000b term, fully explained on pages 190–7 of that book).

24 *Paradoxical theory of change*: Beisser (1972) in the Gestalt school developed a set of ideas, derived directly from Fritz Perls, which have been found to make a lot of sense by Gestaltists; also found in focusing, experiential psychotherapy, psychodrama, person-centred work and so on; change occurs not by trying to go somewhere you are not, but by staying with what is; this is very different from the common idea of self-mastery.

25 *The real self*: the chart in *The Reality Game* (Rowan 1998a: 74) shows that the idea that there is a centre and a periphery to the personality, and that the centre is true and the periphery false, is popular in the centaur stage; the real self seems to me a crucial part of centaur thinking, because without a real self the notion of authenticity collapses. It is a skin-encapsulated self. It is the ultimate, pure sense of 'I', considered as a separate being. That is its essence. It is quite different from the mental ego, however. It does not need all the props, the support, the boosting, the confirmation that the mental ego needs. It is a centred gyroscope with its own power supply.

26 *'I create my world'*: one of the great discoveries of the centaur stage is that it makes sense to take responsibility to the limit, and to say that we are responsible for everything. People like Will Schutz and Alvin Mahrer have spelt this out in great detail. There are some common misunderstandings of this view, but this is not the place to go into them (see Rowan 1998a: 110–12).

27 *Intentionality*: at the centaur stage, just because we take responsibility for our actions, we are fully behind what we do; this enables real commitment; intentionality and commitment go very closely together.

28 *Intimacy*: intimacy between two people is made possible only at the centaur stage because it is only then that roles can be laid aside; you can't be intimate and playing a role at the same time.

29 *Presence*: to be genuinely present with another person is a rare ability – Ronnie Laing could do it and Carl Rogers could do it but it cannot be done through role-playing. To try to portray presence is not to be present.

30 *Openness*: it has been suggested (Mittelman 1991) that openness is in fact the key element in the centaur experience and it is certainly important in humanistic management theory.

This is the fullest explanation of the centaur level of consciousness, and we shall be able to summarize the other versions more briefly. However, it should be pointed out that these other versions (which follow) are based on much better research than that of Maslow.

Postconventional moral positions arise from Kohlberg's (1981) research, conducted mainly on men and boys, which found that this was not a common way of thinking, and in fact in our own culture it represents only a small percentage of the population. The person at this level is able to think and feel beyond the conventional judgements of the mass, and has a unique ethical position based on personal experience. The key concept is justice.

Carol Gilligan found in her research (1982), conducted mainly with women, a similarly mature sense of independence from the common herd. However, she stresses that while men are centrally concerned with justice, women are centrally concerned with non-violence – that no one should be hurt. The key concept is care. Both with men and women, what we find here is true personal conscience. Again Gilligan indicates that people who reach this level are in a small minority. However, people who have been through their own therapy process of self-discovery are much more likely to be part of this minority.

Jane Loevinger (1976), in her research on women and girls, speaks of autonomous and integrated ego development at this level. One of the characteristic things she found was that internal conflicts are faced and recognized. Of course, psychotherapy is very good at working in this area, which fits with our general appreciation of the centaur level.

Jenny Wade's ambitious work (1989) has an important place for this stage of development, which she calls 'authentic consciousness'. She says it is 'free from commonly recognized forms of ego-distorted cognitive and affective perception' (p. 160). And it is largely free from the common ego defences described by Anna Freud and others. Her own research found that 'the most significant shift in this arena is disappearance of the fear of death' (p. 162).

Mary Belenky and her associates (1986) found that at this level women advanced to what they called 'constructed knowing'. At the previous stage of development men and women were different, men using a 'separated' mode of thinking and women a 'connected' mode, but at this level they come together again. Here again is the integration so characteristic of this stage of development.

As previously noted, Ken Wilber describes it as the centaur stage. Using this word does not mean that he is seeing things from an archetypal point of view, but simply that body-mind integration is very characteristic of this state of consciousness. At the previous stage, the basic mental model was of a horse and rider: the rider being the rational intellect, which is and ought to be in charge and make all the decisions. But at this present level, the two are not seen as separate, but as fully integrated and unified. Wilber (1999: 540) says, 'To find centauric meaning in life – fundamental meaning – is to find that the very processes of life itself generate joy'.

So again there is a mass of research supporting the importance of such a level of development. There is also a rich variety of philo-sophical thinking which illuminates our knowledge of this level. Martin Heidegger (1962) makes the distinction between authentic and inauthentic, which has been so influential here. Jean-Paul Sartre (1948) has been even more pointed in his insistence that authenticity is very special and has to be taken seriously in its existential implica-tions. He says: 'Authenticity consists in having a true and lucid con-sciousness of the situation, in assuming the responsibilities and risks that it involves, in accepting it in pride or humiliation, sometimes in horror and hate. There is no doubt that authenticity demands much courage and more than courage. Thus it is not surprising that one finds it so rarely' (1948: 90).

It is becoming clear that the concept of centaur consciousness can never be popular or widely marketed. It is actually different from mental ego consciousness, but since most of the literary critics and psychologists and politicians and sociologists and economists and philosophers are exponents of the mental ego way of thinking, they are going to reject any such idea, in humour or disdain, or most usually in silence.

The person who has done most, perhaps, to naturalize the notion of authenticity into the realm of therapy is Jim Bugental (1981), although Ludwig Binswanger (1963) and Rollo May (1980) have also made important contributions. Psychoanalysts tend to deal with the question of authenticity by relabelling it as countertransference awareness, which seems quite accurate. Just as we can see body and mind as separate or unified, so we can also see conscious and unconscioius as separate or unified. Thus Money-Kyrle (1956) can say that the analyst who has dealt with immature or damaged parts of himself or herself is enabled then to understand the corresponding parts of the patient and treat them by interpretation. Further, 'by discovering new patterns in a patient, the analyst can make "post-graduate" progress in his own analysis' (p. 341) This way of being (the centaur) is within the range of experience open to all of us, and has become much more familiar in recent years.

The **transpersonal 1**, as laid out in Column 3, is less familiar than the other two possibilities, and many of the writers mentioned just now do not go this far; but an increasing number of therapists find it necessary. From the vantage point of what Wilber calls the 'subtle', it becomes clear that the authentic way is limited by having strict boundaries. At the subtle level, talk about boundaries becomes much more problematic. What is this subtle level?

It was introduced by Ken Wilber (1996) in his book entitled *The Atman Project*. He identifies it with the Buddhist term *sambhogakaya*, the realm of symbolic visions. In other words, it is the realm of a kind of mysticism which relies on images and symbols of the divine. To put it in words which are more familiar to us in the West, and in the world of psychotherapy, it is the realm of the high archetypes described by Jung. In recent years, James Hillman (1975) has described it as the realm of soul, and as the 'imaginal world'. It is basically, he says, polytheistic. Indeed, he has tried to suggest (1981) that we need a polytheistic psychology if we are to do justice to what is now called a postmodern world. He says eloquently:

> Therefore, polytheistic psychology does not focus upon such constructs as identity, unity, centredness, integration – terms that have entered psychology from its monotheistic background. Instead, a polytheistic psychology favours differentiating, elaborating, particularizing, complicating, affirming and preserving. The emphasis is less upon changing what is there into something better (transformation and improvement) and more on deepening what is there into itself (individualizing and soul-making).

> (Hillman 1981: 124)

If we take this statement as it stands, it is of course an arrogant attempt to reform the language, but if we regard it, as I do, as a brilliant statement of the subtle state of mind, which we have to acknowledge if we are to enter that state, it makes perfect sense.

Another Jungian has made a useful contribution to our understanding. Thomas Moore (1992) again regards the word 'soul' as useful in entering the subtle realm. He has many good things to say, as for example: 'Soul is the font of who we are, and yet it is far beyond our capacity to devise and to control. We can cultivate, tend, enjoy and participate in the things of the soul, but we can't outwit it or manage it or shape it to the designs of a willful ego' (p. xvi). This fits very well with the model of the subtle we have adopted here. In therapy at the subtle level, it is more a question of surrendering to intuition than of managing anything. It is not the deployment of a toolchest, but rather of going to a place of not-knowing, and waiting.

Unlike the world of the centaur, and of the causal, which we shall be meeting later, it is not about unity, but embraces multiplicity. Another Jungian who has made useful contributions on this level of work is Nathan Field (1996). In his book he has a number of useful things to say, based on his own experience in the field, and emphasizes the extraordinary modification of boundaries that takes place at this level:

> In the selfsame moment that the patient has connected with me they have connected with themselves and I with myself: a totally new *Gestalt* has come into being where separateness and togetherness are simultaneously experienced in all their depth and richness. If I insist on calling it four dimensional it is to acknowledge a relationship beyond the therapeutic alliance, beyond the depressive position, beyond object relationship, beyond secondary process into something which incorporates, underlies and transcends the ego.
>
> (Field 1994: 73–4)

From our perspective here, it not only transcends the ego; it transcends the real self (centaur self) as well.

Looking further into the Jungian field, Schwartz-Salant has spoken in his own terms of this phenomenon, having to do with what he calls the 'subtle body': '. . . a realm that is felt to be outside normal time sense and in a space felt to have substance. This space, long known as the subtle body, exists because of imagination, yet it also has autonomy' (1984: 10–11). He also uses the term *conjunctio*, taken from alchemy (and from Jung), meaning a joining, such that two become one. Elsewhere he speaks even more deeply of this experience, in discussing a particularly difficult client:

> The process is difficult to describe because it exists within an imaginal reality in which one's attention flows through the heart and out toward another person. In the process imaginal sight emerges, a quality of consciousness that perceives the presence of the archetypal level. This sight can be experienced through the eyes, the body or the emotions, but it is a level of perception that gently penetrates in ways that a discursive process fails to achieve. To the abandoned soul, knowledge without heart feels like abandonment. The heart offers a way to connect without violating the soul.
>
> (Schwartz-Salant 1991: 211)

Samuels (1989) indicates that this all takes place in the imaginal world. This imaginal world is a subtle state, where images take the place of language (Corbin 1969; Hillman 1975). Jungians say that it is between the conscious and the unconscious, but we can now see that it really belongs to a quite different realm. It is still true that it is between the therapist and the client. Both persons have access to it and can share it. It is the therapist's body, the therapist's imagery, the therapist's feelings or fantasies; but these things also belong to the client, and have been squeezed into being and given substance by the therapeutic relationship. Samuels (1989) emphasizes that these are *visionary* states, concluding that such experiences may usefully be regarded as religious or mystical. Given the Jungian concept of the collective unconscious, it is perhaps not surprising to find this recognition of the way in which therapist and client are 'joined' at a deeper level. But we can now see that it is more than this: we are really talking about what Assagioli (1965) calls the superconscious.

All the time we have to be clear that we are still in the realm of soul, not in that of spirit. I have called soul 'transpersonal 1' and spirit 'transpersonal 2' in order to clarify this, but most writers on the transpersonal are not at all clear about this distinction, and veer back and forth without any awareness that these are two quite different things.

This becomes particularly clear in the area of gender. The world of the subtle is a gendered world, which is why feminists have been so happy to enter into it. At this level it makes perfect sense to say that the great goddess is different from, and not to be merged with, the personal god of the main orthodox religions. In the world of the subtle, full of images and symbols, permeated by the positive use of mythology as newly-forged to meet the divine challenges of this level of consciousness, we often meet deity figures and other sacred personages. And of course, once we are meeting a spiritual entity which is personalized, there is no way it is not going to be gendered. And once we admit this, there is an incredibly rich territory to be explored. One of the best critical guides to this territory is Barbara Walker (1983), who has taken a point of view informed by feminism.

The realm of the centaur was in part hard to describe because so few people have developed to that level. This difficulty is made worse at the level of the subtle, because fewer people again have much experience of it. However, many people, and probably most in the field of therapy, have had glimpses of it. There are even exercises used in transpersonal workshops which are well calculated to give people glimpses of it. The most famous of these, perhaps, is the journey up a mountain to meet a wise being at the top. This wise being is of course the person's own soul (higher self), though this is not always explained: it is an inhabitant of the subtle world. We are now in the area of psychosynthesis, and Roberto Assagioli is one of the great pioneers, testing out and charting ways of using subtle consciousness in therapy. His follower, Piero Ferrucci (1982), is particularly helpful in this regard. His Chapter 6 of *What We May Be* maps out the superconscious, and we see at once that entering into the superconscious is entering into the country of the subtle. The same book offers a number of exercises which are highly relevant to this endeavour. It would be a great mistake, however, to think that Assagioli is lesser than Jung just because he comes later. He is in fact more sophisticated than Jung in making distinctions within the field of the transpersonal.

Because the transpersonal is not a well-trodden field, it is still possible to make egregious errors in regard to it. One of these is to confuse it with religion, and many researchers are still doing that. Another is to confuse it with psychosis, as for example in the work of Isabel Clarke (2001). We find eccentricities like the article by Rodney Bomford (2002), in which he tries to show that God and the unconscious are one and the same. Even the usually reliable Petruska Clarkson (2003) veers all over the place when it comes to the transpersonal, and instead of relating to the mainstream work of people involved in transpersonal psychology, tries to hack out her own version, based on the notion of physis.

So now we come to Column 4, or **transpersonal 2**, the realm of the spirit. I used to say that this was mainly relevant to the therapist's self-development, rather than directly usable in therapy. It is a realm where there are no problems, and therapy is the realm of problems, where the client wants to be recognized and acknowledged. But since late 2001 I have been changing my mind about this, and it now seems to me that therapy can be carried on at this level. Several writers, quite independently of one another, have drawn attention to this.

Mark Epstein, coming from a psychoanalytic base, found that his Buddhist practice of meditation began to affect his therapeutic work: 'By offering the tools of *how* to stay in the present, meditation aids both therapist and patient; by teaching people how to identify and contain past material, therapy can free a meditation of emotional travail. Both work toward a greater ability to face life as it is; both begin, often enough, in silence' (Epstein 1996: 184). At once we can see the kind of connection that is being made here. Many forms of therapy advocate staying in the present, and most forms of therapy acknowledge this to be difficult. What is being said by Epstein is that meditation has a great deal to offer in this endeavour. And it does this in a full and extreme way, by putting us in touch with the causal level of consciousness.

Another point which Epstein makes he puts in this way:

> Psychotherapy requires a silence that permits a patient whatever she is otherwise out of touch with, or to say what she has not previously allowed herself to think. We are all hungry for this kind of silence, for it is what allows us to repossess those qualities from which we are estranged. Meditation practice is like a mine for this healing silence, which is an untouched natural resource for the practice of psychotherapy.
>
> (Epstein 1996: 187)

Again I believe that the kind of silence which is being talked about here is to be found mainly at the causal level of experience.

It seems clear that the therapist has to lead the way here. One cannot assume that the client has the years of meditative practice which have led to the opening up of the causal. But once the therapist has made it, the client can get the benefit of that, and can get genuine glimpses of the causal. David Brazier, another person writing about this level of work, says:

Within this conventional framework, the sacred work must be created beginning with the therapist's surrender of self-concern. Zen begins with the emptying of the therapist. The best therapy is completely empty (*shunya*). Empty of what? Empty of ego. *Shunyata* (emptiness) means the therapist is wholly there for the client, the other. As therapy proceeds the client also becomes *shunya*. Then they can examine their life without ego getting in the way. The client's ego is getting in the way of their life. The therapist's ego gets in the way of the therapy. To love is to surrender the ego. Therapy, at best, is an experience of *shunyata*.

(Brazier 1995: 205)

But of course the Buddhist approach is not the only one to speak of the causal.

One of the best-developed therapeutic approaches in this area is that of Almaas (1988), who has written extensively about what he calls the diamond approach. He comes from a Sufi background and his main concept is that of personal essence, which seems to be equivalent to what we have called the subtle self. But he also speaks at some length about what he calls cosmic consciousness, which is more like what we call the causal. The diamond approach enables the person to work through all the obstacles to experiencing this level of consciousness. It involves work at a body level, including breath-work, as well as at emotional and intellectual levels. Almaas sees his work as a spiritual path, not only as a form of therapy. And this is a radical departure from the more conventional view that meditation is the only way to the causal.

This question of the difference between therapy and a spiritual path arises again in the work of Amy Mindell (1995), who says: 'Each discipline [in the East] is simply a path to spiritual attainment. Perhaps becoming a therapist, then, is also a spiritual path, if we learn to allow our underlying beliefs to surface through our work' (p. 50). I think the word 'beliefs' is ill-chosen, because at this level we do not have beliefs *about* the divine, we *know* the divine. But one thing which is well emphasized by Mindell is creativity. Of course, as we have seen, creativity is important to some extent at the centaur level, and even more at the subtle level, but at the causal level it is present all the time: 'In his interpretation of the term *mushin*, the Zen master Keido Fukushima called it "free mind" or "creative mind" in contrast to the traditional translation "no mind". His concept of "free mind" is very close to the metaskill of creativity' (Mindell 1995:

141). Mindell's concept of 'metaskills' seems a useful one, to remind us that although work at this level does involve skills, they are not drawn upon in the usual way from our toolchest (instrumental), or from the riches of our experience (authentic), or from our stock of intuition (subtle), but emerge from a realm which is beyond any of these. We could perhaps say that we are not even doing therapy, but a form of metatherapy.

Obviously, as with all forms of therapy, appropriateness is all. We may offer a generous empty space, but if the client is not ready for this, it is just boring. And the general position taken in this book is that the instrumental level is fine – in fact, it may be that all therapists use it most of the time – and so is the authentic level, and so are the transpersonal levels. They are all useful in their various ways, at the right time, with the right client. This is an integrative vision, but it differs from some attempts at integration in not trying to reduce everything to a common pattern. There are different levels and different patterns involved here, and from now on we shall have to take cognizance of this.

DIALECTICAL INTERPOLATION 0: THERE IS AND IS NOT A DIFFERENCE BETWEEN COUNSELLING AND PSYCHOTHERAPY

Michael Jacobs said in 2001 (personal communication) that the question is not: '*What is the difference between counselling and psychotherapy?*', but rather goes further back to: '*Is there a difference between counselling and psychotherapy?*' He also says that we have to go back to that prior question, because there are some who deny the distinction, and say that there is no difference between the two.

This argument goes back a long way. One of the best statements on it that I have come across goes like this:

> There has been a tendency to use the term counselling for more casual and superficial interviews, and to reserve the term psychotherapy for more intensive and long-continued contacts directed toward deeper reorganization of the personality. While there may be some reason for this distinction, it is also plain that the most intensive and successful counselling is indistinguishable from intensive and successful psychotherapy.

That comes from Carl Rogers in 1942, and I think it is as true today as it was then. It is also true that if we were to take an extract from a typical session from the work of a counsellor and a similar extract from a typical session from the work of a psychotherapist, it would be difficult to see any difference between the two: they are doing the same thing. However, if we want to do justice to the question at greater length, I think we have to ask those who think there is no difference to consider certain issues more deeply.

I would say to such people that they are of course entitled to any view they wish on the matter, but they are going to have to contend with the real world out there, where the distinction is not only taken for granted, but also fostered for various reasons by various parties who seem unlikely to go away. *In other words, even if they do not believe in the distinction, they have in practice to act as if they did.* For example, they have to write to the British Association of Counselling and Psychotherapy (BACP) at one address, and the UKCP at another. In fact there are similar differences within psychotherapy, such that they would also have to write to the British Confederation of Psychotherapists (BCP) if they wanted to reach the older established branches of psychoanalysis – or indeed psycho-analysis complete with a hyphen!

When the UKCP was set up, there was a great deal of optimism that we could create a single profession of psychotherapy. Michael Pokorny, as a psychoanalyst, could go between the various organizations in a statesmanlike way, and invite them to work together. After a crisis, it was put forward, again by a psychoanalyst, that the way out would be to have sections within the UKCP which were more specialized. This resolved the crisis for the moment, but it returned later with renewed force, and the BCP emerged as a separate organization with a much narrower focus and identity. For the BCP, it is not the case that psychoanalysis is a subset of psychotherapy. If it is not even true that there is one profession of psychotherapy, because psychotherapy and psychoanalysis are two different things.

It is also worth remembering the story about the Lead Body. The idea of the Lead Body was that instead of talking about labels like counselling, psychotherapy and psychoanalysis, we could set up a series of levels of competence in each area, and provide objective measures of each level. So instead of asking about training and experience, we go direct to competence to perform. When this thinking was applied to advice, guidance, counselling and psychotherapy, all looked well at first. The competencies were divided up into units: A1 Establish contact with the client; A2 Establish working relationship with the client; A3 Operate within agreed codes of practice; A4 Monitor and evaluate own work; A5 Identify, monitor and review progress with client; A6 Develop and maintain interaction with clients; A7 Operate referral procedures; A8 Manage the process of referral; A9 Collect, process and manage information. These were all basic. Added to them were various specialist units: B1 Enable clients to access and use information; B2 Offer advice to client, and so on. These specialist units differed from one speciality to another, and were not common to all. The process of refining these units was proceeding apace in 1994. It was found in the years following that it was indeed possible to specify such competencies at Levels 1, 2 and 3, and indeed up to Level 4. However, when it came to Level 5 – the level at which experienced therapeutic counsellors, psychotherapists and psychoanalysts reckon to practise – it all fell apart, and seven years later we have to admit that Level 5 has still not been established.

There are of course a number of historical facts which bear upon this. Psychotherapy was associated in a fairly loose way with medicine from late in the nineteenth century, and continued to be so in the twentieth. It has that kind of origin, actually in the hypnotic practice of a number of people around the turn of the century, as very clearly described in the Ellenberger (1970) book which is well known. Of course the major influence in its development in the twentieth century was psychoanalysis, although other forms of psychotherapy came along later. The coming of behaviourism in about 1910, not at first called psychotherapy, linked therapy with academia and with psychology, and with science generally.

Counselling, on the other hand, did not come into being until the twentieth century, first of all in America and later in this country. In the USA it was linked with the mental hygiene movement. It was associated with education a great deal, and in this country with the Church as well. For a long time it was associated with advice and guidance (including marriage guidance, as it used to be called), and one of the major journals in the field still bears the marks of this link in its title, the *British Journal of Guidance and Counselling*. Connections with medicine and with psychology came later – possibly not until after World War II. So there is a very different historical background to the two disciplines.

There are other differences, too. Counselling is more of a frontline activity, and often access to counselling is immediate. Psychotherapy is more in the background, and often requires a wait before someone can be seen. Counselling tends to be carried out in the context of an organization, while psychotherapy tends to be carried out independently. In the eyes of most people, counselling is more ordinary and accessible than psychotherapy, which is seen as more to do with serious and long-standing problems, and therefore to carry more stigma and more commitment. The consumers are seen as different too, with the poorer ones going to counsellors and the richer ones going to psychotherapists. The richest ones may perhaps go to psychoanalysts. There are a lot of differences like this, which mean that although there may be only small differences in the activity as witnessed in the therapy room, there are large differences between the personnel involved, and the locations in which they work. Not many counsellors in Harley Street.

Even in the activity performed, I think there are some important differences. For example, psychotherapists have a wider range of interventions than counsellors. I don't know of any counsellors who carry out bodywork, for example, while I do know a number of psychotherapists who do. My impression is also that psychotherapists do more confrontation than do counsellors, and in general are willing to put more pressure and more demands upon the client (Rowan 1998b). The general point is that psychotherapists have more therapeutic tools in their kitbag than do counsellors. Some forms of counselling are of course very limited, as for example bereavement counselling, crisis counselling and so on. On the other hand, many counsellors have to know much more than psychotherapists on such topics as access to legal advice, the addresses of specialized agencies on narcotics or alcoholism, the reconstruction of debt, the addresses of refuges for battered women and so forth.

There are differences in the frequency of sessions: very few counsellors see people twice a week, for example. This is of course partly related to the fact that they often work for agencies which forbid this, but even where this is not the case there seems to be a reluctance on the part of counsellors to see people more frequently than once a week, though I have to admit I have not seen any statistics on this.

To sum up, then, what I am saying all the way through is that, in the eyes of the world (both lay and professional), counselling and psychotherapy are *different*. Anyone who says they are not is therefore giving themselves a hard row to hoe, and are unlikely in my view to carry the day. *Such people are going to have to act as if there were differences between counselling and psychotherapy, whether there are any or not*. So they have to take seriously that other question: supposing that there are differences between counselling and psychotherapy, how can we name them?

The way I put it in a letter to *Counselling* (12(7)) was this:

> On reading the piece by Gabrielle Syme on psychotherapy and counselling, it occurred to me that the issue can be summed up quite succinctly by saying that there is a paradox involved here. On the one hand psychotherapy and counselling are different – they have different histories and associations, for example; while on the other they are the same – for example, they have many identical interventions and involvements. This contradiction – they are the same AND they are different – has to be held and maintained. Let go of either end of the antinomy and we fall into mere dispute and argy-bargy.

So for the present, my summing up is that those who think there is no difference will have to abandon this one-sided position, and act as if there is a difference. So they cannot ignore the question of how to distinguish between the two, much as they would wish to. The obvious fact that there is no difference between what most counsellors are doing every day and what most psychotherapists are doing every day is also part of the picture, and has to be acknowledged. In fact, with the coming of counsellor accreditation in the early 1980s (first by the Association of Humanistic Psychology Practitioners and then by the British Association for Counselling) the real differences in daily practice have been eroded still further. Increasing professionalism has made bedfellows of us all.

Chapter 1

Do we need training?

Therapy generally is not in a happy state at the moment. A few years ago a book came out entitled *Psychotherapy and its Discontents* (Dryden & Feltham 1992), and in the years that have followed matters have not improved, as Howard (1996) and others have pointed out. If we are to find answers to these discontents, we have to dig deep.

Research findings

One of the most curious things about training, and the one we should look at first, is the research showing that untrained people can do just as good a job as trained ones. For example, Hattie *et al.* (1984) found 43 pieces of research in which professionals and paraprofessionals were compared in their effectiveness when treating patients. The conclusion was that the paraprofessionals were actually more effective than the professionals. A later critique of this paper by Berman and Norton (1985) went over the data afresh, and found that there was actually no difference between the performance of the two groups.

To cut a long story short, Roberta Russell (1981: 6–7) surveyed the research literature very thoroughly, and her six main conclusions were the following:

1 Comparative studies show that the outcome of psychotherapy does not depend upon the school to which the therapist adheres.
2 Experienced therapists are generally more effective than inexperienced therapists, and experienced therapists resemble each other to a greater extent than they resemble less experienced therapists trained in their respective disciplines.

3   Paraprofessionals consistently achieve outcomes equal to or better than professional outcomes.
4   A professional training analysis does not appear to increase the effectiveness of the therapist.
5   Therapists who have undergone traditional training are no more effective than those who have not, but microcounselling and skills training appear to be useful procedures in the training of therapists.
6   Congruent matching of therapist and patient increases the effectiveness of therapy.

This survey was later updated (1993) to take account of more recent research, but the basic results did not change.

These are quite striking findings, but the reason for them appears to be basically quite simple. Of all the influences making for success in therapy, the greatest is the readiness of the client for change. Art Bohart and Karen Tallman have shown at length that the client is highly active in the process of therapy, and that most of what happens depends on the activity of the client rather than that of the therapist. They urge us to think of the therapist not as a medical doctor with a set of cures, but rather as an existential-humanistic person who intends to work with the client in ways which the client is ready for: 'We further argue that all therapy is ultimately self-help and that it is the client who is the therapist' (Bohart & Tallman 1996: 9). If this is the case, how can it matter what the training of the designated professional is?

In a striking piece of research, Svartberg and Stiles (1994) found that the strength of the therapeutic alliance correlated positively (r = +0.48) with outcome in brief psychodynamic therapy, whereas the therapist's expertise at using brief dynamic therapy procedures correlated negatively (r = −0.55). Again it does not appear to be the trained skill of the therapist which is crucial.

In recent years, Barry Duncan and his colleagues (Duncan & Moynihan 1994; Miller *et al.* 1995) have based their whole approach on the idea that the client is the primary change agent and that therapists would do well to work within the client's framework. In a later book, Scott Miller and his colleagues (1997) have presented this argument at greater length. They also point to the importance of factors other than those within the consulting room:

Researchers estimate that as much as 40% of the variance in

psychotherapy outcome can be attributed to the operation of extratherapeutic factors (Lambert 1992; Lambert *et al.* 1986). As such, they contribute more to outcome in psychotherapy than the therapeutic relationship (30%), the theoretical and technical orientation of the therapist (15%), or the operation of placebo factors (15%).

(1997: 36)

They remark that there is very little research evidence as to how these findings can be integrated into practice. Jerry Gold (1994) has presented a number of examples of the active, creative and innovative efforts of clients. Maureen O'Hara (1986) has suggested that the therapist can function something like a research assistant, providing support for the active change agent, the client.

And yet it stands to reason that training must do something. Perhaps part of the issue here is that most of the research has always been on short-term therapy. Yet it is common knowledge that most of the difficulties in the therapeutic relationship emerge in long-term therapy. If we look at the stages which are gone through in a typical long-term therapeutic relationship (see Table 1.1) it seems clear enough that the first five stages (the commonest and best researched) are the ones least likely to throw up interpersonal problems. And if the therapy finishes at or before Stage 5, as mostly it does, of course the effects of training will hardly have had time to show themselves.

Table 1.1 What happens in therapy? The alchemical sequence together with the research of William Stiles (Stiles *et al.* 1991, 1992; Leiman & Stiles 2001) (*italics*), the suggestions of Jocelyn Chaplin (1988) (normal script) and the research of Meier and Boivin (2000) **(*bold italics*)**

1 Materia prima and nigredo (colour black)
Presenting problem. Establishment of working relationship.
Level 0 – warded off
Getting started and building trust
Problem definition

2 Fermentatio
The therapy process takes hold. Deepening of relationship with therapist.
Level 1 – unwanted thoughts
Identifying themes: separating out the opposites
Exploration (1)

3 Separatio (colour blue)
Internal conflicts and family of origin. Emotional release. Deeper patterns being recognized, accepted and dealt with.
Level 2 – vague awareness
Exploring the past: understanding the opposites and inner hierarchies
Exploration (2)

4 Calcinatio
Increased trust. First changes noticed. Feelings of movement which may be positive and negative.
Level 3 – problem statement or clarification
Dissolving the inner hierarchies and facing ambivalence: accepting the opposites
Awareness/insight

5 Albedo (colour white)
More experience of emotional release. Symptom relief. Feelings of success experienced.
Level 4 – understanding or insight.
Making changes: living with the opposites
Commitment/decision

6 Conjuctio
For men, dealing with connectedness. For women, dealing with assertiveness. 'Joining the human race.' A stage of practice out there in the world.
Level 5 – application or working through. Level 6 – problem solution.
Connectedness: expressing the opposites
Experimentation/action and integration/consolidation

7 Mortificatio and second nigredo (black again)
End of first phase, beginning of second. May leave therapy, may continue with greater commitment and deeper understanding.
Level 7 – mastery.
Endings and new beginnings
Termination

8 Solutio and third nigredo (black again)
The long haul where the deeper difficulties have to be dealt with. Everything is in the melting pot again. Doubts and complications. This is where we leave behind the research already published and forge on into new territory. Very little research goes this far, partly because the numbers tail off, and partly because long-term research is quite expensive. But see Blomberg *et al.* (2001).

9 Coagulatio (colour yellow)
Relationship with the therapist may be problematic. Deepest material emerges. Feeling of real engagement.

10 Sublimatio
Death and rebirth. A breakthrough. Something remarkable happens. Some kind of shattering of previous assumptions. Sense of initiation.

11 Rubedo (colour red-gold)
The chymical wedding. Emergence of the Self. Ability to handle relationships in the best way. Full contact with all or most of one's potentials. Ability to suffer in a genuine way. Ecological consciousness.

In the case of psychotherapy, this is often followed by a phase of working through, designed to integrate the new person with the existing environment. For the full version of this, see Rowan (2001c).

The threefold division

But these matters can be clarified considerably if we take seriously the threefold breakdown introduced earlier. If we follow the *instrumental* way, training is absolutely necessary in order that therapists be held accountable for their actions. How can we do objective research on therapy if we do not manualize and specify correctly what is being attempted? Skills must be specified, honed and practised in order that correct procedures are followed.

Not only must therapists be trained, they must be trained very specifically in one named method. Otherwise we do not know how to test, or what to test for. Ideally, as Thomas Daniels and his co-workers have urged, trainees are tested repeatedly and at short intervals throughout the training: 'Only one skill at a time is taught in a given microtraining situation. A single skill is learned to a predetermined criterion, and over time the trainees gradually develop and integrate a repertoire of helping behaviours. This proposition appears to be essential for beginners' (Daniels *et al.* 1997: 279).

We must also make sure that different trainings are comparable. Windy Dryden (1994) has argued that a situation where a diploma in one institution is equivalent to a certificate in another, where an advanced diploma in one is equivalent to an MA in another, is too messy to be tolerated.

But it is people at the instrumental level of working who are most enthusiastic about training. They insist that many problems brought by clients (such as a fear of flying) can be cured in one session if the therapist is properly trained. Listen to this: 'Years ago it took me an hour to work with a phobia. Then when we learned more about how a phobia works, we announced the ten-minute phobia cure. Now I've got it down to a few minutes' (Bandler 1985: 45). That is how instrumental people talk. They really want to win.

Perhaps the most striking example of this is to be found in the work of Milton Erickson. Listen to this:

One of the author's most capable subjects required less than 30 seconds to develop his first profound trance, with subsequent equally rapid and consistently reliable hypnotic behaviour. A second remarkably competent subject required 300 hours of systematic labour before a trance was even induced; thereafter, a 20–30 minute period of trance induction was requisite to secure valid hypnotic behaviour.

(Erickson 1980: 143)

Can you imagine the determination of a hypnotist who would persevere for 300 hours rather than admit defeat? Only someone sure of his or her rightness could do anything like this.

One of the characteristics of the instrumental approach is that its proponents tend to be very loyal to the model adopted. This means in practice that strong emotions and personal needs may hold the therapist locked into a way of thinking that cannot be challenged. Lovinger (1992) details several reasons, both professional and personal, for a therapist's inflexible allegiance to a particular theory. Malcolm Robertson tells us that 'when emotion is invested in a theory the theory becomes a personal mystique' (1995: 22). He says that too often an adversarial stance develops in which proponents of the orientation adopt a protective posture and invest their energies in defending instead of challenging the status quo (Robertson 1986: 419).

We may say, in fact, that as soon as we find someone with an unswerving commitment to a single orientation, we have probably found a therapist with an instrumental position. This could be in any school of therapy, whether it be psychoanalytic, humanistic-existential or cognitive-behavioural. But it may be that such an adhesion is more common in the cognitive-behavioural schools, because their whole outlook tends to be black and white rather than relaxed and colourful. Someone who relies on research a great deal is very likely to feel that rightness goes with that.

And of course it is well known that some of the psychoanalytic schools are very particular about their boundaries. The Institute of Psycho-Analysis (founded in 1910) will not recognize anyone as a psychoanalyst who is not a member of the International Psycho-analytical Association, and they are in fact the only organization in the UK which has this membership (Morgan-Jones & Abram 2001). This has caused a great deal of criticism and resentment among people with a perfectly good psychoanalytic training not obtained at the Institute. Similarly, several of the senior psychoanalytic institutes withdrew some years ago from the UK Council for Psychotherapy, which is the broad umbrella organization for all forms of psychotherapy, and founded a breakaway organization, the BCP, all of whom consider themselves to be psychoanalysts. These statements of narrowness are quite remarkable and suggest an instrumental approach, even though many of the therapists involved may not be instrumental at all.

Nor are other schools immune from this sort of tightness. There are Gestalt organizations which refuse to acknowledge the legitimacy of other Gestalt organizations. There several different schools of transactional analysis which are not on speaking terms. Which of them are instrumental and which not is a matter of dispute.

One of the things which is particularly emphasized in the humanistic approach is communication, and many communication exercises have come from this orientation. One of the areas which is particularly important is what happens when we need to criticize someone. Life is not always smooth, and we may have to confront someone at times – someone who is offending us, or irritating us, or making us feel bad in some way. In deciding how to do this in the best way, we are often unsure. Let's look at seven different types of communication we could use.

Silence

This is a very powerful mode of communication. It says, 'I am superior to this discussion. I am making my judgements and observations privately, and there is no way in which you can influence me.' It reserves our position and saves us from making mistakes. But in fact it is always seen as making us distant, withdrawn, unfriendly and faintly menacing. The reason seems to be that it reminds people of God. As the 93rd Psalm says:

> How great are thy works, O Lord!
> Thy thoughts are very deep!
> The dull man cannot know,
> The stupid cannot understand.

Another version of this is to leave the room. This can often be a very powerful mode of communication. The basic problem is that no one knows what we think about the issue – they are supposed to guess and work it out for themselves. But this is made difficult. This is of course very akin to certain Skinnerian techniques of extinction (behaviour modification techniques), though it seems doubtful whether Skinner ever quite realized some of the more subtle ramifications of this method. In therapy, the therapist often uses silence, and this needs to be done carefully if it not to give the wrong impression. On the whole, silence in therapy is better adapted to the later sessions when trust has been built up.

Labelling

Here we put a mark on someone else by saying, 'You are a pain in the neck'; 'You are intelligent'; 'You are a hair-splitter'; 'You're being very defensive, aren't you?' This again puts us into a superior position. We just happened to come along, and there was this fellow sitting there with a card hung round his neck – all we did was to read it out. There is this perfect objectivity about it. It is like a scientist describing a new bug. It may sometimes develop into a whole lecture about what is the case. At other times it can turn into exhorting, moralizing or preaching. And at other times again it may turn into warning, admonishing or threatening. In these cases we are RIGHT, and the other person is WRONG. But labelling is always seen as a put-down, ultimately. It puts the two parties into a superior/inferior relationship, even when it is ostensibly favourable ('What a good cook you are'), and so it always diminishes the person addressed, and takes away a little of his or her autonomy. When it is unfavourable, it arouses great defensiveness, and makes further communication very difficult. When it is favourable, it often comes across as patronizing, and leaves the other person with no answer. So essentially it is not a mode of communication at all, since all real communication is two-way. Some interpretations in therapy can seem like this to the client, and the therapist should always be careful not to give this impression.

Hostile questions

This is really very close to the previous approach. Here we ask the person questions, often using the word 'Why?', which take for granted some kind of label in the process. 'Why are you so selfish?'; 'Why do you keep making these terrible mistakes?'; 'Why can't you listen when I tell you these things?'; 'Why can't you be more thoughtful?'; 'Do you realize what a mess you've made of this whole thing?' This covertly says that we have a number of pre-prepared boxes with all the possible answers on them, and we are only waiting for the signal as to which box to put the answer into. But all the boxes are uncomplimentary, so it doesn't really much matter. It is a set-up. A variation on this is when we interpret, analyse or diagnose the other person. Here we don't even wait for the person to answer a question – we just pop them straight into a box in any case. Again the result is resentment and defensiveness, and again communication is cut off rather than encouraged. Psychoanalysts sometimes wonder why there is always a deathly silence after they have made a strong inter-pretation; perhaps this is now a little easier to understand. These kinds of intervention should always be made in a tentative and ques-tioning way, rather than as statements which may seem dogmatic at times (Egan 1976).

Blaming

Here we admit that we are parties to the relationship, but put all the responsibility onto the other person: 'You give me a pain in the neck'; 'You've put me in a very difficult position'; 'You make me laugh when you say that!'; 'This isn't the first time you've done that to me.' Blame always tends to float downwards in organizations, and again these statements imply a superior/inferior relationship. They again bring resentment and defensiveness on the part of the recipi-ent. Again, further communication is closed or blocked by this kind of accusation. Closely connected with this is sarcasm. Like the other versions of Type 4, this often feels like a very satisfying form of communication, because it allows emotion to come in, but it is no better. After being left alone for an hour: 'You certainly know how to make someone feel wanted!' After seeing someone behave very rudely toward someone else: 'You do have terrific tact, don't you?' After a child has wrecked the whole room: 'You certainly have pretty good control over that kid, don't you?' This is a recipe for ending a dialogue, not for beginning one. But it is only dialogue and nego-tiation which can get us what we want without adverse side-effects. In therapy, some forms of diagnosis can seem to the client like blaming (Spear 1968).

Advising

This is seemingly very positive, but in fact it is still based on the top-down model. Here we give suggestions or offer solutions to the other person: 'Couldn't you be a bit kinder to Jenny?'; 'Why don't you count to ten before you speak?'; 'If you'd only pay attention, you would learn a lot more.' Or it may take the form of reassuring, consoling or sympathizing with the other person: 'You're obviously having trouble with that – let me do it for you'; 'Don't take on so – have a cup of tea'; 'I had a problem just like that, and I surmounted it!' These approaches can actually make the person feel worse, because they assume that the person is a kind of weak child in need of help, unable to cope on their own. Badly-run clinical groupwork is full of this kind of patronizing pseudo-communication, where people seem to be helping but in fact are putting the other person down. It all too easily turns into the kind of rescuing which has been analysed so acutely by the transactional analysis people in their 'drama triangle' of persecutor, victim and rescuer (James 1995). Petruska Clarkson (1992) has argued that there is always a fourth position – the bystander – and this is particularly noticeable in groupwork.

Commanding

Here we tell the other person what to do: 'Shut up!'; 'Now listen to me for a change!'; 'Stop doing this to me!'; 'Don't keep asking me how I feel, and then not listening to the answer!' This again has a great potential for making the other person feel resentful and even less inclined to cooperate. The louder and more forceful it is, the more it tends to paralyze the other person. It is slightly better than the others, because it is at least clear and unambiguous, but it falls considerably short of being a good kind of communication. It almost always implies some kind of labelling, and this of course would take it right back to Type 2. Its main justifiable use is when there is an emergency and something drastic has to be done urgently. Therapists do sometimes have to use this mode, but it needs to be done carefully, as Bugental (1987: Ch. 4) has argued.

Real communication

Real communication is only possible between equals and always implies that the parties are on the same level. It may be spontaneous or it may be deeply considered, but it usually comes out as sounding spontaneous in any case. It can best be achieved by keeping up an awareness of our own emotions and bodily states: 'When you say that, I must admit my stomach turns over'; 'When you got to about the middle of the lecture, I fell asleep'; 'When I am with you I experience my own ability to dramatize things'; 'My fantasy is that you feel very scared about that possibility.' All these are criticisms or potential put-downs, but they don't have the same quality of automatically producing a defensive reaction. The other person can say 'That's your problem!' The options are much more open. Both parties are quite explicitly involved, and on a more or less equal basis, so channels of communication are opened up, rather than closed down, as with the other types. The speaker has to be non-defensive to express this kind of communication, and this helps the listener to be non-defensive too. There is a 'we' quality about real communication which pays attention to the 'between'. Martin Buber ([1923] 1970) introduced the idea of an 'I-thou' relationship as distinguished from an 'I-it' relationship: the former more useful with human beings, the latter more useful with things. In the 'I-thou' relationship, real communication is possible, because we are recognizing the common humanity between us. One way which has been suggested of remembering the crucial distinction between this form of communication and all the others is to make the contrast between giraffe language and jackal language. Real communication is giraffe language ('the giraffe has the biggest heart of any animal in the jungle') and all the others are various forms of jackal language. It is giraffe language which is most useful to the authentic therapist (Hycner 1993).

It is surprising how often we adopt one of the less adequate forms of communication, but the penalty is to not get what we want. If we are to get what we want from the other person, without adverse side-effects such as resentment or actually getting hit back, we have to use real communication. This can make us feel more vulnerable, but it is the strong kind of vulnerability which makes genuine human dialogue possible.

If instead we follow the *authentic* way, the whole thing takes a step and a jump and turns around completely. Instead of seeing training as learning a number of skills which can then be practised, we are more likely to see it as a process of unlearning assumptions and attitudes which we thought were obvious or necessary before. In other words, all students tend to enter training with so many false beliefs that the main work of training is unlearning them. It seems best to put these points in a paradoxical form, because at this level the Aristotelian or Newtonian or Boolean logic we found in the instrumental way gives way to what Wilber (2000a) calls 'vision logic'. Vision logic, which Wilber elsewhere makes it clear, is very much the same as dialectical logic, thrives on paradox. Some of the paradoxes we deal with at the authentic level of work are featured throughout this book as dialectical interpolations. These can be read as they come up, but as a whole they add up to quite a strong statement of the authentic position.

Coming on now to the *transpersonal* approach, the question of training takes another turn. There is much more emphasis now on the *being* of the therapist, and less upon what the therapist does or does not do. So training has to involve some direct psychospiritual input. Students need to be initiated into a whole world of symbols and images, archetypes and myths, gods and goddesses, and the whole imaginal world described so well by people like James Hillman (1990).

It was of course Jung who opened up this whole area in a ground-breaking manner. He was always very modest about this, and always tried to be a conscientious psychologist rather than a guru or spiritual teacher of some kind, as Clarke (1994, 1995) has made clear. The whole issue about Jung as a cult leader has been well examined by the historian Shonu Shamdasani (1998). But he had an extraordinary knowledge of mythology and symbology, and made it clear that this was rich territory for psychotherapy to conquer.

Students need to be initiated into the whole idea of the super-conscious, as described by Roberto Assagioli. This is the realm of intuition, creativity, altruism and the transpersonal generally: 'Transpersonal experiences have a reality which many feel to be more profound than normal everyday existence. They embody an intrinsic value, a noetic quality, leaving the individual with a deepened sense of value and meaning' (Whitmore 1991: 10). There is a further expansion of consciousness here.

Putting all this together, it now seems that there is a point to training. It is not so much about the acquisition of knowledge, but rather the gaining of wisdom. It is not so much about accumulation, but rather of discarding unwanted assumptions and beliefs. Having seen that we can find a point in training, then, and that the making of maps seems to be important, we can move on to the content of a good training – the question of theory.

DIALECTICAL INTERPOLATION I: WE ARE AND ARE NOT DEALING WITH A DISTINCT AND SEPARATE INDIVIDUAL

All the attention paid to boundaries of time and place and relation-ships takes for granted that we are dealing with the one person in front of us. It is important to realize, however, that this is only a partial truth. It is also true that we are just parts of a social field which includes the two of us but also includes much more. Some cultures pay much more attention to this field, and regard the person as part of a family and part of a community, and do not really see the person as an individual quite separate from all this.

There are a number of people now saying that the whole idea of postulating or assuming a separate personality is barking up the wrong tree. There is no such thing as a person, separate and distinct and atomic. There is just a social field, largely constructed out of language, in which there are nodal points – sometimes individuals, sometimes couples, sometimes groups, sometimes larger com-munities. The therapeutic couple is one such nodal point: it is the field they jointly create which is the reality. They create this field through dialogue and discourse, and especially through narrative.

These people variously call themselves intersubjectivists, post-modernists, constructivists, deconstructionists, dialogical theorists and field theorists: '. . . all meaning, including the meaning of one's self, is rooted in the social process and must be seen as an ongoing accomplishment of that process. Neither meaning nor self is a pre-condition for social interaction; rather, these emerge from and are sustained by conversations occurring between people' (Sampson 1993: 99).

This is a very different way of seeing the therapeutic situation. What emerges is a mutual creation, not a bit of archaeology, nor a piece of evidence-gathering. One of the pioneers of this stance was Nietzsche:

> That the value of the world lies in our interpretation . . . that every elevation of man brings with it the overcoming of narrower interpretations; that every strengthening and increase of power opens up new perspectives and means believing in new horizons – this idea permeates my writings. The world with which we are concerned is false, i.e., is not fact but fable and approximation on the basis of a meagre sum of observations; it

is 'in flux', as something in a state of becoming, as a falsehood always changing but never getting near the truth: for – there is no 'truth'.

(Nietzsche [1901] 1967: sec. 616)

This radical doubting of the idea of truth is very characteristic of the position. It cannot matter whether we get back to the truth of abuse or trauma, because there is no truth to get back to. There is only the story we produce between us. This is the point of view of Paul Stenner and Christopher Eccleston, when they say that the more the distinction between the real and the discursive is examined, the more it becomes obvious that it is precisely the meaning something has for people and what it matters to anyone (both discursive questions) that constitute its reality. So their approach, which they call textuality, sees the usual objects of psychological inquiry as so many texts which we read and discuss as opposed to entities or essences which we strive to know:

> Another way of putting this is that textuality serves to worry or trouble the commonly held dichotomy between subject and object or knower and known. For us, neither subject nor object is accorded the status of already existing fact or pre-given essence. Rather, both are viewed as socially constructed: as continually (re)produced in discursive practices in the course of social activities.
>
> (Stenner & Eccleston 1994: 89)

This enables them to question in a radical way the importance and even the existence of such things as attitudes, emotions, memory, personality, prejudice and thought: 'It is a deconstructive strategy which serves to dissolve the very "thingness" of the entity by drawing attention to the discursive work necessary to constitute and uphold the impression of "thinghood" ' (p. 94).

This vision of contexts within contexts within contexts is a difficult one to get hold of, and these authors are careful to distinguish themselves from various misdescriptions and misunderstandings which have been imputed to such a position. Much more accessible is the work of Lolita Sapriel, in the Gestalt tradition. She takes up an either-or position, contrasting the idea of an autonomous self with intersubjectivity theory, which 'posits that one's sense of self is an emergent phenomenon of intersubjective relatedness' (Sapriel

1998: 42). Another writer in the Gestalt tradition who has moved in this direction is Gary Yontef. One example he chooses is the simple one of the client having a feeling: 'Showing that "having a feeling" is a Newtonian mode of thinking and that the oneness of us and our feeling is a field theoretical mode of conceptualising is helpful in making the connection between the more abstract and concrete levels of theorising' (Yontef 1993: 345–6). Here he is saying that we have to give up 'Newtonian thinking' and go for a dialogic field instead: 'The dialogic view of reality is that all reality is relating. Living is meeting. Awareness is relational – it is orientation at the boundary between the person and the rest of the organismic environment field . . . We grow by what happens between people, not by looking inward' (p. 33).

It is important to know about this approach to therapy, because it seems to be on the increase at the moment. One of the most influential texts has been Stolorow and colleagues' (1987) book *Psychoanalytic Treatment: An Intersubjective Approach*. This was followed up by Stolorow and Atwood's (1992) book *Contexts of Being: The Intersubjective Foundations of Psychological Life*. They say that if two people are intensely involved in their common enterprise (the psychotherapy of one of them), they create a phenomenon which is greater than the sum of the two. This creation may be termed the intersubjective.

An interesting book which examines some aspects of this is John McLeod's (1997) *Narrative and Psychotherapy*, particularly Chapter 5. He warns against looking for a unified constructivist view of therapy: 'The second reason for not expecting a unified school of constructionist narrative therapy ever to emerge is that the idea of discrete schools or theories of therapy is itself a modernist notion. The pluralism and reflexivity of postmodern thought run counter to the formation of "grand theory" ' (p. 84).

Here, then, is something which is more of a challenge than a substitute. It tests us by asking us a number of awkward questions about our assumptions in therapy. It gives us some more things not to take for granted. It seems to me that training is all about not taking things for granted. If we assume that we are dealing with a separate individual, we have at the same time to assume that we are not. This dialectical vision is more defensible than either the view that there is only the person or the view that there is only one field. We have to hold both views in suspension if we are to do justice to what is there. As Maurice Friedman (1964: 169) put it, 'The self experiences the vertigo of being a free and directing consciousness, on the one hand, and an "eddy in the social current" – to use George Herbert Mead's phrase – on the other'. To take just one horn of this paradox to the exclusion of the other is not justifiable, and one of the functions of training is to enable us to deal with it.

From an instrumental point of view this does not make sense, and it is better to ignore the whole thing.

The authentic view does not entirely endorse the postmodern dogmatism, but takes it seriously as something to keep in mind when tempted to fall into that other dogmatism which says that there is a thing called a real self. From a dialectical point of view, the self is a process rather than a thing. But it does need to be taken seriously, because the client may discover it in quite dramatic ways, and does not need to be told it is illusory. It is not a virtue to eliminate it in favour of a social field. The postmodernists are more at home in academia than in the consulting room.

From a transpersonal point of view there is nothing new here. The whole idea of boundaries is radically questioned in any case at this level.

Chapter 2

Theory

One of the most extraordinary things about training is that historically it has been so narrow. Trainees have been indoctrinated with the teachings of a particular school and left with the conclusion that this is enough. It is not.

Psychoanalysis is not enough because it is so weak on the question of varied technique. Humanistic theory is not enough because it is very weak on the question of countertransference, and particularly on the question of negative countertransference. The cognitive-behavioural approach is not enough because it is so weak on the whole question of the unconscious. All three are weak on the question of pre- and perinatal experience, and also on the question of the transpersonal.

What I would like to suggest here is that there are at least three quite different approaches to this question, based on different notions of the self. In order to focus this discussion, let us look again at Table 1 in the Introduction (see pp. 6–7).

A map of the realm

This is based on the work of Ken Wilber (2000a), though he is in no way responsible for my application here. He says that there is a process of psychospiritual development which we all go through, though most of us do not go all the way with it. This process starts before birth, and there are definite waystations as we go on from there. In early childhood we have a body self, which is very much attached to our experiences of being a body, or being in a body. In later childhood we have a membership self, which is very much attached to our experience of being a family member. We see ourselves as part of a family, and are identified with that. In adolescence, we move out of this conception of the self, often with the help of the peer group as a stepping-stone, and eventually end up with a mental ego. This is where we have got to in the first column of our chart. There is plenty of research and plenty of support from developmental psychology for the story so far (Craig 1992).

The point Wilber makes, however, is one which is not often found in the standard texts: it is that the whole notion of the self changes with each of these transitions. And it is not just a smooth process: we have to abandon the previous stage in order to go on to the next one. Each of these transitions feels risky and dangerous, not just automatic. Perhaps the most obvious example of this is adolescence, where there is often a quite traumatic break from the family, which is sometimes not completed until years later.

Let us now begin to see how all this mapmaking applies to psychotherapy. It will be useful here to apply the ideas to all the existing forms of psychotherapy, to see where they fit in to Wilber's schema.

The mental ego

It can be seen that there are four columns in Table 1 (see pp. 6–7). The first is labelled mental ego. This is the level at which most counselling and psychotherapy is carried out. It has to do with adjustment to consensus reality. The client at this stage is going through some very unpleasant emotional experiences, and wants to get back to the status quo. Or perhaps the client has been experiencing incapacitating feelings for a long time, and just wants to be able to love and to work. The client may be presenting with depression, eating disorders, anxiety, shyness, bereavement, exam nerves, being made redundant, fear of flying, loss of a partner, persistent headaches, any one of the thousand symptoms and problems which plague our daily life.

Virtually all practitioners are able to handle this level of work, because virtually all practitioners are familiar with this level of development in their own experience. Probably the vast majority of the work done in this field is at this level, and the vast majority of the research carried out is also at this level. Language is extremely important for this kind of work, because it embodies the consensus reality which the person wants to get back to.

Psychoanalysis is included in this column because classical Freudian psychoanalysis explicitly says that it is restricted to this level. (There are of course some neo-Freudians and groups who are not so restricted, such as Horney, Fromm, Guntrip, Balint,

Fairbairn, Winnicott and so forth, who do have some notion of the real self.)

This is very much the level of symptom removal, and of working directly on the problem in a focused way. But we are not aiming at liberation, and may indeed at this stage regard it as something dangerous: 'Indeed, it is clear to me that society needs men to have unresolved Oedipus complexes; that we continue to live with the fear of the father (the Law). A truly free man would represent a real threat to social organization' (Jukes 1993: 114). There is a fear here, a fear of social disorganization. If the boundaries of control were broken, all kinds of bad things might happen. It is catastrophic expectations on the part of therapists which make them restrict their work to what is safe and unexceptionable. One of the favourite slogans at this stage is 'We don't pretend to know better than the client. We let the client set the agenda and the aims.' This assumes, of course, that there is just one client – the conscious and rational one who makes the contract. But perhaps it is sometimes the irrational one, the neurotic one, the unconscious one, who makes the contract, with the rational one nowhere to be seen. This sort of suggestion is often resisted, at this stage, with a sort of robust common sense, which says things like: 'When the going got tough [in restricting his rituals], George typically suggested that it might be better for us to explore the meaning behind his symptoms. I would react, using my "tough army sergeant stance" by pointing out that he had devoted six years of his life to exploring meanings and dynamics to no avail' (Lazarus 1989: 234).

It may be surprising to some to find psychoanalysis in the same box as all this, but of course in recent years there has been a good deal of exploration of brief psychodynamic psychotherapy, as well as a more eclectic approach by many psychodynamic psychotherapists. Some of the most interesting developments have been the integration of psychoanalysis and behaviour therapy by Wachtel (1977, 1982), and the integration of cognitive and dynamic therapy by Schwartz (1993) and by Ryle (1990). We shall return to this topic at the end.

The centaur level

The movement from Column 1 to Column 2, from the mental ego to the centaur or real self, is another of the wrenching moves mentioned earlier. It usually happens as a result of some crisis, such as a partner leaving, loss of a valued job, death of a loved one, and so forth, which brings us into therapy. This very often happens about the age of 30, but it may be considerably later.

It is the stage where we say in effect, 'I know how to play my roles very well, and to get esteem from others to quite a reasonable estate, but it all seems to be about playing a part: how about me? How about the person behind all the roles? I know all about playing parts in other people's dramas: how about writing my own dramas?' Usually this thought does not occur at the beginning – at the start we are very often lost in some problem which seems overwhelming – but it starts to dawn as the journey progresses.

However, the movement does not have to start like that. Nowadays it can start in a much more positive way, where we say in effect, 'I know I can do my stuff adequately, but maybe I can do more than that. I am able, but maybe I can be more able.' This is the line of personal growth, rather than of problem-solving. It can also be linked with starting to take training in counselling or psychotherapy, and finding that one's own therapy is obligatory. But however it starts, the movement is away from role-playing and towards authenticity.

The second column is the one which has been of most interest to humanistic practitioners and to some others (although of course most of them work most of the time in the first column, just like everyone else). At this level, the emphasis is on freedom and liberation (Schneider & May 1995).

It is very important to note, however, that this centaur, this real self, is still regarded as single and bounded. It has definite limits, a habitation and a name. People at this level often talk about community, but their actions are in fact very individualistic. Wallis (1985), in a sociological analysis, describes this whole way of looking at the world as 'epistemological individualism'. A good critique from a feminist point of view is to be found in McLellan (1995).

What is also important to note is that no one can bring someone else to this level who has not reached it themselves. This is an amplification and extension of Freud's original statement that the therapist can only move the patient to the limit of the therapist's own resistances. What we are now having to go on to say is that as well as resistances, the therapist also has contractions. These contractions are drawings-back, avoidances, distortions of growth. But someone who has never contacted their own real self, because of this kind of contraction, cannot enable someone else to contact his or her own real self. In fact, they can obstruct it.

The actual experience of the real self is, I have argued, a mystical one. This is the feeling of being in touch with my own centre, my inner identity, my true self, my authenticity – that self which lies behind or beyond all self-images or self-concepts or subpersonalities. It is what Assagioli (1975) calls the 'I' – the centre point of the whole personality. It is what Wilber (1996) calls the 'centaur' – the complete body-mind unity. The discovery of this self often happens in primal work, whether individual or group, but it can also happen in many other ways. It is a developmental step, principally discontinuous, involving step-jump rather than gradual form (Boydell & Pedler 1981). We can now say 'I am I', and it means something to us. The existential tradition has a great deal to say about how it works. Martin Buber quotes from the tales of the Hasidim: 'Before his death, Rabbi Zusya said: "In the coming world, they will not ask me: 'Why were you not Moses?' They will ask me: 'Why were you not Zusya?' " ' (1975: 251). This is the classic existential insight, that we are responsible for being ourselves, and that is a high and deep responsibility indeed. If we take responsibility for ourselves, we are fully human. Rollo May (1983) has some excellent things to say about this.

This seems to me a very important step in psychospiritual development, because it is a gateway to the realization that we *must have spiritual experiences for ourselves*, we cannot get them from someone else. This is the basic attitude of the mystic in all religious traditions – to get inside one's own experience, to commit oneself to one's own experience, to trust one's own experience.

At this stage, too, comes the typical breakthrough experience. It often involves some sense of death and rebirth: as Perls used to say, 'To experience one's death and be reborn is not easy'. Death and rebirth are quite crucial concepts here, as Stanislav Grof has shown at great length and in some detail (1988). At each point where we leave the level of the mental ego for a higher or deeper or more inclusive state of consciousness, we experience a breakthrough – a peak experience where we suddenly seem to be in contact with the truth. It is like a kind of initiation. All the previous effort now seems dust and ashes, quite irrelevant or even handicapping. Everything now seems clear and true, and there is no fear any more. Alvin Mahrer, the great theorist of this level, says:

> The following words apply to the nature and content of the good feelings of experiential actualization: aliveness, vitality, physical-body lightness, tingling, buoyancy, 'high', excitement,

exhilaration, ecstasy, joy, happiness, satisfaction, pleasure, power, force, energy. Each word is to be taken as referring to events of the physical body.

(Mahrer 1978: 585)

This often happens after a cathartic experience. The phrase which often comes in at this stage is, 'I create my world'. This is the stage where we start to take responsibility for our own development, rather than allowing ourselves to be moved on as if up an escalator. Symbols may be used deliberately for growth. This is the highest point in the existential realm. Blissful states or peak experiences may be encountered. Fritz Perls, who specialized in working at this level, talked of the 'mini-satori', which is quite explicitly a mystical experience. Again, however, as before, it may be very scary to move on from the previous stage, with all its certainties and all its familiarity.

This is a particularly paradoxical stage, because of this quality of being the end of one process and the beginning of another. It is a spiritual stage which may be totally atheistic.

The subtle level

Let us now look at the third column, labelled subtle (self or soul). There is more than one spiritual experience, and some of these are very different from others. One of the most common, I suppose, after contacting the real self, is contacting what used to be called the higher self. This is the sense of being in touch with my transpersonal self, my deep self. This often comes about in transpersonal therapy or groups, or in psychosynthesis therapy or groups, but again it can happen in many other ways. (see Ferrucci 1982; Starhawk 1982; Vaughan 1985). At first it appears to be outside of us, and may even appear to have a three-dimensional reality. Essentially it has a touch of the divine – it is a symbolic representation of the sacred.

My own view is that the transpersonal self is best represented, in most cases, by a person. But it does not have to be so. I have known cases where the transpersonal self was represented by a dome, or flowing water, or a jewel, or a flower, or a light of some kind. For example, Emmons (1978) quotes the example of a 20-year-old woman in a therapy session who said this:

It was as if there were a bright light encompassing my whole body. My body seemed to inflate and balloon out and 'I', the

'me-ness' of my body, seemed to be filled and carried with this
light . . . The light then narrowed into a stream of an intensity I
would imagine a laser beam to have and focused deep down
somewhere, no place physical that I can point to, just deep in my
'me-ness' . . . After a while the light seemed to be focused on the
lump in my throat where I'd tried to hold down my tears . . . The
lump in my throat dissolved . . . I feel great.

(Emmons 1978: 111–112)

This symbol of the laser beam was used in later sessions as a guide,
helping to awaken more of the client's potential. This again does
seem like a mystical experience of some kind.

After having had such an experience I may follow it up in various
ways: I may take religious advice and instruction, and most mystics
do (Moss 1981), but even so, I have to decide which instruction and advice to take and which to follow, and there is no way I can
put the reponsibility for this outside myself. Even if I say that it is a
voice inside me, I still have the responsibility for which voice to listen
to. John Klimo (1988) has a good discussion of this point in his book
on channeling.

Roger Walsh speaks well about the shamanic stage of consciousness. He says that shamans go in for controlled ecstasy: 'For
example, the shaman seeing power animals, the Christian contemplative envisioning angels, and the Hindu practitioner merging with
her *Ishta deva* are all clearly having different experiences. Yet at a
deep structural level they are all seeing archetypal spiritual figures'
(1993: 127).

In the same journal, in an earlier essay, more is said about the
actual details of shamanism. Of course many people recently
have been involved in sweat lodges and other shamanistic practices.
Larry Peters tells us that there is a connection between this and
yoga:

Another parallel between shamanic practice and yoga is the so-
called 'Deity Yoga' of Tibetan Buddhism. Here the yogin first
visualizes the Buddha, then becomes one with him, embodying
the values of compassion and wisdom. After merging, the yogin
(like the shaman) moves and acts like the embodied deity
(Hopkins 1974). Yogin and shaman both experience and possess
the qualities of the transpersonal.

(Peters 1989: 122)

So yoga values and works with imagery and ecstasy, and uses ritual to do so. Which brings us on to tantra. Quite a few people have now been involved in tantric workshops or other events. Tantra too has this character, as is well explained by Philip Rawson (1973: 116): 'Each individual, by performing Tantrik yoga, can discover that the central column of the radiating world is identical with his own subtle spine'.

It is worth making the point that imagery is very powerful in all these traditions, and imagework, which Dina Glouberman (1995) has argued is a better term than visualization, is used a great deal. As Coomaraswamy says: 'To have lost the art of thinking in images is precisely to have lost the proper linguistic of metaphysics and to have descended to the verbal logic of "philosophy" . . . This is primarily due to our own abysmal ignorance of metaphysics and of its technical terms' (quoted in Campbell 1988: 73). He is clearly talking here of transpersonal, rather than prepersonal, imagery. Images and symbols have this extraordinary ability to communicate, because they span some of the lowest and some of the highest levels of development. They can be less than words: they can go beyond words. And again, they can be invoked in rituals where a group participates.

The causal levels

The fourth column is put in not so much because it is of great relevance to psychotherapy (although it can be of high relevance to therapists in their own development), but because it indicates that the third column is not the end of the road. Again it is possible to hold back, the familiar contraction ensuring that one will stay at an earlier level rather than advancing to this, the deep water of spirituality. Here at the level of the causal self, the level of spirit, we have to give up all the symbols which were so useful and got us so far at the previous level. This is the realm of religion proper, and of the deepest kinds of mysticism – the sage rather than the saint or yogi.

But in fact it has been discovered that we can do therapy at this level, which I call transpersonal 2. Examples of this are to be found in Epstein (1998), Rosenbaum (1998), Brazier (1995), Shore (2000) and Almaas (1988).

Psychotherapy integration

Now what is the relevance of all this for what is possible and what is impossible in psychotherapy integration? The table summarizes briefly much of what has just been outlined, and what I would like to say is that *integration* within *a given column is always possible, though there may be all sorts of historical and other reasons for making it difficult. Integration* between *columns, however, is impossible, because the actual notion of the self is different in each case.*

This may sound like rather a dogmatic statement, but it follows strictly from the arguments given up to this point. It would be helpful here if we could look at the psychotherapy research literature to see what it has to say about this problem. But a careful reading of texts such as Dryden and Norcross (1990), which is a compendium of all the research arguments about integration and eclecticism, shows that there is no research which directly bears on this question. What this book does give, however, is a list of which combinations of therapies are most popular. The study of Norcross and Prochaska (1983) showed that cognitive and behavioural approaches were the most favoured team-mates. This fits with Column 1. So does the third favourite, which is psychoanalytic and cognitive; there is a practical difficulty here about the unconscious, but it seems that this can be overcome. This again fits with Table 1. But what about the second favourite, which is humanistic and cognitive? According to the argument above, this would be impossible.

What I would suggest here is that when an attempt is made to integrate the humanistic and the cognitive, one of two things will happen. Either the cognitive will be transformed into a mere adjunct to the humanistic, or the humanistic will be transformed into a mere adjunct to the cognitive. In other words, one will be assimilated into the other, rather than staying with the assumptions of its own heartland in one column or the other. For example, take the Erskine and Moursund (1988) book. In it they put together the theory of transactional analysis with the techniques of Gestalt therapy. But in doing so they force transactional analysis to remain within Column 1, and the same with Gestalt. None of the outcomes in the case histories so fully given in the book are discoveries of the real self. They are all triumphs of adjustment, whereby the person is rendered able to take up customary roles with greater success. There is no ecstasy in this book, though they mention magic a couple of times in a hopeful sort of a way.

The implication of this is that therapists, in their own training, need to have moved at least into Column 2 before doing much work there, and preferably need to have moved into Column 3 as well, if they are not going to be thrown by some spiritual emergency (Grof & Grof 1989; Bragdon 1990; Grof & Grof 1990).

All I am contending for is that we be clear about what we are doing, and don't confuse ourselves or our clients.

Implications

Some of the implications of what I am saying are quite surprising. For example, I am saying that it should be possible to combine classical psychoanalysis and behaviour therapy, the Kleinian and the cognitive, because they are both in Column 1. This means, of course, that the development of cognitive analytical therapy was to be expected, and has now arrived on the bookstalls. And the Brussels programme of an integrative model in psychotherapy training (Roose *et al.* 1991) also fits well with this analysis, combining as it does the psychodynamic, the behavioural and the systemic approaches. The relatively new approach of cognitive analytic therapy is of course now well known (Ryle 1990).

It is very revealing that both psychoanalysis and cognitive-behaviour therapy relate very well to the NHS and to medicine generally. This is because they share with medicine the basic model of restoring people to health, by one means or another.

On the other hand, it also explains why people in Column 2 find it so difficult to relate to medicine, unlesss it is complementary or holistic. They do not hold to the basic medical model, and indeed criticize it regularly. I myself have been known to say things like, 'Anyone who wants to cure a client is deeply into countertransference!' (Rowan 1994).

It also explains why psychoanalysts of the classical school in Column 1 often say that everything that happens in therapy is transference or countertransference, while psychoanalysts of a more liberal kind in Column 2 want to make clear distinctions between different relationships which are going on in therapy, of which transference and countertransference are only two. For example, it is crucial for people in Column 2 to have a notion of authenticity, and if everything is transference or countertransference there is no room for this (Clarkson 2003).

It is of course always possible to alternate methods, but that is not the same thing at all. Some of the attempts at integration which have been made, as for example Douglas (1989) and Fonagy (1989), seem to me to fall into this trap, and to believe that they are integrating when they are only alternating. By alternating I mean that the same therapist uses one approach with one client, and another with another, or with the first on another occasion.

It may also be possible to devise some very subtle forms of integration, where the attempt is made to see different approaches as complementary rather than unified, or where bridges are built between disparate schools of psychotherapy. There is a very full discussion of all these matters in the magisterial book by Mahrer (1989a). Of course I am not saying that there are not all sorts of interesting questions as to how, when and why a therapist would want to move from one column into another. All I am trying to say is that there are certain approaches which cannot be melded, moulded or fused into one, and that there are others which can.

Some objections have been made to this view by Michael Wilson (1994). He says that someone working at the highest level can operate eclectically at any other level. He says that too many things are mixed up together in my Column 4, so that it looks as if I am lumping together types of pure spirituality which are really rather different from each other, such as Christianity and Taoism. This is quite true. The reason for this is that I wanted mainly to talk about Columns 1, 2 and 3, which I believe are the main ones which therapists actually use – mostly Column 1, in fact, Column 2 to a lesser extent, and Column 3 only occasionally. I don't think many therapists use Column 4 much in their actual work, though they may find such a spiritual discipline very useful for their own development. If we wanted to talk more about Column 4 as such, as I believe Wilson is trying to do, we should have to distinguish, as Ken Wilber (1995) does, between the lower causal, the higher causal and the non-dual. But for that the rubrics on the left of the table which I have used to distinguish between the different levels actually used in therapy would be more or less irrelevant. So a different approach would have to be used, and a different article written, which would be very interesting to those embarked upon a spiritual quest, but not so interesting to the everyday therapist I am trying to address.

All in all, then, there is much to agree with in what Michael Wilson has said, and in fact I find his views quite compatible with my own. It seems to me that we have here more a difference of emphasis than a real difference of opinion.

To sum up, then, what I have been saying is that if two forms of therapy in a single column want to come together, they may construct something which may look as unlikely as a duck-billed platypus, but which may well be viable and productive. From such a union a new school of integrative psychotherapy may spring up. But if two forms of therapy in two different columns try to come together the result will be more like a sphinx, with parts which never quite fit, and do not lead to any successful school or training. The only apparent exception to this would be a training which assimilated something in one column to something in another, changing its nature in the process.

Ken Wilber (1986, 1995) has argued that integration has much wider implications. A fully integral therapy would somehow bring in the ignored quadrants in his four-quadrant model. It would include neurophysiology from the upper-right (Feinberg 2002); it would include sociological components from the lower-right (Samuels 1993); and it would include intersubjective components from the lower-left (Stolorow & Atwood 1992). In this book this argument has been regarded as too far ahead of where anybody actually is at the moment, but for the future this has to be a hot area.

DIALECTICAL INTERPOLATION 2: WE KNOW AND DO NOT KNOW HOW CHILDREN DEVELOP

We in the West see developmental psychology as something very necessary for the therapist to know about. In this way the therapist can ask about the different ages at which different events happened, and have a background of knowledge about that phase in a person's life. There are several assumptions bound up in this. One is again that we are talking about a single individual. Another is that children in all nations and cultures have the same developmental sequence. Another is that levels of development build on one another in a causal way, so that what happens early in a child's life can cause things to happen at a later point. All these beliefs can be questioned. How far back do we have to go in therapy? Is it necessary to delve back into the past? Is it even possible to excavate the past?

Some say that we do not have to go back at all: 'Cognitive therapy does not assume that therapeutic change is based on a reconstruction of developmental experiences in the context of a supportive therapeutic relationship' (Freeman & Reinecke 1995: 195). Nor is there any concept of an unconscious in this aproach. This is clearly at the instrumental level.

Most people in the psychodynamic field say that mostly we do not have to go back before the Oedipal stage at about 5 years old, though there can be disturbances which go back to the phallic, the anal or the oral stages:

> The optimal interpretation . . . would take the form of 'what you are doing (feeling, thinking, fantasizing, etc.) now is what you are also doing with your significant other (spouse, child, boss, etc.), and what you did with your father (and/or mother) for such and such reasons and motives and with such and such consequences'.
> (Wolitzky 1995: 28)

The concept of an unconscious is central here. This approach can be instrumental or authentic, depending on how far the therapist goes in paying attention to the countertransference.

Academic psychology says that we cannot go back too far in life, because the brain is not well enough developed to have any proper memories before that age:

> The conscious conceptual system begins to operate from about 10 to 12 months of age, corresponding to the consolidation of cognitive abilities such as 'object permanence' and symbolic play. At this time infants begin to distinguish between various adult reactions or attitudes and appreciate that these can be different from their own. It is only with this elementary self-awareness that children can have *subjective* feelings. And it is only subjective emotional experiences that could conceivably have an impact on our subsequent emotional and social interactions.
> (Cunningham 1999: 28–9)

Academic psychology like this has no use for a concept of the unconscious.

Kleinian psychoanalysis and object relations psychoanalysis generally say that the first year of life is crucial for development and that many important decisions are made at that stage:

> Let us look again at the moment when a baby arrives in this world, in a parlous state, weak, helpless, and at the mercy of the

terrifying anxiety of annihilation. Initially, little can be done to confront this anxiety, some parts of which are split off, relegated for the time being to the unconscious, but which remain always on tap and potentially active. Anxieties about murder and madness may remain forever in the mind, impoverishing the personality, while others can be safely examined and confronted as the ability to think and act is strengthened.

(Cooper 1990: 46)

Primal therapy and holotropic therapy say that the birth trauma can be very important: 'Grof (1992) is very clear that early trauma can be very real and very important, and relates it particularly to the process of birth. He distinguishes four stages of birth, and says that adult neurosis is very frequently based upon traumas suffered at one or other of these stages' (Rowan 1999: 20–1).

Primal integration says that conception, implantation and foetal life can all be important, and need to be taken seriously. There are such things as muscular memory and cellular memory:

[These slides] simply show very clearly that not all sperm go in head first. And in fact you get these arms of cytoplasm coming out and engulfing the sperm. In fact, that word was used by the IPF doctor when I went to ask him for some slides to show you. He said, 'You know, when I look down the microscope and see that egg put her arms out and take the sperm, I feel as if she's engulfing, devouring, and destroying,' and I fell off the chair because I have a tape of myself saying those three words after my very first sperm primal in 1976. Engulf, devour, and destroy. Incredible that the same words are used so many years later when he sees physically down the microscope what the egg is doing.

(Farrant 1986: 7)

It is hard for some people to accept the truth of such statements. All we are saying at this point is that any training which totally ignores all this is hardly likely to be adequate to the world of the future: 'The person starts early. Memory can go back before language is acquired. People can often remember their own births. The foetus is conscious. All these statements are empirically checkable, and in recent years more and more evidence has been appearing about them' (Rowan 1988: 15).

Past-life therapy says that we may need to go back into previous lives to get the answers to present-day problems: 'From nearly a decade of taking clients and colleagues through past life experiences and continuing my own personal exploration, I have come to regard this technique as one of the most concentrated and powerful tools available to psychotherapy short of psychedelic drugs' (Woolger 1990: 15).

There are credulity problems with every one of these approaches. It is quite permissible for you to say, 'I can accept some of these but not others'. None of them is certain, none of them is sure. We have to make up our own minds, based on our own understanding and experience, as to which of these we are going to accept and which reject. It may be that as we advance in knowledge and experience, our credulity level will shift, and we should allow for that possibility.

It certainly seems to be true that we have to recognize more than one form of memory in therapy. The controversies about memory in therapy might be eased if we accepted that there were four memories, not one:

1   Intellectual memory, cognitive memory, is located somehow in the brain, mostly in the cerebral cortex. The details are not yet worked out, but nearly all of the work in memory in psychology has to do with this type of memory. See any good textbook for this.

2   Emotional memory also has a great deal to do with the brain, but here it is mainly in the limbic system, and takes the form of images rather than words. It is difficult to reach other than by actually re-experiencing the events concerned. This also applies to memories held in the muscles, as Reich and other body therapists have discovered. See Babette Rothschild (2000).

3   Bodily memory is held all over the body, and has also been called cellular memory. Again it has to be re-experienced or relived, rather than called up verbally. Graham Farrant (1986) calls it cellular memory, and has written a good deal about it. Much primal work depends upon this level of memory.

4   Subtle memory or soul memory is not located in the body or brain, but in the subtle body. It holds memories of previous lives and of lives lived at other levels of the transpersonal realm. It is not difficult to tap into once one makes the effort, as Roger Woolger (1990) has argued.

Each of these four has its own rules and its own mode of investigation. But 2, 3 and 4 are hardly studied in academic psychology. Hence therapists interested in the subject, because it comes up in their work with clients, find it hard to read much about it, and the word gets passed down from therapist to therapist in informal ways. It would be better, in my opinion, for all four to be opened up properly in academia. If these things exist, they should be studied in all their complexity, and not left to the few therapists who have taken the trouble to write up their findings.

The main point I am making here is that training has to unlatch the consciousness of the trainee from too great a dependence on any one of these positions. It is better to be uncertain than to be certain of the wrong thing. The secret again is to hang on to the paradox that we both do and do not know a great deal about human development.

Here it does not seem to matter very much whether we take up an instrumental, authentic or transpersonal way of doing therapy. These issues will arise in any case. Any form of training which ignores them is ignoring important parts of the client which may come up for treatment or meeting.

Chapter 3

Skills

Instrumental

Looking at the question of skills from our threefold perspective, we can see at once that in the instrumental level skills are all-important. It is skill that makes the difference between a therapist and a friendly listener. Therapists must therefore be highly trained in the necessary skills. Of course different traditions emphasize different skills, and the differing ways of imparting them. At the most basic level, the instrumental approach favours micro-skills to be taught and played back in short bursts. Allen Ivey is the big name here, and he has been advocating the use of micro-skills in training since the 1960s. He has suggested that the same six steps should always be used if the maximum benefit is to be obtained from the method (Daniels *et al.* 1997: 278). In cognitive-behavioural circles, such skills as functional analysis, brief therapy, assessment and the assignment of homework are seen as crucial. The person-centred approach has long been thought of as abjuring all skills training, but in recent times this has begun to shift, and books are starting to appear on the use of skills in person-centred work. Similarly with psychoanalytic training: there has long been a tradition of avoiding skills training, but in recent years it has been understood that the training analysis embodies a great deal of skills training – putting flesh on the bones of abstract theory.

Up and coming in this field is the use of manuals, and the books now coming onto the market include some which suggest that there is a set of skills suitable for each diagnostic category. Adhering to these is likely to result in success. This seems quite clearly an instrumental approach.

Therapeutic interventions

But of course there are some general skills, and the instrumental approach attaches great importance to these. There are certain basic interventions which are common to all orientations, and these need to be addressed. It has been suggested (Rowan 1998b) that there is a wide spectrum of interventions which can be made by therapists (see Appendix for details). But out of the 56 named, some are very rare and some are quite specialized. It seems that for practical purposes it might be more useful to name and exemplify the most common and often used (see below). The aim is to make therapists more aware of the range of interventions open to them, so that they do not restrict themselves unnecessarily through mere ignorance. It is a common experience with trainee therapists that they restrict themselves much more than they are aware, and one of the objects of skills training is to increase the range of interventions used, so that they become second nature and are permanently available in the session with a client.

1   *Silence*. The therapist doesn't speak, but by body language can still show interest and caring. Rapport can be achieved even if the therapist says nothing. Silence is not so much used in the early part of therapy, because it can be quite threatening to the client, but once the course of therapy is well established, it can be quite welcome and quite appropriate. It is something the therapist needs to be able to use well. Compulsive filling of the silence is not appropriate.

2   *Bridging*. These are the little noises the therapist makes to indicate interest and presence. 'Uh-huh' or 'Mmm' is the classic example. Nodding also counts as a kind of bridging. They can sometimes be expanded into sentences such as 'Can you say a bit more about that?' Be aware that these things can become an irritating mannerism, and vary them from time to time. I heard tapes once of a therapist who always said 'Mm-hm, mm-hm' in quick sequence. It drove me crazy, I don't know what it did to the client.

3   *Reflecting, restating, summarizing, clarifying.* The therapist repeats some of what the client has just said. Or the therapist draws together some related thoughts from the client's presentation and feeds them back to demonstrate understanding. There is no attempt, however, to make a new message emerge from this.

This is a simple intervention which can be very useful: it is important to realize, however, that it does not go very far. It can, if well done, make the client feel understood, and as if the therapist is 'at home'.

4   *Empathy*. This entails entering into the client's world and making oneself at home there. It should always be accurate. This is hard to achieve at the instrumental level, because empathy is more of a personal quality than a teachable skill. Empathy may be shallow or deep, and is most effective when it is deep: the therapist needs to drop a great deal of the usual separateness for this, and to be much less defensive than usual. There is some further discussion of this in the book by Rowan and Jacobs (2002), and in the section 'Dialectical Interpolation 7' in the current volume (see pp. 150–157). One important aspect of this is that if the therapist is criticized by the client, an empathic response often has the power to bring the session back on track.

5   *Questions*. This is a very tempting intervention, but it should be used sparingly, because it may have the effect of seeming to put the client on the spot. The client immediately feels that the answer *should* be known somehow. 'Why' questions are particularly suspect, because they tend to drive the client up into the head, instead of down into the whole being. Questions come under the heading of 'necessary but dangerous'. They should normally be open rather than closed: in other words, the client should not be able just to say 'Yes, that's right.' And even with open questions, it is better, for example, to say 'Is there a feeling that goes with that?' rather than 'What is the feeling?' The first question is more open than the second: in other words, it takes less for granted.

6   *Confrontation or challenging*. At times the therapist may pick up a contradiction. For example, there may be inconsistency between the verbal statements and the body language, or the client may say just the opposite of what they said earlier, or the body language may speak louder than the words. The therapist can then bring this to the client's attention, and invite the client to explore this discrepancy. This has to be done with care if it is not to seem like an accusation or a criticism, but it can open up very important material and increase awareness. In the authentic approach, special attention is paid to this, as we shall see below.

7   *Repetition*. If a client says something possibly emotional in a quiet voice, the therapist may invite them to repeat it again, only

louder. When this is done several times, a deeper emotion may appear. Again, it is important not to push the client who is not ready for this. It is an invitation, not an instruction (see the discussion of directiveness, below). It can also be done on a body level: if someone is doing little kicks with the foot, they can be asked to repeat this or exaggerate it, to see what emerges.

8 *Subpersonalities.* When a client uses phrases like 'On the one hand I want this, but on the other hand I want that, which is incompatible' the therapist may invite them to set up and have a dialogue between these two positions, as if they were the voices of two different people. It may turn out that these two voices come from different ages, or different parents, or submerged parts of the person. This can then be explored further. Sometimes archetypal figures may emerge, and be very significant. The Shadow may sometimes be important here. The Topdog and Underdog of Gestalt therapy may emerge spontaneously, and play their self-torture game. Subpersonalities may also take the form of another voice emerging when certain topics are discussed.

9 *Affect bridge.* If a client is feeling something in the present, and is puzzled by it or worried by it, it is often a good idea to try to trace it back to its manifestations in the past. It is often useful to go back to an earlier time where the same feelings were experienced, say what could not be said at that time, and then go back to an earlier time again, similarly. Sometimes this produces a whole sequence, a sort of ladder going back into the past, and sometimes the earliest item in the sequence is the key to it all. Grof (1992) describes this as the COEX (condensed experience) system. It can sometimes lead to deep regression, and the therapist needs to be able to handle this if it happens. It has also been called spot imaging (Gordon-Brown & Somers 1988), where the emphasis is on an image which has emerged somehow, and which is followed back.

10 *Filling in gaps.* Sometimes the client may miss something obvious. The therapist may then suggest alternatives or considerations which have not been mentioned. For example, if the client and therapist have been exploring self-support in a difficult situation, the therapist may introduce the idea that external support could be explored as well. Never ignore the obvious, while remaining aware that what is obvious to the therapist may not be at all obvious to the client. Never bully or try to dominate the client.

11 *Maps*. Sometimes clients are using inadequate maps. For example, a client may think that the only alternative to domination (power-over) is submission (powerlessness), and may miss the possibility of cooperation (power-with). Or a client may think that they have to be strong or vulnerable, and miss the possibility that someone could be strong and vulnerable at the same time. Or a client may think that they either have to be aggressive or placating, and miss the possibility of being assertive. The therapist may then offer an alternative map of the situation. This is an educative function, which is quite legitimate even in the non-directive modes of therapy.

12 *Self-disclosure*. Sometimes it makes sense to say what you as the therapist are thinking or feeling. There is a real danger in this, as it may turn the session into being about the therapist rather than about the client, but at times this kind of straight talk is valuable, particularly if it seems as if the client is mystified about the therapist. Like all interventions, it needs to be judged carefully and used at the right moment. Disclosure of the therapist's own life is sometimes of value, and some therapists use this a good deal (Kramer 2000; Shadley 2000).

13 *Imagery*. Instead of asking 'How do you feel about that?' the therapist may say 'If you could come up with a visual image representing that, what would it be?' This can also be done with people in the client's life – if the person turned into something else, what would they turn into? Then the image can be worked with in the same way as a dream image, or an artwork. All therapists need to cultivate the ability to work in this way, as it offers a great deal of flexibility, and can also open up the regressive and the transpersonal.

14 *Interpretation*. This is something from the therapist's understanding, which is offered to the client in case it might be relevant and helpful. It is often better to offer this in a tentative way, rather than as a conclusion or a truth. The phrases most used are 'it seems that' or 'it is as if' – both used with a questioning inflection, rather than as a hard statement. This may lead to some further work in exploration.

Of course there are many more interventions which may be used, most of which are to be found in the book by Seiser and Wastell (2002).

Directiveness

An important issue which needs to be discussed is the question of directiveness in therapy. The instrumental appproach is quite happy with directiveness, and does not reject it at all. But the authentic approach abjures directiveness. However, there is a seeming paradox here.

It is common in the literature of psychotherapy to say that one of the main differences between psychoanalysis and humanistic psychotherapy (person-centred, Gestalt, psychodrama, bioenergetics, encounter, primal integration, psychosynthesis, etc.) is that psychoanalysis relies on interpretations, while the humanistic approach is more directive. Most texts which are psychoanalytically orientated say that psychoanalysis is the least directive mode of therapy, psychodynamic psychotherapy is slightly more directive, humanistic forms of psychotherapy are more directive again (with the possible exception of person-centred psychotherapy), and behavioural and cognitive psychotherapy (including things like functional analytic psychotherapy) is the most directive of all.

I want to argue that this is a radically and importantly wrong way of putting the matter.

What is being said is that a psychotherapy which mainly or entirely restricts itself to interpretations is the most non-directive form. It waits for the patient to deliver, rather than hurrying or pushing the patient in any way. The main point I am making here is that humanistic interventions are of the same nature as interpretations. They arise in the same way, and they have similar effects, enabling the client to go deeper into their own experience. They carry forward the movement of the psychotherapy. And they are not directive.

Let us then look at the nature of an interpretation. I have argued elsewhere (Rowan 1998a: 123) that there are two steps in making an interpretation:

Step 1: notice that something is going on under the surface
Step 2: draw it to the client's attention

The first step is to notice that something is going on which is not obvious to the client, to decide that here is an area worth probing. For example, a young man may refer to his girlfriend in very dependent terms, which may make the therapist think, 'I wonder if he is seeing his mother in her, and trying to get from her what he couldn't get from his mother?' It is a possibility which is worth exploring, because if it were true, this could go back to very early material in the Freudian oral stage. This is, then, the first essential stage in interpretation – picking out something which is worthy of attention, in terms of the theory being employed.

Step 2 is to get the client to pay attention to it too. Unless both therapist and client are paying attention to the same thing, no interpretation is going to be at all effective. So the therapist takes the last thing the client did which was relevant, and holds it up for the person to see in some way. If you are a person-centred therapist, you might say, 'You're kind of *imploring* her to pay some mind to you'. If you are a Gestaltist, you might say, 'On this chair is sitting your mother. Try saying the same thing to her'. If you are a co-counsellor, you might say, 'Try saying that again a few times and see what comes up'. If you are working in the area of regression, you might get the person to lie down and hold up their arms and repeat the last request a few times, such as, 'I want more from you'. And if you are psychoanalytically-oriented, you might say, 'It is as if you were really talking to your mother'. Or possibly, 'I wonder if you feel the same way about me?'

Now only the last two of these interventions are interpretations. But all of them are of the same nature as interpretations. They all put the therapist's guess into the client's mind in some way or other, more or less directly. Of course there are many different types of moves one might want to make between Step 1 and Step 2. One might want to get the client to focus more on the general area before deciding exactly how specific to get, for example. But this is just as true of the psychoanalyst as it is of the humanistic practitioner.

If one calls the humanistic interventions 'directive' one falsifies this truth. These interventions are much more like interpretations than directions. Directions normally mean things like, 'I want you to go to the doctor about that,' or 'I think the time has come now to bring the lawyers into the picture.' Things like this are often not regarded as part of psychotherapy at all, and certainly most practitioners of all persuasions would be very cautious about ever using them. By calling all the interventions mentioned above 'directive', one is therefore giving quite a wrong impression.

The main point I am making here is that humanistic interventions are of the same quality as interpretations. They arise in the same way, and they have similar effects, enabling the client to go deeper into their own experience. They carry forward the movement of the psychotherapy.

Of course, Mahrer (1985) has argued very cogently that interpretations are more prescriptive than they seem, and that even the interventions of person-centred counsellors are more prescriptive than they seem. For example, the question, 'What are you feeling right now?' implies that: the client should be feeling something; the client should be in touch with his or her feelings; the client should be able to name the feelings; the client should be able to trust the counsellor enough to share these feelings; the client should be present in the here and now; and so forth. All I am arguing here is that the kinds of humanistic intervention we have been referring to are no more prescriptive than any other intervention or interpretation. As Hanna and Ottens (1995) have argued, all these things need to be used with wisdom if they are to be effective.

A great deal of research in therapy is spoilt, in my judgement, by having an inadequate set of categories for assessing the interventions used. This is one of the many ways in which research ignores the practitioner, and hence is ultimately no use to the practitioner. And this particularly applies to the humanistic practitioner, who has a wider range of interventions than most, and who sees most of them left out of the picture. There actually seems to be a bias among researchers against humanistic psychotherapy.

Take for example the Hill (1985) manual, which offers nine categories of intervention. Researchers will be very familiar with this approach. But none of the categories offered has to do with experiments which the client might carry out within the session, in order to explore their own experience more deeply. Yet such experiments are of prime importance in Gestalt psychotherapy ('Try talking to your mother instead of about her'), in psychodrama ('Now be your father and talk back'), in co-counselling ('Try saying the opposite of that'), in primal integration ('Try lying down and breathing'), in psychosynthesis ('See if you can bring to mind an image which expresses that'), in transactional analysis ('What does your Child say about that?'), in bioenergetics ('As you say no, bring down the racquet'), and in fact in most of the humanistic approaches. These items just quoted are humanistic interventions which I am arguing are of the same character as psychoanalytic interpretations.

Similarly with the Stiles (1986) taxonomy of verbal response modes, again familiar to most researchers. The nearest category is 'advisement', but this is not really about encouraging the client to explore his or her own experience; it is more about telling the client about something from the therapist's experience.

Elliott *et al.* (1987) compared six such taxonomies of therapeutic interventions, and found that six categories were common to all: interpretation, reflection, questioning, advisement, information and self-disclosure. It can be seen that this again misses out the essential category, which I would label as 'experimenting'. How curious it is to find this apparent bias appearing so regularly and consistently.

In examining these scales, and many more, I came across the Bugental (1987) book with its 'Keyboard of Interpersonal Press', containing four octaves of interventions. Again these missed out the essential material, and I was even more surprised at this, because Bugental was a humanistic practitioner himself. I wrote to him suggesting some additions, and he was interested and helpful. The eventual result was the list of seven octaves to be found in the Appendix. I now believe that this is a much more complete list than I have seen elsewhere, and that anyone who ignores much of it is not going to be doing very good research. The difficulty with such a sophisticated and excellent discussion of the many variables involved in psychotherapeutic change as that provided by Fred Hanna (1996) is that it is hard to remember. So much is covered that seems relevant and good, but the ordering is not very helpful to anyone who wants to use the information. One of the advantages of arranging these interventions into octaves is that they are easier to keep in mind.

Let me make it clear that two extra dimensions can come into the picture with many practitioners. These are the lower unconscious and the higher unconscious (Hardy 1987; Rowan 1993). Each one of the interventions mentioned may be carried out with an awareness or an unawareness of either of these two dimensions. The seven octaves may be played in a completely cognitive way, or in a way which pays a great deal of attention to the unconscious material emerging, or in a way which lays emphasis on the transpersonal elements in what is coming forth. For a deep discussion of some of these differences, see Wilber (1981).

In all these cases transference, countertransference and resistance will be present and important, though the humanistic practitioner handles these things rather differently from the psychoanalyst (Brammer *et al.* 1993 – see also Fordham 1979 and Gottsegen & Gottsegen 1979. On resistance, see particularly Wachtel 1982, who includes material about behaviour therapy in this context).

It will be seen in the Appendix that there are seven octaves, and that they are arranged in order of intrusiveness. The last note of one octave is the first note of the next octave, as in music.

The first octave is called 'listening' and covers the basic non-intrusive forms of interaction with a client, which form a part of every kind of therapy. The second octave is called 'experimenting' and covers the non-directive but more intrusive forms of intervention, including interpretation. This is the one which contains most of the humanistic interventions referred to above. The third octave is called 'bodywork' and includes all those modes where the therapist refers directly to the body of the client. It includes not only touching but also inviting the client to take up some posture or perform some exercise. The fourth octave is called 'existence' and comprises all those interventions which refer to the here and now. It includes exposing transference, and authentic interactions. It is very important in many forms of therapy. The fifth octave is called 'guiding' and includes asking open questions, giving information, structuring of the session and so on. Many therapists do more of this than they realize. The sixth octave is called 'instructing' and covers many of the interventions used in supportive forms of therapy, including suggesting alternative courses of action. The seventh octave is called 'requiring' and is not often used. It is the most directive, and is included for completion of the scale. In saying that humanistic interventions are not directive, I am referring particularly to the second octave. It seems obvious to me, as soon as it is laid out, that the humanistic interventions in this octave are no more (and no less) intrusive than psychoanalytic interpretations.

It also seems clear enough that the third octave is less intrusive than the fourth. As actually carried out in practice, bodywork is facilitating rather than directing. It is following the client's needs and the client's energy, rather than imposing the therapist's ideas or wishes. The therapist who uses bodywork is just as aware of transference and countertransference as any other practitioner. The journal *Energy & Character* is a good place to find the fullest information about such matters (see also Chapter 10).

The most intrusive and directive octaves are the fifth, sixth and seventh. These are common to most forms of psychotherapy, including cognitive and behavioural, and are not peculiar to any one school. To repeat, then, the main contention: humanistic interventions are facilitating rather than directive. They very often come into the same octave as interpretations, and should not be contrasted with interpretations as if they were something very different.

What I am saying is that the majority of the most frequently-used techniques in psychotherapy fall in the second octave, and to an appreciable extent in the third and even more in the fourth octaves, yet the second octave is not often talked about in the way I would like. Let us pay it some detailed attention.

The second octave

Going now through the second octave in detail, because it would be tedious to go through them all here, let us look at each of the interventions in turn.

1 *Repetition: inviting the client to repeat something louder and louder until some catharsis takes place. This only works if the statement is affect-laden in the first place. Contradiction: encouraging the client to contradict a statement, and to see what that feels like – often combined with repetition. Usually used in the case of self-putdowns.* This intervention is taken from co-counselling, but it is also used in many other humanistic approaches, such as Gestalt and psychodrama. It is used when the client says something which is obviously affect-laden, such as, 'And then she left, and closed the door.' There is a slight quaver in the voice, and the therapist says, 'I wonder if you could try saying that again, and see what comes up?' After two or three repetitions, the client may burst into tears, or perhaps explode into anger, if that is what they needed to do in the first place. The other half of this – contradiction – is used when the client says something like, 'I'm just the worst person who ever lived.' By asking the client to try saying 'I'm the best person who ever lived' and to repeat that a few times, the client will either go deeper into the bad feeling, or experience a new feeling. Either way something more definite and less repetitious emerges, and often this has to do with previously repressed or warded-off material.

2 *Direct talking: asking the client to talk to someone, rather than about someone. This can be done either by talking to an empty chair or cushion, or by talking to the therapist in role.* This is used when the client keeps on referring to a person not in the room, in a descriptive way, but obviously with quite a head of emotional steam behind it. By asking the client to speak to, rather than about, this person, a greater degree of emotional involvement usually emerges. It often helps the interaction if the client is assured that this is for him or her, not for the other person – considerations of tact can be dropped for the moment. This is

not a rehearsal for a real conversation, but an attempt to take the psychotherapy forward. It is an opportunity to say what has been unsaid up to now. Repressed material may emerge. Gestalt therapy, experiential therapy and psychodrama are full of this kind of intervention, and it is unnecessary to give fuller examples here.

3   *Regression/recession: encouraging the client to go back in time, and also deeper into that experience, based on some feeling or bodily sensation in the present. Going back down the COEX (condensed experience) ladder (Grof 1992).* This is often called 'using the affect bridge' (Feltham & Dryden 1993). It has also been called 'spot imaging' (Gordon-Brown & Somers 1988). The counsellor says to the client something like, 'See if you can get a little deeper into that feeling you just mentioned: how does it affect your body, your breathing – see if you can be more aware of this felt experience' (see also Bohart 1993). Then when the client has done this, the counsellor says, 'And now let that feeling take you back in time to another time when you had that same feeling, earlier in your life.' To get the client off the idea that he or she has to search the memory banks, the counsellor may say something like, 'Don't search your memory, just stay in touch with the feeling, go back in time, and stop when you come to a scene or situation where you are having that same feeling.' When some suitable scene is reached, the therapist invites the client to explore it in detail, and to express whatever could not be expressed at the time. Then the process is repeated, going further back again in time. Often deeply repressed material or transpersonal material, as Grof (1992) has emphasized, will emerge from this process. This is a popular move in many forms of therapy, including some of the psychodynamic approaches, and perhaps most of us are familiar with it. Laing (1983) makes the point that we must also talk about recession, by which he means a move from the outer to the inner world. Going back is no use unless at the same time we are going deeper into our own experience. Regression without recession is of little use or interest. Petruska Clarkson (2003) has some excellent remarks to make about this aspect of therapy.

4   *Imaging: letting the client find an image of the person, thing, experience or situation which they have been talking about. This can then be taken as a metaphor and worked on in various ways (Glouberman 1995).* This is a very productive way of working,

because it enables more of the client's consciousness to come into play, and hence makes the maximum use of the resources present. It may be particularly useful where early trauma is involved, because it avoids the use of words, which may be too direct and hurtful at first, particularly in the case of sexual abuse. The trauma may even sometimes be worked through entirely by means of metaphors (Grove & Panzer 1989). Where someone is referring to an intimate, it is often productive to ask what that person would turn into, if they turned into something else, in the manner of a fairy story. All imagery can be worked with in the same way as one works with dreams; most forms of dreamwork are well described by Mahrer (1989b).

5 *Artwork: the client is invited to use art materials such as paints or Plasticine to express something about where they are. Sandplay can also be used in this way.* This is not to be confused with art therapy, used as a separate modality, as it often is in mental hospitals and other institutional settings. This is the introduction of artwork into the therapeutic process itself (Rogers 1993). For example, if the client has a vivid dream, he or she may be invited to draw or paint the image or scene which forms the heart of the dream. This can then be worked with in detail (McClelland 1993). One of the simplest forms of this, and one of the most effective with a stuck client, is the squiggle game invented by Donald Winnicott: the therapist draws a squiggle on a piece of paper and hands the paper to the client, with the words 'Please make a picture out of that.'

6 *Subpersonality work: the various conflicts or other voices within the client can be brought to life and treated as persons (see Rowan 1990 for details).* This is an important resource, which is now used in many apparently quite different therapeutic approaches (Stein & Markus 1994). The new self can talk to the old self, or the Topdog may talk to the Underdog, etc., etc. Perls pointed out that Freud had a lot to say about the Topdog (superego), but not much about the Underdog – a very important partner in the game being played. Many ways of working with subpersonalities are explained by Cooper and Cruthers (1999).

7 *Interpreting: the counsellor makes a link with the unconscious material which the client has not seen yet.* This can be a very powerful intervention, when it is timed correctly. The client has to be just about ready to see the connection being alluded to. It is of course very important for the therapist to be open to being

wrong, and not to insist on always being right (Plaut 1993). Interpretation is the intervention in this octave which has been most often written and talked about, all through the history of psychoanalysis.

8   *Touching: reaching out to the client to underline something the client has said – for example, if the client says there is a weight on his or her shoulders, pressing down on the shoulders.* There are obvious dangers of sexuality intruding here, and this is particularly true for male therapists working with female clients. But surprisingly often this approach does no harm at all, and the touch is received as just another intervention, much like the others. It can be very useful, particularly where the muscles have retained early memories, and pressing on them releases repressed material (Boadella 1988).

Let us now sum up the implications of all this. The main point seems to me to be that each psychotherapist, however trained, will make use of some of these interventions and not others. But all of us should know of the whole range that is possible – otherwise our interventions are not principled, but merely stem from our training. Whatever is done must be done from choice, in order to be an adequate expression of the person of the therapist.

Similarly, each researcher must make some selection from these possibilities in coding interventions carried out in their research. It is not good enough to use old scales simply because they are there. Any research must allow relevant differences to appear, and not lump together things which belong in quite different octaves.

It seems to me that unless these things are taken seriously, far more than they are now, psychotherapy itself must suffer from sheer lack of information. The time has passed when we can take for granted that our training was enough, just because it was the best available at the time. We have to make choices as to what further training to take, and what further interventions to admit to our practice. But these choices cannot be valid unless they are based upon good information. It is a little of that information which I have tried to convey here.

It also now seems to me that one of the ways in which psychotherapy differs from counselling is precisely in this wide range of interventions. Typical counsellors often pride themselves on being non-directive, in other words restricting themselves to a relatively narrow range of interventions. In psychotherapy we have this whole wide range of possibilities at our disposal. Obviously, different practitioners will always make use of only part of this range, but we should know what is available and ask ourselves questions as to exactly why we restrict ourselves in the way we do. And those who run training courses might ask themselves the same questions. Are we preparing the new young psychotherapists of the future adequately for the tasks in hand, or are we depriving them of some of the tools they may need?

Of course there has been a good deal of discussion of the similarities and differences between psychoanalytic approaches and humanistic approaches, to be found for example in Stricker and Gold (1993) and Norcross and Goldfried (1992). But I think the seven-octave approach is illuminating and useful in showing how all these approaches contribute to filling up each octave, emphasizing some and ignoring others.

This also fits in with the whole movement towards integration in psychotherapy, which I favour. It seems to me that the days of the single approach, the single narrow training, are over, and the new horizons which now appear are challenging indeed.

Authentic

Coming on now to the authentic level, there is again a continuum running from more emphasis on skills to the positive avoidance of skill training. Gestalt therapy used to place a great deal of emphasis on skills, and the common stereotype of people outside the field is that it is very directive. However, in recent years it has become clear that techniques may not only be downplayed but may even become irrelevant (Yontef 1993). Psychodrama is still the home of a multitude of skills, but even here the emphasis in training is not so much on the possession of all these skills, but more on the qualities of spontaneity and creativity which Moreno always emphasized (Jefferies 1998). The most extreme position is taken by existential analysis, which sets its face against the acquisition of skills, and indeed no namable skills emerge from such a training. The emphasis is all on presence and authenticity. As Mick Cooper (2003: 144) tells us, 'All of the existential therapies – apart from logotherapy – tend to be at the relatively spontaneous end of the spontaneity-technique dimension'. Experiential therapy is quite open to skills, and indeed people like Eugene Gendlin (1996), Kirk Schneider (Schneider & May 1995) and Alvin Mahrer (1996) go a long way towards laying down very specific skills in focusing, in tuning in to deeper potentials and so forth.

Interesting questions arise because different schools have different names for the same thing. Let us look at just two examples of this. These are: (a) what is the humanistic/existential equivalent of the unconscious; and (b) what is the psychodynamic equivalent of authenticity?

The unconscious

The existential view, shared by most humanistic therapies, is that there is no need for a concept of the unconscious, and that indeed the whole notion may be mystifying (Spinelli 2001: Ch. 4). But as I have pointed out at length elsewhere (1990), there is in fact an equivalent idea already well established in the literature. It is the concept of a subpersonality. Many existentialists do not use this concept, but there are some who do (Cooper 1999). The recent work on configurations of self in the person-centred tradition (Mearns & Thorne 2000) takes forward the work of Carl Rogers and is now well accepted. And it turns out that there are great similarities between configurations of self and subpersonalities. Of course there are many synonyms for this (about 25 of them in fact), but it answers to the purpose very precisely. The psychoanalyst might say, 'My holiday may be perfectly acceptable to your conscious mind, but at an unconscious level you may feel abandoned or abused.' The humanistic therapist might say, 'My holiday may be perfectly acceptable to your adult self, but your inner child may feel abandoned or abused.' Similarly, the analyst might say, 'At an unconscious level, you may resent me.' The humanistic therapist might say, 'There may be someone within you who resents me.' I am suggesting that these are equivalent statements, which refer to the same thing in different words.

Authenticity

The humanistic concept of authenticity, considered as a quality of the therapist and an aim for the client, is not to be found in the psychoanalytic literature. However, the analytic concept of counter-transference, considered as something positive to be aware of and used, is quite equivalent (Rowan & Jacobs 2002: Ch. 3). Just as the work on oneself is considered essential in humanistic work, leading to an ability to be genuine, so in the same way the work on oneself is considered essential in analytic work, leading to the ability to open up and use one's own countertransference. In both cases there is an increase in self-knowledge and self-awareness which is considered essential for the therapist.

It is impossible to read the work of someone like Harold Searles (1979) without realizing that here is someone who has a deep self-knowledge, which he is using fully in his work with his difficult clients. Similarly, Donald Winnicott (1971) breathes a deeply authentic sense of relationship with his patients, such that he is fully present with them in an authentic way.

Of course, the whole question of the relationship comes in here. At the authentic level, the idea of a genuine meeting is central, as we have seen, and so for these people the relationship has to be considered in detail. There is much research to show that it is a critical variable in all therapeutic work. Whether we look at the classic book of Smith *et al.* (1980) or the classic chapter of Lambert and Bergin (1983), or Lambert's fine paper of 1986, or the updating chapter of Lambert *et al.* (1986), or the later fine paper of Hans Strupp (1989), the message comes across loud and clear, and of course the magisterial book of Petruska Clarkson (2003) puts the capstone on the whole edifice.

Transpersonal

At the transpersonal level, there is a paradoxical position on the question of skills. On the one hand one is expected to have all the toolbox of skills acquired on the developmental path; on the other hand one is expected to go to a place of not knowing, and wait. So while there is no emphasis on skills as such, the trainee is expected to pick up all the skills required for appropriate measures to be taken in each individual case. One of the skills which becomes extremely important at this level is the use of imagery and symbolism. Even here, however, it is more a case of improvising in the moment rather than bringing out the correct image or technique. And again, as at the previous stage, there is a lot of emphasis on getting deeply involved with the client.

One of the main characteristics required at this level is intuition. And it is a particular kind of intuition – what I have called 'surendered self-intuition'. Now it is in a way quite wrong to call this a skill. Nevertheless, in the same way that empathy can be regarded both as a skill and as a personal quality, so here intuition can be regarded likewise. Peter Heinl (2001), in his interesting chapter on intuition, refers to it as 'the icon of a new thinking about thinking', and comments upon its frequent mention by scientists. He quotes a survey (Marton *et al.* 1994) of Nobel laureates which showed that all 72 of those questioned recognized the importance of intuition in their work.

So if it is so important, surely it must be possible to imagine ways of cultivating it. But in my view this is a paradoxical quest, which requires just as much the letting go of such an aim as its earnest pursuit. This in fact does parallel the equivalent paradox of mysticism, where one has to seek the ultimate by letting go of all attempts to reach it.

Listening

Listening is difficult for the new therapist because there is a lot of unlearning to be done. In most conversations, we are formulating a reply when the other person is talking, so as to be ready when he or she finishes; we are going back and forth between what is being said and our reply, so that we never really hear properly all that is said. The therapeutic meeting is very different:

Ordinary listening	Therapeutic listening
Interest in the content of the statement – what it is intended to convey	*Interest in the statement itself as a symptom of things the client did not intend to say*
Trying to relate the other person's experience to your own	*Not paying attention to your own previous experiences*
Thinking of interesting replies to carry on the conversation and keep one's end up	*Not being concerned with replies or conversations, only with the client's efforts at self-exploration*

It would be tedious to enumerate all the ways in which therapeutic listening differs from ordinary listening; all that is intended here is to underline the point that there is a good deal of unlearning to be done. But the other important thing to realize about listening is that there are a number of different levels involved.

Content

What is being said. The thing here is continually to push the client into being more specific. If the statement is 'People don't like me', the next question is 'Which people? Name one'. If the statement is 'I know you have to make allowances', the client might be asked to change it to 'I know *I* have to make allowances', or asked the question, 'Who exactly says you have to make allowances?' This gentle urging in the direction of being more specific and more personal is one of the most basic moves of the therapist, as Bandler and Grinder (1975) have pointed out. It always has the effect of moving the client into deeper levels of experience.

Feelings

The feelings behind what is being said. These come out most prominently in the *way* things are said. If the whole tone of voice is flat and depressed, for example, that may be more important than anything the client is saying. Sometimes you can hear a kind of suppressed panic in the voice which is very characteristic once you can spot it; in such a case I would want to get the person to relax more before doing anything else. Feelings of anger (resentment, irritation, antagonism, rage etc.) and feelings of hurt (pain, suffering, injury etc.) can be very important, because either one can cover up for the other: in men I have noticed that it is more common for anger to cover up for hurt, while in women it is more common for hurt to cover up for anger, but it can happen either way in either sex.

It is impossible really to listen for feelings without having feelings yourself. Hence this kind of listening (sometimes called empathy) can be hard on the therapist unless they have fully worked through the same level of feelings in themselves. This is one of the main reasons why humanistic therapists need to go through the whole process of psychotherapy themselves. Another reason is that therapists tend to stop clients from going into a level of feelings deeper than those which they have experienced and worked through themselves. Thus clients can be cheated of part of their own experience if the therapist has blocks still remaining.

The body

It is possible to listen to body language. The way that a person is sitting may be all screwed up even when what they are saying sounds perfectly reasonable. Persistent gestures can be very revealing. Expressions *may* tell you something, but the hands and feet are much harder to keep under control: the actual movement may be disguised, but the moment when it starts can say a lot. The breathing can be very important: often by breathing at the same rate and the same depth or shallowness as the client, you can pick up something worthwhile. How the person moves may be revealing – do they talk bold and act timid, or vice versa? Many clients have a stiffness or rigidity somewhere in their body. Where is it exactly, and how do they keep it stiff or rigid, and how come it is so important not to let go of it? How does the client sit – are they tense or relaxed, or tense at some times and relaxed at others; what do they do when they are tense, what do they do when they are relaxed? And what are the moments at which they switch? The body is a rich storehouse of memories and experiences, and it can tell us a lot if we can only pay attention to it (see Chapter 10).

Sexuality

A lot can be going on at a sexual level between therapist and client. Freud pointed out many years ago that the client can virtually fall in love with the therapist, and experience this as falling in love with a parental figure; hence, feelings about incest and castration can arise, which can go back to the family situation at about 5 years old. In this area it is important to realize that in fact the therapist can appear to be a mother or a father, irrespective of what actual sex they may be. But of course other and much more directly sexual feelings may arise. The therapist may seduce the client, the client may seduce the therapist, and spontaneous mutual falling in love cannot be ruled out. All these things are harder to sort out if the therapist is not clear in this area, so again it is important for the therapist to have worked through his or her own sexual material first. A therapist who is still engaged in a personal 'search for the beloved' can be a menace to all and sundry (Russell 1993). This is made doubly difficult by the fact that the humanistic therapist often touches the client in some way, and may ask the client to take off some or all of their clothes at certain times. For these reasons it is even more important for the humanistic therapist to have gone through the full process of psychotherapy than it is for the psychoanalyst. Otherwise there is likely to be a trail of broken hearts rather than a trail of real meetings.

Spirituality

A client is a spiritual being on a spiritual path (even though they may not be aware of it yet) and some of the material they bring up may be at that level (Boorstein 1996). Jung showed long ago how dreams might reveal spiritual directions and spiritual longings which could be quite surprising to the person at a conscious level – and in recent years James Hillman (1990) has been following up this insight. Unless we are listening for these things, we are quite likely to miss them. We can in fact help the client to get into this area by using symbols. It is often possible to ask the person to put forth their problems in the form of a drawing, or by the use of a sandbox, or through a guided fantasy, or by just asking for an image or symbol of their problem. This deliberate use of symbols does not necessarily lead in a spiritual direction, but it is very compatible with spiritual exploration, and if the person is needing to go in that sort of direction, this is likely to show up and become workable.

Again it cannot be overemphasized that the therapist who has not worked through this material in the course of their own development is likely to stop the client going through it. As always, the therapist needs to be at least a few steps ahead of the client in order to work effectively (Rowan 2002). And this spiritual area is likely to be particularly important for creative people, or those who want to be creative or more creative. It can open a whole new way of being creative which the person did not have access to before.

The great clarifier in this area has been Ken Wilber, who has written with enormous clarity about the exact way in which psychology and psychotherapy relate to spirituality. Anyone who wants to sort out this area of listening would do well to read Wilber (1981).

The political

Sometimes the things that are bothering people are just as much political as personal. In such cases it may be advisable to suggest action other than therapy, such as joining a women's group, doing some community organizing, blowing the whistle on an employer, going on a demonstration, duplicating a leaflet or whatever. It may also at times be desirable to join with the client in changing a situation which is politically oppressive (Freedman & Combs 1996). So it is necessary to be able to listen at this level, and to be able to hear the political element in what is being said. (We shall be looking at this further in Chapter 10.)

The emotional

Of all the levels of listening, it is the emotional level which is the most important. It links, in a unique way, the earliest and the latest experience, the deepest and the shallowest, the most refined and the most earthy. If there is one thing the therapist has to learn, it is how to listen, and how to encourage the client to relate, at this level. And it is in the initial interview that this listening needs to start.

The transcultural

Training for crosscultural, intercultural, transcultural work is of course important, because there is so much ignorance and prejudice about, even among therapists. But again it looks different at each of our three levels.

The instrumental level is full of hints and tips. We learn that in some cultures it is a sign of disrespect to give full eye contact. We learn that some cultures prefer a closer or more distant presence. We learn that using first names is a choice to be checked out carefully. There are plenty of these rules. They can help us to avoid the most obvious pitfalls.

But at the authentic level, we are expected to work on our own racism in order to eliminate or at least reduce it. If we are to meet someone genuinely, then we need to take care that there is nothing getting in the way.

And at the transpersonal level, where we rely so much on intuition, our intuition may lead us astray. It always works best on familiar territory, and where the territory is too unfamiliar, it can lead us astray. However close we feel to a client, we still need to check out even our most cherished assumptions (see Chapter 4 for more on this).

Sexual politics

The same applies in the field of gender. We are all more sexist than we think we are, and if we are with a client who is sensitive to these things, as many are, it is easy to make mistakes which may be quite offensive. See McLellan (1995) for the basic critique here. We are also more heterosexist than we think we are, and our prejudices about lesbians and gay men, not to mention transvestites and transsexuals, are not to be underestimated (Davies & Neal 1996).

DIALECTICAL INTERPOLATION 3: WE MUST AND MUST NOT HOLD ONTO OUR MODEL OF THE PERSON AS BEING THE CORRECT MODEL.

There are important differences in different models of the human being (Maddi 1996). Growth models say that there is a common process of psychological growth, and that one of the tasks of the therapist is to enable the client to grow further. Conflict models say that there are basic conflicts which cannot be avoided, such as the conflict between the individual and social norms, or the conflict between the conscious and the unconscious, and that these cannot be avoided or grown out of. There are also balance models, which say that people continually seek for a cognitive balance between different needs and tendencies, and find rationality a big help in doing this. We should know what we are taking for granted here, and what we are excluding.

One of the most useful ways of looking at personality is that put forward by Salvatore Maddi (1996). He distinguishes between the core and the periphery of personality, and says that different theories can be best understood by looking at the ways in which they treat each of these aspects.

The core of the personality refers to the basic things which are common to all people, do not change much in life, and have general effects. The periphery of the personality refers to things which are more concrete and readily observable, which are usually learned or modified considerably through life, and are much more specific in their effects. They are mainly used to describe the differences between people. Using this framework, Maddi says there are three main types of personality theory: the conflict, the fulfilment and the consistency models.

The *conflict model* says that life is in the grip of a clash between two great, opposing, unchangeable forces. There are two versions of this: the psychosocial version, where the individual is opposed to society; and the intrapsychic version, where both great forces arise from inside the person.

The advantage of a conflict model is that it is very dynamic. It offers a concept of the person which is in movement, which is never at rest because the conflict is never fully resolved. On the other hand, by the same token, it is negative and depressing, because it offers only the prospect of further struggle: there are no breakthroughs here, no sudden revelations of truth or finality. It is also somewhat intolerant of approaches which do offer such things, on the grounds that they are only leading people up the garden path and offering them false promises of resolution. So there is a tendency toward dogmatism built in here. Authenticity is somewhat suspect, because it sounds like something which can be achieved. The transpersonal is even more suspect, because it bespeaks an end to conflict, or an ability to rise above it. The only exception to this would be where a person has such an incursion from the world of the soul or spirit that he or she has to somehow accommodate that experience. This is what happened, of course, in the case of Jung, who in his early work was very down to earth and conducted scientific experiments to prove the existence of the unconscious. It was not until he had spiritual experiences which shook his whole world that he expanded his notions of what was possible in therapy.

The *fulfilment model* says that there is only one great force, which is inside the person. Again there are two versions: the actualization version, where it is all about the realization of potentials which are present from the beginning; and the perfection version, where the force is striving towards ideals of what is fine, excellent and meaningful in life. Such a model breathes a spirit of optimism: breakthroughs are possible, high or deep goals can be reached, the whole is more than the sum of its parts. In particular, authenticity is possible, and in fact highly desirable. The existential view is of course that one of the main tasks of the therapist is to question the inauthenticity of the client. And the transpersonal is a possible realm, merely requiring an expanded sense of fulfilment. It is easy to see the transpersonal as a natural progression from the authentic. And in fact Maslow was the great figure who led the way in moving on from the authentic to the transpersonal in his own work.

In the *consistency model* there is little emphasis on great forces, but rather an emphasis on feedback from the external world. The two versions here are the cognitive dissonance model, where the basic urge is to overcome inconsistency between two thoughts, or between an expectation and a perception of occurrences; and the activation version, where the basic urge is to overcome inconsistency between the degree of bodily activation that is customary for the person and that which actually exists at the time. Here both authenticity and the transpersonal are hard to reconcile, and so this approach tends to be restricted to the instrumental. Table 3.1 shows how Maddi lays out the schools. This seems to make a great deal of sense, and Maddi has a very sophisticated way of comparing and contrasting these theories, really bringing all the evidence to ask the question – which is the best theory?

Table 3.1 Maddi's three types of personality theory

Conflict		Fulfilment		Consistency	
Psychosocial	Intrapsychic	Actualization	Perfection	Cognitive dissonance	Activation
Freud	Rank	Rogers	Adler	Kelly	Fiske/Maddi
Murray	Angyal	Maslow	Fromm	McClelland	
Erikson	Bakan	Costa &	Allport	Epstein	
Object-	Perls	McRae	White		
relations	Jung		Existential		
Kohut			Ellis		
Berne					

The main point here is to convince the trainee that no one model has all the answers. There are many partial truths here. A general attitude of optimism or pessimism also seems to be relevant. The fulfilment models tend to be optimistic; the conflict models tend to be pessimistic. The consistency models are also pessimistic, in the sense that they offer nothing beyond adjustment.

It is interesting to see where the existential approach comes in here, as for example in the work of Emmy van Deurzen (2002). There is a disowning of the idea of a personality. There is certainly a personal world, an *eigenwelt* in the original terms, but what might be called a personality in other philosophies is labelled as a sedimented set of beliefs about oneself in this one.

We cannot avoid having some model at the back of our minds, but it is important not to be too attached to it. Perhaps it is true, or perhaps it is only part of the truth, or perhaps it is totally misleading.

Chapter 4

Supervision

There is now a sizeable literature on supervision, some of it very good. There are courses in supervision, qualifications in supervision, accreditation in supervision. Instead of being something one got landed with at a senior stage in one's development as a therapist, it has become a speciality within the whole field of psychotherapy and counselling. The point has been made many times in this book that if we take seriously the idea that there is such a thing as psychospiritual development, then therapy can be adapted to various stages within that. But this way of thinking has never, to the best of my knowledge, been applied to supervision. This chapter attempts to fill the gap.

Instrumental

The general description of this level is to be found in the work of Ken Wilber, and I have summarized the relevant parts of the theory in Table 1 (see pp. 6–7).

The supervisee at the instrumental level is seen as a learner technician, who has to be helped to improve the technique. Michael Carroll tells us that the supervisor is seen as an educator more than as a counsellor or facilitator (Carroll 1996: 27). As Douglas Forsyth and Allen Ivey explain, the supervisor may sometimes teach skills in a well-defined way, quite concretely (Forsyth & Ivey 1980: 246). Model application and even model building will be a focus. Alan Lidmila (1997) suggests that the supervisor at this level may behave like a detective, an inquisitor or a librarian.

The supervisor evaluates the supervisee, as Elizabeth Holloway makes clear, and corrects any tendencies to deviate from good practice (Holloway 1995: 3). Similarly, the supervisor is regarded as someone who has to be carefully watched and kept in line. Monitoring is felt to be a major concern. A single model of the therapeutic process is generally favoured.

In psychodynamic supervision at this level, according to the classic work of Ekstein and Wallerstein (1972: 16) it is understood that the supervisory experience is often inhibited by intrapsychic conflicts and resistances of the student and occasionally the supervisor. It is believed that the primary commitment of the supervisor should be directed toward the patient, in keeping with the principle espoused by Robert Langs that once a physicianly responsibility is established on any level, it takes precedence over all else (Langs 1980: 105). Within this level, a great deal of importance is given to the unconscious, but my own view is that the depth to which the unconscious is plumbed makes no difference to the level on which the work is practised. In other words, someone working well with the unconscious may sometimes be quite instrumental about it, using specific techniques such as interpretation, with the aim of curing the patient.

There is an emphasis on the insight of the supervisee, and occasionally the supervisor may use his or her own insights to supplement those of the supervisee. There are great dangers of narcissism, infallibility and inflation for the supervisor who does this. The main focus is often on the client, and on the supervisee's relationship with them. Is the supervisee getting it right, or is some correction needed? Notes and tape recordings are very important aids in this respect, and rather full notes are encouraged at this level.

In cognitive-behavioural work at this level, as Richard Wessler and Albert Ellis (1980: 188) have argued, supervisors try to remain especially alert to times when supervisees agree with their clients' irrational beliefs, thereby becoming co-sufferers; and when they help their clients avoid rather than work on their disturbances. Clarity about aims is a major value.

The basic goals of therapy supervision, as Marsha Linehan (1980: 149) has told us, regardless of therapeutic orientation, are to assist the therapist both to do effective therapy in the present and to achieve the capability to carry out effective therapy independent of the supervisor. There may be a good deal of challenging of the supervisee. The word 'effective' is often a clear sign of an instrumental approach.

There is thus an emphasis on competence and doing what is correct, and making sure that both supervisor and supervisee do not stray too far from good practice. When the supervisee gets it right, there may be praise and confirmation. There is a good deal of attention to being helpful and getting good results. There may even be some interest in the question of right-brain thinking as opposed to left-brain thinking, but this does not mean that we are leaving this level by so doing, as Phil Mollon (1997) makes clear.

There is little interest in the social or political aspects of the work, and what there is tends to be restricted to established political parties or single-issue campaigns. There is of course no problem about ethics, adhered to conscientiously at this level, however, it is noticeable that some books at this level (e.g. Shipton 1997) do not mention ethics at all. A good basic guide to ethics has now been published by the BACP and has become very influential in the field (see Chapter 7).

Many of the concerns of supervision at the instrumental level are, of course, shared by the other levels. All therapists have to take account of such things as note-taking, possible litigation and so forth. Sometimes the rules are not clear, as in the following example.

Many years ago I was instructed on behalf of a psychiatrist. She had treated one of the parties to a matrimonial suit and had been subpoenaed to give evidence by the other party. I saw her in conference. She believed, passionately, that to disclose what had passed between her as psychiatrist and her patient would destroy the fundamental professional relationship between them, not only in that case but generally, and she was adamant that she would reveal nothing, whether or not that meant an unwelcome sojourn in Holloway. My job was to warn her of the likely consequence of refusing to answer, which I did, and then to try and procure that her sojourn would be as brief as was necessary to vindicate the majesty of the law. We arrived in the High Court. She entered the witness box and gave her name, address and qualifications. Counsel then asked about the psychiatric history of her patient. She refused to answer. The question was repeated. So was the refusal. The judge repeated the question. She said she would not answer. I awaited the inevitable explosion. The judge asked her why she would not answer. She explained. The judge listened carefully. When she had finished, the judge turned to counsel and said: 'Well, Mr X, I am not going to order this lady to answer your question. What do you propose to do about it?' There was of course nothing he could do about it. My melody remained unheard, although (if the poet was right) all the sweeter for that.

(Bingham 2003: 471–2)

On the other hand, there are many ways in which a therapist can fall foul of the courts, such as: excessive or inappropriate self-disclosure (which can amount to unprofessional domination of the session); business relationships with clients (if anything goes wrong, the therapist may be held to be at fault as the dominant partner); using techniques without proper training (especially invasive techniques such as massage); using incorrect diagnosis deliberately (particularly important where there is a contract with a third party); avoiding the medical model (the courts seem to find this hard to understand); believing that true love makes sexual relationships all right (this applies to all therapeutic relationships, whether current or in the past); inadequate notes (may be held to indicate a lack of professional care); failure to obtain an adequate history (may be particularly important where psychiatric conditions emerge in the course of the therapy); uncritically accepting what a client says (a good therapist has to combine intense gullibility with intense suspicion); use of inadequate syndrome testimony (making up syndromes is not an indication of creativity); out of the office contact, particularly where there is some verbal interaction (careful notes should always be taken in such cases); and failure to obtain supervision or other peer consultation (important when a therapist seems to be out of his or her depth).

These are not the only things which can lead to trouble, but they are all very important and need to be understood (Caudill 1999).

Authentic

The general description of this level of work is to be found in Table 1 (see pp. 6–7), in Column 2. Much of it is usually described as the humanistic type of work, though recently Leslie Greenberg and others have moved to the term 'experiential' (see Greenberg *et al.* 1998).

Here the goal is seen, certainly by Ernst Beier and David Young (1980: 196), as helping the supervisee in the work of encouraging the client to question and vary his or her routines and accept the uncertainty which is a byproduct of interpersonal exploration. Freedom to explore is regarded as important. Questioning rather than acceptance is what is asked of the supervisee. Confrontation may become very important if the supervisee becomes too passive or uncreative.

Creativity, or the ability to make effective personal changes, is regarded as very important, and can be seen as starting with this freedom to explore. Spontaneity is regarded as important both in the supervision and in the therapeutic work itself, and this is strongly encouraged. The vision of the supervisee is regarded as very important. This means that notes are quite suspect, and some supervisors at this level do not allow the use of notes in the supervision session. The argument is that notes are mostly about what happened, whereas what we are most interested in here is the *meaning* of what happened. For the psychodynamic supervisor, where the main interest is in the countertransference, this can be accessed just as much by what the supervisee forgets as by what he or she remembers. For the humanistic supervisor, it is again what lies beneath the surface that is of more interest than what was recorded more or less accurately. For an authentic meeting between supervisor and supervisee, notes can only get in the way, and the same applies to tape recordings.

There is a continual questioning of narrowness. The body is included; the social system is included; the family of origin is included; traumatic experience is included; different kinds of relationship are included. It is regarded as important not to leave things out. There is an experiential and holistic approach all the time.

Above all, it is said by Peter Hawkins and Robin Shohet (2000: Ch. 4) that supervision is a place where both parties are constantly learning, and to stay a good supervisor is to return to question not only the work of the supervisee but also what you yourself do as supervisor and how you do it. And Gaie Houston (1995: 95) asks the question: is the supervisor taking the supervisee forward at the right pace towards self-confidence based on reality, and towards abundance motivation?

Supervision is often seen at this level as a containing and enabling process, rather than an educational or therapeutic one. According to Steve Page and Val Wosket (1994: 39) supervision, to be effective, must be exploratory. This is because it is believed, as Laura Rice (1980: 138) tells us, that for both supervisor and supervisee there is the basic growth motivation, a push toward differentiation, authenticity and new experience. The growth and development of the supervisee is most important.

What is regarded as central is not education or correction or monitoring, but as Margaret Rioch and her colleagues (1976: 3) insist, increased self-awareness both for supervisor and supervisee. There is little emphasis on correct technique, or the precision of one theory. It is more important for supervisor and supervisee both to be fully present in the supervision session, which will help to enable the therapist to be fully present with the client in the therapy session. There is often an emphasis on integration and/or eclecticism. Often the question of aims is deliberately disregarded or de-emphasized; where aims come in, they tend to be long-term rather than short-term.

Simplicity is encouraged. The main focus is on the supervisee rather than on the client. A peer relationship is aimed at as the ultimate goal.

There is often a real concern for the social and political implications of the work, and both the therapist and the client may be encouraged to take action in the direction of liberation, particularly in the case of oppressive regimes. The supervisor may draw attention to the need for more heed to be paid to the social/political/economic context. The question of racial prejudice must also be taken into account (Lago & Thompson 1996). Luckily, the whole field of multicultural counselling is now much better understood, and Palmer and Laungani (1999) and others have offered ideas which are very easy to incorporate into training courses.

It must not be assumed, however, that this level of supervision is only to be found in the humanistic/existential field. In the psychoanalytic field it takes the form of a very insistent emphasis on the awareness of countertransference. Racker (1968) and Fordham (1979) have both commented on the importance of this for supervision. Paying attention to one's internal processes is precisely the kind of self-awareness which is so characteristic of the authentic level.

Transpersonal

The general description of this level of work is to be found in Table 1, Column 3 (see pp. 6–7).

I am going to refer to four of the six schools of transpersonal psychotherapy, split up the insights about transpersonal supervision between them, and then make some remarks about multicultural work. First of all, then, the Jungian school.

The Jungian school

So far as supervision is concerned, there is a lot of emphasis on the further development of the supervisee, and on the enlargement of the supervisee. There is an encouragement of the subtle perception and intuition of the supervisee. Joe Henderson says the supervisee may need further education in the whole field of mythology and of archetypes, as part of the work of developing the ability to use the superconscious in therapy. The term 'soul' may be used (Henderson 1995: 156), not as suggesting a 'ghost in the machine' but rather as referring to what is deepest within the person.

It could also be said at this level, as Valerie James suggests, that the supervisory situation is a *temenos*, a sacred space within which transformation may take place. The supervisor is responsible for the integrity of the container within which the therapist may be transformed (Valerie James, unpublished Minster Centre dissertation 1996). The supervisor, like the therapist, is a wounded healer.

The whole interaction may be seen in archetypal terms. At any one moment of time, as Petruska Clarkson has suggested, any supervisor may need to be a Cerberus guarding the territories and boundaries, or a psyche-sorter of the wheat and barley of primary and secondary realities, or a Zeus-like referee between warring internal or external factions, or a Chironic mentor teaching and modelling the skills of healing, or even a Hestian flame of spiritual direction (Clarkson 1998: 143). John Beebe (1995: 103) feels that the trickster archetype may certainly become involved in the double existence of the therapist being healer and healed at the same time.

Crittenden Brookes (1995: 122) has pointed out that the supervisor may need to encourage the therapist to educate the client in confronting the numinous and archetypal layers of their own experience. Lionel Corbett (1995: 75) wants to say that numinosity, like transference, may not be noticed until it is drawn to the therapist's attention. Also it may be noted, as Noel Cobb (1997: 275) has critically suggested, that many schools of therapy teach therapists how to run sessions with clients in such a way that they actually prevent any incursion of the sublime.

From this point of view, instead of a focus exclusively on the personalistic aspects of the transference, the supervisor would also be interested in its archetypal aspects. As Lionel Corbett says, there is a deep interest in how the Self manifests itself in the therapeutic field (1995: 70).

Or it may be seen in shamanic terms. Some supervisors, such as David Henderson, believe that the shaman is the original expression of the archetypal intent in human society, but that over time some aspects of the shaman's identity have split off and developed a character and autonomy of their own (Henderson 1998: 65). From this kind of imaginal perspective the significance of fantasy is discovered not so much through analysing or unmasking it, as through elaboration and following its lead. In other words, as David Maclagan

(1997: 63) has suggested, fantasy is treated less as an object of suspicion, more as a resource to be tapped. And this is true whether we are talking about individual or group therapy.

Analysis may be regarded as a mysticism of persons – and hence polyvalent, pluralistic, many-headed, many-bodied. As Andrew Samuels (1997: 158–64) has insisted, the *Mundus Imaginalis* is given due weight in the thinking of both supervisor and supervisee. This is the imaginal world so well described by the Sufi scholar Henry Corbin. In this case supervision would also partake of this character. It would involve the superconscious. At this level, intuition ceases to be a chancy thing, and starts to become the basic way in which one thinks. It would involve a regular opening up to contact with the divine, the sacred. As Joe Henderson (1995: 157–8) has told us, this may then be experienced as an initiation.

There may well be an interest in the social and political context, as Samuels (1993) has suggested, and here the concern tends to be towards the long-term good, rather than briefer campaigns.

Psychosynthesis

You could say that when the therapist comes for supervision, he or she is going on retreat. They come to stop and listen, to open their awareness. Diana Whitmore (1999: 3) has told us that the supervisor is providing the space for retreat, the holding for retreat and the transpersonal context for retreat.

It is sometimes felt, certainly by Whitmore, that supervision from a transpersonal context requires an act of will on the part of the supervisor, to affirm that all supervision begins with the supervisor's internal state of consciousness and a commitment to work from the 'inside out' before even meeting the supervisee. This is a contrary attitude to 'outside in', where the supervisor is regarded as the expert and as doing something to the supervisee (Whitmore 1999: 1). This would emphasize the transpersonal frame of the work as important. From this point of view, notes are sometimes useful and sometimes not.

Buddhism

I have not been able to find much on supervision from the Buddhist school, but one document from the Naropa Institute suggests that meditation may help. Sometimes it is found, say Bonnie Rabin and

Robert Walker (undated), that it is helpful for both supervisor and supervisee to have a personal mindfulness-awareness meditation practice, although this is not absolutely necessary.

The academic school

There is a further side to all this, which is best examined through the concept of the spiritual emergency, as described by Emma Bragdon and the Grofs (Bragdon 1988; Grof & Grof 1990). A very important issue which has come to prominence in recent years is the appreciation of the difficulties which can arise when people move into the transpersonal area. This is particularly difficult when people are suddenly exposed to spiritual experiences which they are not ready for. Energies which have been activated in the higher levels as a means of awakening the sleeping mental ego may be just too much, and go over the top. Christina and Stanislav Grof (1990) have outlined ten specific problems which can come out of such events.

1 *Peak experiences*. These can be so overwhelming for someone who has never been ecstatic before that there can be fears of going crazy. To be out of touch with ordinary reality, even for a short period of time, is for some people an impossibly worrying event. It is important at this point not to get into the hands of a psychiatrist or a mental hospital. A supervisor can help an uncertain therapist here.

2 *Kundalini energy awakening*. Sometimes through yoga, body-work or even quite spontaneously, the energy of the *chakras* can combine to give an overwhelming experience, as John Nelson and Lee Sanella have told us (Sanella 1987; Nelson 1996). This tends to be at the level of the sixth or seventh *chakra*. Probably this is worst for people who have no conception of such a thing, and who live in a social context which is unsympathetic to it. But it is essentially a healing experience if it can be contained and lived through. Even the trained transpersonal therapist may find this disconcerting and need support.

3 *Near-death experiences*. These are the experiences when people are declared physically dead, and are then revived. Even an approximation to this, through an accident, for example, can result in a full-blown near-death experience. This is often at the subtle level. The difficulty may come from the people around at the time, who may be very worried by what the person says, and

perhaps later for the person involved, in owning it and in talking about it. This is quite well-trodden territory now, and should not give too many problems.

4 *Past-life memories*. If a person has, for any reason, a vivid memory which appears to refer to a previous life, this may be very disturbing for the person, particularly if they do not believe in reincarnation. Often such memories have a life-or-death quality to them, which may make them hard to take, at the same time as they make them very meaningful. They can be at any level from the lowest to the highest. All therapists need to know the work of Roger Woolger (1990) just in case a client comes with this sort of material. And the transpersonal supervisor certainly needs to be able to help the supervisee who is confronted with such material.

5 *Opening to life myth*. Here the person seems to go on a journey to the centre, to the central meaning of life. But because it takes place on a psychic or subtle level, the whole process can be dramatic and overwhelming. The person may feel that they are at the centre of global or even cosmic events. Death and rebirth, masculine and feminine energies – these can be central concerns on a grand scale. There are here great dangers of ego inflation, and this state needs to be handled very carefully and with real understanding, so as not to fall into the error of assuming that it is a manic episode. It can be healing and very positive, if handled correctly. Emma Bragdon (1988) makes the point that these experiences, usually last no more than 40 days. Interestingly enough, they often last *exactly* 40 days.

6 *Shamanic crisis*. This is an initiatory crisis often involving a visit to the underworld, where annihilation takes place, followed by a rebirth and perhaps an ascent to heaven. Power animals are often involved, sometimes in quite horrifying ways. But if the person can be encouraged to stay with the experience and work through it, it can be genuinely initiatory, taking the person to a psychic or subtle level of consciousness. This is a realm which the conscientious transpersonal supervisor needs to explore, and in fact many do go on workshops and courses led by people like Leo Rutherford (1996).

7 *Psychic opening*. This is the arrival of psychic powers of one kind or another, perhaps quite suddenly and surprisingly. All sorts of paranormal phenomena may be involved here, including poltergeist phenomena. Out of body experiences are quite

common – apparent journeyings through space, leaving one's solid body behind (Grof 1988). Loss of identity may be experienced, and this can be frightening, too. There may be experiences of synchronicity, which may be confused with delusions of reference. The psychic level has to be handled here.

8 *Channeling*. The arrival of spirit guides or discarnate entities offering to use one as a channel for communication can be very disconcerting. This can be a healing and transforming experience for the recipient, and other people may also feel benefited. The dangers of ego inflation are large here, and so it is very important to discriminate what is prepersonal from what is transpersonal. Jon Klimo (1988) has written well about this.

9 *UFO encounters*. Contact with UFOs can be frightening and challenging, and such an experience often carries with it, as do many of these other experiences, the feeling that one cannot talk about it. One might be regarded as crazy, or at least as self-deluding. Yet such experiences can be genuinely illuminating for the person involved. However, therapists may be faced with difficult decisions as to what to say when the client asks: 'Do you believe me?', and a supervisor may be helpful here. In general, it is unwise at the transpersonal levels to ask questions such as 'Is this true?' Again, ego inflation for the client may result, and has to be watched out for.

10 *Possession*. Here there is a sense that one has been taken over completely by an entity which may be good or evil. If it is voluntary, as in some rituals where the participant is supposed to be taken over by a god or goddess, there is usually no problem. But if it is involuntary, and particularly if the entity seems to be evil, it can be very frightening, both to the person and to those around them. But 'when the person is given an opportunity to confront and express the disturbing energy in a supportive and understanding setting, a profound spiritual experience often results, one that has an extraordinary healing and transformative potential' (Grof & Grof 1990: 99).

There is now a worldwide network of therapists who are willing and able to handle such states, and this is something which all those involved in the transpersonal may be able to help with.

Multicultural work

What we have here, therefore, is an awareness of the spiritual context within which all supervision takes place. The notion of the Self (in touch with the divine, the numinous, the holy, the sacred), as opposed to the self, is often stressed. It has often been suggested that a brief period of meditation before the therapy session is desirable for the client, and also for the therapist. What I think we ought to now say, in the light of some of the multicultural material, is that prayer before the session may be indicated for some people – again both client and therapist. The supervisor might on occasion want to suggest this.

It has been pointed out that there is a particular role for the transpersonal therapist in the field of multicultural work, because of the increased respect for all religious experiences which comes with transpersonal development. The research paper by Cinnirella and Loewenthal (1999) for example, shows that members of communities such as White Christian, Pakistani Muslim, Indian Hindu, Orthodox Jewish and Afro-Caribbean Christian have many different attitudes to counselling and psychotherapy. Some of these make them particularly suspicious of western types of therapy. It is the transpersonal approach (not mentioned in that paper) which would be the most likely bridge for such people to use, in order to get the benefit of adequate therapy. The supervisor's role in this can be to encourage the transpersonal therapist to look for such experience and to make his or her presence known to the relevant people.

Not quite in the same category, but offering the same kind of disconcerting experiences, is the multicultural work involving discarnate entities of one kind or another, ranging from gods and goddesses to demons and devils, and from *loas*, *orishas* and *zar* to ghosts and witches. A great deal of fear may be aroused by such material for the client, and may be picked up by a therapist who is not well versed in this area. The excellent book by Fukuyama and Sevig (1999) can be very helpful in such cases. The transpersonal therapist is of course much better able to handle this material than other therapists, because their experience of the psychic and the subtle realms, and the transformations of consciousness, will stand them in good stead (see Wilber *et al.* 1986). Also, the whole idea of the pre/ trans fallacy may be important, in placing the phenomenon into the right place. Again the work of the supervisor may be much needed here. Indeed, the supervisor may get out of their depth too, and have to refer to a specialist. But the simple fact of having been opened up to that level of spiritual reality may well be enough to deal with most problems.

What I am now saying, therefore, is that every transpersonal supervisor has also available to them the earlier formations and abilities. Every authentic supervisor has also available to them the instrumental techniques in Column 1 of Table 1 (see pp. 6–7). And there is no reason why these should not be used in an aware way. If a trainee simply does not know a certain technique, and the supervisor considers that it would fit very well with a certain problem, there is no reason why the supervisor at any level should not introduce it. If the trainee has made an obvious mistake, and is blind to it, a supervisor at any level has to make a decision as to what to do about it. The manner might be different; the language might be different; but the problem will still need to be tackled.

As always with this kind of model, it seems worthwhile to utter the caveat that we cannot jump levels at will. We cannot will ourselves into the second column unless and until we have done the work on ourselves which can take us there. We cannot become transpersonal supervisors without doing the transpersonal work on ourselves. There are some huge challenges here, as well as some amazing opportunities, as William West (2000) has pointed out.

But at least it seems clearer now, to me at least, where we are going and what we have to do to get there, and what the new world looks like at least in general terms.

DIALECTICAL INTERPOLATION 4: WE ARE AND ARE NOT LOOKING FOR THE ORIGINS OF DISTURBANCE IN OUR CLIENTS – WE ARE AND ARE NOT LOOKING TO SEE HOW THE PROBLEMS ARE BEING MAINTAINED IN THE PRESENT

Some forms of therapy are mainly concerned with the origins of disturbance in the person. They talk about the roots or the foundations or what is primary. However, it also turns out that they do their main work in therapy, like other forms, in the present, in the here-and-now. They are interested in what happened to the person in the past – what some people have called a form of archaeology – but only in the service of bringing into the present what can be dealt with in the therapy room. All therapies seem to agree with the basic proposition that *the present is the point of power*.

Other forms are mainly concerned with how the person is keeping their disturbance alive in the present. They are therefore more interested in how to manage the disturbance in the present, so that it does not give problems to the person. This is often done by modifying the person's behaviour, or by modifying their thoughts and beliefs. Such approaches will use things like homework and behavioural exercises to link the therapist's consulting room with the everyday world. They are very keen to point out self-defeating patterns in the client's thoughts and actions.

But what we are saying here is that both are always necessary, and each by itself is inadequate. What is the use of finding out the origins if it has no connection with the present day? What is the use of finding out how to modify actions in the present if what produced them is untouched and will produce more problems in the future?

Some forms of therapy focus on the origins of disturbance. Let us call them the O-therapies. Other forms of therapy focus on the way in which disturbance is maintained in the present. Let us call them the M-therapies. Of course these two aspects of disturbance are not mutually exclusive: in fact, they are complementary. It is a shame if one of these forms of therapy appears to exclude the other, but historically they have grown up rather separately, as shown in Table 4.1.

As can be seen from the table, O-therapies tend to be longer, and to be more emotionally orientated. Going into deep origins requires a lot of trust to be built up between therapist and client, because there is potentially a lot of pain involved. We discover things about ourselves that are not complimentary and things about our early life

Table 4.1 O- and M-therapies

O-therapies	M-therapies
Psychoanalysis	Behaviour therapy
Reichian and neo-Reichian	Cognitive therapy
Primal therapy	Cognitive-behavioural therapy
Many forms of bodywork	Neuro-linguistic programming
Past-life therapy	Solution-focused therapy
Transactional analysis	Rational-emotive behaviour therapy

that may be hard to take. Trust takes time to build up and is easily threatened. Training therefore endorses the value of therapy for the therapist, because this is where the issues involved in the question of trust can be experienced and absorbed most readily.

M-therapies tend to be shorter, and to avoid these painful areas. In many (probably most) cases they work very well, and cause no problems, because the original forces producing the problems have weakened or dropped out of the picture in some way. The offending symptoms were simply remnants and survivals with no real functions left. In some cases, however, this is not so, and it is hard to predict in advance which problems will fall into which category. Training for the M-therapies often avoids therapy for the therapist, believing it to be unnecessary.

There are a number of therapies, of course, which are committed to a more integrative approach, and try to deal with both of these aspects of the work. They include:

- Psychosynthesis
- Primal integration
- Some Jungian approaches
- Core process therapy
- Process-oriented psychology
- Experiential psychotherapy
- Relational approaches

These integrative therapies offer a wide range of opportunities for work at all levels, and are much to be preferred if the therapist is up to them. However, they do require a good deal more in the way of training, because they need much more flexibility on the part of the therapist, and much more acquaintance with a variety of techniques. To be genuinely integrative requires a great deal of commitment.

There are other therapies which focus very much on the here-and-now, but are prepared to go into the past if it seems that the past is actually impinging very much on the present. These include person-centred therapy, psychodrama, Gestalt therapy, focusing, personal construct therapy and existential analysis. All of these require the trust which we have seen is so crucial for deep work.

For going back into the past, regressive techniques such as breathing, lying down and imagery are useful. Any therapy which absolutely refuses to go into such things will probably turn out to be an M-therapy. For dealing with the maintenance of problems in the

present, cognitive techniques such as reframing, disputation, homework exercises and behavioural rehearsal are useful Any therapy
which absolutely refuses to go into such things will probably turn out
to be an O-therapy.

Because the psyche-soma is a system, any change at any level in
any area will produce changes in other levels and other areas. It is not
necessary to deal with each problem directly – changes will come
about indirectly so long as something is moving. This is one of the
reasons why it has been impossible to prove one approach superior
to another in psychotherapy. The other reason is that most of what
comes into the process of therapy comes from the client, not from
the therapist. If we want to do justice to the person and to the field
we must not let go of either horn of the dilemma: both origin and
maintenance need to be held in paradoxical suspension.

Chapter 5

Own therapy
and groupwork

Own therapy

The instrumental approach

Here is an extract from a brochure produced by Mindfields College in Sussex:

> **WHY PERSONAL COUNSELLING OF STUDENTS IS NOT NECESSARY**
> One of the many myths that grew up in counselling is that counsellors need to undergo many hours of being counselled themselves to become good at it. We are very clear about this 'requirement'. Extensive research shows conclusively that therapists who have received personal counselling are *not* more effective (Russell 1993). Moreover, the type of counselling that many trainee counsellors are required to undergo, if it is excessively emotionally arousing, can actually be harmful to them (Griffin & Tyrrell 1999). (Some people undergoing long-term therapy value it because they are getting their attention needs met through it, but this is a different issue.) People only need counselling when their lives aren't working. Just as we only need to take medicine when we are ill – and then in the right quantity and at the right time from someone who really understands our condition.
>
> Research from various sources has established that much counselling and psychotherapy training has a detrimental effect, both on the trainees and the distressed members of the public they would like to help (Dineen 1996). (This is rarely acknowledged by academic organisations offering such courses.) Instead

of lifting depression, for example, some counsellors may inadvertently deepen it (antidepressant bills often rise in surgeries that employ counsellors (Fletcher *et al.* 1995; Sibbald *et al.* 1996)). Instead of defusing traumatic responses, counsellors frequently make them more incapacitating. And, instead of teaching missing social skills that enable people to move on with their lives, many counsellors disempower and further depress their clients with the psychological archaeology they indulge in. Some clients are so disappointed with their treatment that they never return after the first session, while others, vulnerable and easily indoctrinated, become dependent on the attention they get by being counselled. Naturally there is a growing tide of dissatisfaction with this state of affairs. Soon, in our increasingly litigious society, counsellors will be successfully sued in the courts (as already happens in America) for using inappropriate counselling with anxious, depressed, angry, traumatized or addicted people. This is because the research findings (Danton *et al.* 1995; Sibbald *et al.* 1996) are so clear and unambiguous. Effective counselling can be demonstrated. Harmful therapy and counselling can be clearly defined.

This diploma course has been created to correct the situation.
(Extract from *Human Givens Diploma Course* produced
by Mindfields College, Chalvington, East Sussex
BN27 3TD, European Therapy Studies Institute,
Principal tutors: Joe Griffin and Ivan Tyrrell)

Here we have a typical statement from the instrumental level of work. Therapists do not need their own therapy at all. However, things are not quite as clear as the authors say, even from this point of view.

Darongkamas *et al.* (1994) did a fair-sized and quite respectable survey of all the clinical psychologists working in the NHS, altogether contacting a sample of 321 of them. Among other things, they were asked about their own orientation as therapists, whether they themselves went to a therapist and, if so, what was the orientation of that therapist.

For their own orientations, 41 per cent were cognitive-behavioural, 39 per cent eclectic, 14 per cent psychodynamic and 6 per cent others (Gestalt, transactional, person-centred or group). The proportion of the sample who had had personal therapy was 41 per cent. As for their therapists' orientations, the result was psychodynamic

64 per cent, other 20 per cent, eclectic 14 per cent and cognitive-behavioural 2 per cent. Looking just at the biggest group, the cognitive-behavioural psychologists, 44 per cent chose psychodynamic, 22 per cent eclectic, 22 per cent other and 11 per cent cognitive-behavioural therapists. Of the other orientations, not one psychologist chose a cognitive-behavioural therapist for their own therapy. Of the psychodynamic people, 85 per cent went to their own.

I think this is fascinating. It has long been a conviction of mine that cognitive-behavioural therapists do not go to people of that persuasion for their own therapy. What is good enough for their clients is not, apparently, good enough for themselves. The biggest single group of them went to analytical therapists. And the same is true of the eclectic practitioners, 62 per cent of whom went to psychodynamic therapists.

On the other hand, those in the 'other' category, which I suppose would include most of the humanistic people, went mainly to their own – 63 per cent went to therapists with that same label.

If these results are at all indicative of the general position, it is clear that in spite of the Mindfields warnings, many therapists working in an instrumental way do go in for their own therapy, whether as part of a training course or not. And it seems from papers like those of Macran and Shapiro (1998) and others that this is widespread. They quote research from the USA which shows that 'around two-thirds to three-quarters of all therapists have received at least some form of personal therapy.' (p. 15). And they give a concise list of the functions which are served by therapy for the therapist:

1   Supporting the therapist's own mental health, which can be put under strain when the work gets demanding. Therapy gives personal help and also exploration of the way in which some clients can put more pressure on than others. Macaskill (1988) suggests that it is the more disturbed or otherwise difficult client who benefits most from the therapist having been through his or her own therapy. It is also evident that clients in the later phases of long-term therapy may put greater strain on the therapeutic relationship, if negative feelings toward the therapist have to be worked through.

2   Awareness of the therapist's own problems and areas of conflict, which may get in the way of doing good work with clients, particularly clients with similar problems and similar areas of

conflict. The vexed question of countertransference arises here (Rowan & Jacobs 2002).

3   Insight into what it feels like to be a client. Developing empathy and understanding of the various roles which clients may be falling into, just by being in therapy. See Haugh and Merry (2001).

4   Personal experience of a more experienced therapist in action may help in the development of ideas and techniques to be used with the therapist's own clients. Alvin Mahrer (1998) has argued that most training courses do not do enough by way of giving trainees the experience of seeing experienced therapists in action. As we shall see later, it is particularly easy to achieve this through group workshops.

5   Personal experience of the ways in which therapy can be inspiring and encouraging. Instead of seeing therapy as narrow in scope, the therapist as client can experience the way in which it can encompass a wider variety of functions. For this to be really effective, I would argue that trainees need to experience more than one way of working: again groups can be very helpful in this, because of the greater intensity of such experiences.

I could add more, of course, and here is a list which I have compiled from various sources:

- to increase your insight into yourself and therefore your clients;
- to reduce the risk of your being blind to aspects of your client's problems;
- to reduce the risk of your acting out problems of your own on your clients;
- to reduce the likelihood of your projecting characteristics in yourelf, which you prefer to disown, onto your clients;
- to enable you to understand what it's like to be a client in the psychotherapeutic situation;
- to increase the chances of your working in harmony with your associates and setting a good example to your clients;
- to give you first-hand experience of psychotherapy and how problems that arise in it can be tackled;
- to actually experience the difference between sympathy and empathy, rather than just reading or hearing about it;
- to learn how to be comfortable about the expression of emotion, rather than trying to avoid it;

- to make you more resilient and resourceful as a therapist;
- to enable you to grow into more awareness and self-under-standing, so that you are at least one step ahead of the client;
- to process experiences happening on the course you are doing, emerging either from theory or from experiential work;
- to discover all the things you didn't know about your family, your childhood and yourself;
- to enable you to work with clients beyond the limitations of your own initial resistances and misunderstandings.

It has to be admitted that personal therapy may be upsetting to the trainee, and also that issues coming up in the trainee's therapy may adversely affect the work with clients. But these are only possibilities, which seem to affect a minority of trainees (Macran & Shapiro 1998). It does seem to be true that a minority of emotionally vulnerable therapists become practitioners as a means of resolving their own conflicts. Guy *et al.* (1988) found that 62 per cent of practising psychologists had received therapy following their training.

The authentic approach

From the authentic point of view, things look rather different. Perhaps the main thought here is that the therapist should not be too narrow or exclusive. The view is that one does not want to produce the narrow kind of therapist who was trained in one school, analysed by one analyst, and practises in one mode. The view is also that it will not do to become the narrow kind of so-called 'therapist' who has never done any self-therapy at all. Better to aim at the open kind of therapist who has had many teachers and tried many modes, and has then settled on his or her own combination. As Freud said, therapists can only operate up to the limit of their own resistances. These resistances tend to be strongest in the areas which have not been reached by the type of therapy they did in their training. So when they get clients bringing up material which they did not cover in their training, they distort it and treat it as something else, which must be ineffectual.

When we ask people for their own experiences in therapy, they will say that, sure, their own experience shows that their own therapy was very important to them, and did help them become more balanced and more adequate in their work. But they would rather ignore their own experience and indulge in a fractious demand for empirical research evidence. Yet as soon as we really think about this, we can see that such research would be so hard to do that it is no wonder that researchers have steered clear of it and stuck to things which they think are simpler. The research which has been done has been shallow and simplistic, and far from helping us, it has only made us more confused (Matarazzo 1978). Much of it, indeed, has not been done using real therapists or real clients, and this surprises non-researchers when they discover it.

It seems crystal clear to me that the most important influence on any therapist is the personal therapy they have experienced themselves: on themselves and for themselves. The second most important influence is the supervision they have had. And the third most important influence is the clients they have had; but this third one can be crucially and sometimes cruelly limited by the first two.

There are paradoxes here. Own therapy increases objectivity, in that it removes the distortions caused by compulsions to think, feel and act in certain fixed ways. It decreases objectivity in that the hard-won theorietical and practical discoveries made through the therapy itself are held onto in what is often a rigid way. Just because they have been acquired through lengthy and painful experience, they are hard to question.

Perhaps all forms of training entail the losing of some false preconceptions and the acquisition of new rigidities. The deepest and most important role of therapy is to raise the consciousness of the would-be therapist to the appropriate level for the kind of work that has to be done.

At the instrumental level, there is little need for therapy, because the level of consciousness necessary to work at this level is basically already there for most candidates. The everyday rational view has been inculcated into us all the way through our education. We have learned all about objectivity and its importance almost every day.

At the authentic level, however, a good deal usually needs to be done to initiate trainees into the level of consciousness necessary to carry out work. Basically it involves meeting and dealing with the Shadow. Different therapeutic models describe this process differently. In the psychodynamic field the talk is of making the unconscious conscious, so that the therapist may use countertransference in a positive way. In the humanistic therapies the talk is of genuineness – being in touch with one's whole organismic being. In existential therapy the talk is of questioning sedimented assumptions, or questioning all inauthentic responses. The aim is always to reduce defensiveness and increase openness. Richard Hycner (1993) has written well and movingly about this.

So for the authentic therapist, own therapy is central and of unquestionable importance, simply because the authentic state of consciousness can only be reached in that way. The main value of therapy, it seems to me, is to unlearn very many of the things we thought we knew – whether about ourselves or about others. As Eric Whitton (2003) has argued, the self-awareness needed so crucially by the authentic therapist can only be achieved through the therapist's own personal growth.

The transpersonal approach

At the transpersonal level, there has to be initiation into the subtle realm. I used to think that this was best done by following a spiritual path involving ritual and ceremony, but now I believe that therapy itself can be a spiritual path. The kind of work practised in Jean Houston's sacred psychology (1982, 1987), the kind of exercises offered in psychosynthesis (Ferrucci 1982), the pathways offered by the Centre for Transpersonal Psychology (Wellings & McCormick 2000) are just some examples of attempts to initiate participants into the subtle level of consciousness.

One of the most interesting workers in this area is Amy Mindell. She has suggested that therapy itself is a ripe field for psychospiritual development, and has urged that we pay attention to the way in which it is unlearning which takes us further, rather than more and more learning: 'Each discipline is simply a path to spiritual attainment. Perhaps becoming a therapist, then, is also a spiritual path, if we learn to allow our underlying beliefs to surface through our work' (1995: 50). These 'underlying beliefs' are not so much a question of doctrinal content, but more a sense of opening to the divine. Not so much the application of truths, but rather the ability to open up to divine wisdom. And so not so much the learning of truths, but more the letting go of false assumptions. Someone once said to me, 'Kali eats falsities'. This is of course the great goddess of therapy Kali-Ma (Walker 1983), not the purely destructive demon so often confused with the Mother of All. Eating falsities seems to me a highly valued activity, leading directly to spiritual insights: 'Shunryu Suzuki reminds us, "If your mind is empty, it is always ready for anything; it is open to everything. In the beginner's mind there are many possibilities; in the expert's mind there are few" (Suzuki 1970: 21)' (Mindell 1995: 83).

Amy Mindell does not distinguish between the subtle and the causal: many of the things she sees as emerging from the causal are much more like what I call the subtle – in other words, they involve symbols and images, actions and responses, rituals and ceremonies, and so forth. We shall have more to say later about working at the causal level. I used to say that the causal was no use in therapy, because at that level there were no problems, and what the client wanted was to have his or her problems dealt with and taken seriously. But it now seems to me that in causal work we can transform problems in a radical way, not by denying them but by seeing them as part of a process in which they get lost or diminished, or radically redefined: 'There is a layer of process work that notices states and figures, yet ultimately connects to the flow of nature beneath all manifest events. It then goes one step further, not only noticing this energy but creating with it. We do not become passive boat riders on the river but actively create with the river's waves' (Mindell 1995: 147).

All forms of working at the transpersonal level require the basic ability to be fully present, and it is only a question of shedding one or two more layers than usual: 'The combination of fluidity and stillness appears in many traditions. Once again we are reminded of Don Juan's attitude of "controlled abandon". This is a special mood in which a warrior lets go of himself while retaining a quiet centre' (Mindell 1995: 158). Of course we do not have to believe in Don Juan to accept this notion. It is a question of degree. Many therapists would agree with the ideal, but the degree to which it is actually possible may depend, more than anything, on the quality of the work the therapist has done on his or her own consciousness. Just as with authentic consciousness, which cannot be attained simply by wishing to do it, subtle consciousness has its own initiatory demands which have to be met.

Arnold and Amy Mindell have obviously gone a long way in their own work on themselves, and they describe the result rather well:

> But even knowing all of these skills is not enough if we are not connected to a certain transpersonal something, which has to do with belief in what others might call the apparently absurd or impossible. You shall soon see that I look for the absurd, the nonsensical thing in an individual or group, the thing which others ignore. I look for the spirit of the incomprehensible statement, gesture or error and then care for it and let it unfold.
>
> (Mindell & Mindell 2002: 11)

This is work which instead of relating to a toolkit of interventions, lets go of all that, goes into a place of unknowing, and waits. Or as they put it: 'But process work shows the roundness of our universe. It shows that if we have the courage to follow unintentional signals to their edges, we do not fall off, but discover new worlds' (Mindell & Mindell 2002: 11). This puts into words something quite subtle and hard to describe. By 'process work' they mean a kind of therapy which is fully integrative, not holding to any one doctrine or persuasion, and not even organized in advance in any way: 'Earlier I needed to think before acting. Now I trust nature and do less thinking. Instead I follow my feelings. It is my present way to follow the unpredictable. I act now and think later' (Mindell & Mindell 2002: 12). This represents the intuitive approach which is so characteristic of the transpersonal. Similarly, as I and others have urged, the whole question of boundaries comes into question at this level: 'Everyone agrees that you and I are separate, but we also know from personal experiences, from relationships and from modern physics that there are no definite boundaries between you and me. We cannot say exactly where you end and I begin' (Mindell & Mindell 2002: 13).

So what we find at the transpersonal level of work is linking, rather than treating or meeting, as in the previous levels. And it is therapy itself which can be the training ground for this – as time goes by the relationship can change and develop in this direction.

It may even be possible to initiate people into the causal realm through therapy, though this is a much rarer pursuit. Almaas (e.g. 1988) is one of the few to attempt this feat. More usually, meditation is chosen as the preferred method of approaching the causal. But the question arises as to whether it is possible to do therapy at the causal level.

Most work in transpersonal therapy is done, as already indicated, at the subtle level. This is the level of myths, fairy stories, symbols such as the heart, images, deities and other archetypal figures – the whole range of the imaginal world. It relies quite heavily on images, on ritual and ceremony, on directed daydreams and the like. The mode of thinking at this level is basically intuitive. Instead of reaching into one's toolkit, one goes into a place of not-knowing, and waits, as we have said before. It was pioneered by Jung and Assagioli. Many other Jungians have developed it in various ways – Hillman with his emphasis on the soul, Marie-Louise von Franz through her work on dreams and fairy tales, Robert Johnson in his work on the active imagination, and so forth. In psychosynthesis there is not only the well-known work of Piero Ferrucci, but also the very important work of John Firman and Ann Gila. I have gone into this at greater length in a recent paper (Rowan 2003).

But the question I want to raise now is whether it is possible to work at the causal level, as defined by Ken Wilber (2000a). As we know, the subtle level is the realm of symbols and images, while at the causal level there are no symbols or images. Brant Cortright (1997) has called these the soul path and the spirit path. Masters and Houston (1966) call them the symbolic and the integral. Robert May (1991) calls them the archetypal realm and the spiritual self. In Buddhism (Kapleau 1967) we speak of the distinction between the *Sambhogakaya* and the *Dharmakaya*. At the subtle level, to put it another way, we still have thousands and thousands of assumptions, even though vast numbers have been given up, while at the causal level there are no assumptions. How then can therapy be possible? It is even more difficult if we look at it in the light of what we know in psychology about assumptions.

Therapy can often be thought of as a process of giving up our assumptions. So in therapy the best, final, ultimate approach is to encourage and enable the client to question all his or her assumptions without exception. As David Levin says in his essay on Freud, Jung and Tibetan Buddhism: 'All conceptual constructions of the experiential process are defence mechanisms, to the extent that they solidify into patterns of response that obscure a clear perception of one's situation and block an appropriate, effective and spontaneous involvement' (1981: 248).

The ideal therapist is someone who can approach the client in a mood expressed by the phrase 'emptily perfect and perfectly empty'. There is then no distortion of the client's experience, no twisting of it to suit some theory. This enables the client to move in the same direction: that is, towards more openness and less restrictiveness. Levin says: 'The therapist thus prepares a spacious clearing, a comfortable openness, for the other . . . to open out into . . . We might call this quality "spaciousness": the gracious hospitable spaciousness we need to grow, to live, open up' (1981: 254–66). There is no statement here of any stages or levels of development, nor of any person or system by which change takes place. The emptiness in the therapist allows the client to move towards her or his own emptiness.

David Brazier makes the same point in his book on the practice of Zen therapy. This is what he says:

Within this conventional framework, the sacred work must be created beginning with the therapist's surrender of self-concern. Zen begins with the emptying of the therapist. The best therapy is completely empty (*shunya*). Empty of what? Empty of ego. Shunyata (emptiness) means the therapist is wholly there for the client, the other. As therapy proceeds the client also becomes shunya. Then they can examine their life without ego getting in the way. The client's ego is getting in the way of their life. The therapist's ego gets in the way of the therapy. To love is to surrender the ego. Therapy, at best, is an experience of shunyata.

(Brazier 1995: 205)

At first this may sound rather abstract and lacking in content. We shall come back to the question of love later. But this, as Shunru Suzuki (1970) says: 'does not deny the world of multiplicities; mountains are there, the cherries are in full bloom, the moon shines most brightly in the autumnal night; but at the same time they are more than particularities, they appeal to us with a deeper meaning, they are understood in relation to what they are not' (quoted in Wilber 1979: 41). These things do not make us unhappy unless we see them as denying us, frustrating us or unattainable by us. The constant thing in all unhappinesss and distress is that it is 'I' who am unhappy or distressed, and all therapy is based on the premise that it is the 'I' which needs to change, to be worked on. But from our new point of view we can now see this differently. As Wei Wu Wei put it:

Why are you unhappy?
Because 99.9 percent
Of everything you think and
Of everything you do
Is for yourself –
And there isn't one.

(Quoted in Wilber 1979: 53)

This is the equivalent in therapy terms of the statement I made once about Harold Walsby's ultimate ideology, the ideology that enables us to describe and account for all ideologies (Lamm 1984). I said that 'the ultimate ideology must be understood and accepted by nobody', simply because there is absolutely nothing to understand or accept. I went on to point out:

In fact, the metadynamic level [the ultimate ideology] can have no expression at all, except the negative one of showing that all basic assumptions are self-contradictory, each in its own distinct way . . . We have seen through all other basic sets of assumptions, and we have nothing to put in their place.

(Rowan, unpublished manuscript)

Similarly in therapy, as we reject false self after false self in the search for the true self, we discover that there is no end to this process. When we realize that, there is nowhere for unhappiness or suffering to belong to or connect with. To put it in another way, you behold your original face on all sides. Ken Wilber (1979: 58) puts it like this: 'The more I look for the absolute self, the more I realize that I can't find it as an object. And the simple reason I can't find it as a particular object is because it's every object! I can't feel it because it is everything felt'. This is the sort of empty paradoxical talk to which one is reduced when one tries to talk about what cannot really be talked about. But we have said enough to make it clear that from such a point of view the idea of measuring therapy, or of specifying the outcomes of psychotherapy, is absurd.

This is all very well, and very true. I could actually live up to it at times. But when I tried to do this and only this in therapy, I found that I usually could not do it. Always there seemed to be something needed first, some more immediate aim which had to be carried out before we could get on to the real emptiness. This now seems to me the essential paradox of psychotherapy; we can hardly ever do what is the best thing to do because there is always something better to do first.

If we just do the real therapy, the ultimate therapy, we restrict ourselves to the clients who are ready for that, and clients are hardly ever ready for it. This is not in any way to blame the clients; it is merely to recognize that the process of development is long and slow. When I am the client, I am no better than many of my own clients.

It seems that both therapists and clients are equally adept at avoiding the real issue, and perhaps this is necessary. Maybe the periphery is just as important as the centre. Maybe to concentrate on the centre all the time is too pure, too obsessive, too rigid, too arrogant; but at least it seems worth knowing: the difference between the centre and the periphery, the ultimate and the proximate.

Perhaps in the final analysis there are many levels of therapy, and we need to work on all of them at different times with different clients. If so, the sooner we know more about how many levels there are and how to work on each of them, the sooner we shall get out of empty arguments as to which level is the best.

That is all very well, but here we are interested in the practicalities of what happens when we attempt, in all honesty, to work at the causal level. But before we do so, there is another interesting issue we have to face.

What is so striking is that therapists who are obviously familiar with the causal, and able to speak and write in causal terms, usually resort to the subtle when actually doing their work. David Brazier (1995) writes with real authority about causal states, but when he does therapy it often sounds like psychodrama. Amy Mindell (1995) writes with real familiarity about causal states, but when she does therapy it often sounds like Gestalt. A. H. Almaas (1988) writes very well about causal and even non-dual states, but when he does therapy it often sounds like object relations. Mark Epstein (1996) has some very wise things to say about the causal, but when he does therapy it often sounds like psychoanalysis. Robert Rosenbaum (1998) is clearly familiar with causal states, but when he does therapy it often sounds like existential phenomenology. Perhaps it would be over-simplifying to say that the work they do is mostly in terms of their original training or experience, but there is certainly something like that going on.

And I don't want to criticize this in any way. There is a nice quote in Almaas which helps to explain it. It comes from a Japanese therapist, who says: 'The person, the "I am this body, this mind, this chain of memories, this bundle of desires and fears" disappears, but something you may call identity, remains. It enables me to become a person when required. Love creates its own necessities, even of becoming a person' (Maharaj 1981 in Almaas 1988: 449–50). This idea, that therapy is based on love, and that love is an important aspect of the causal, is a powerful one. It helps us to understand that although the juicy compassion of the subtle is very different from the steady compassion of the causal, they do have love in common. And it is this love which makes the bridge between the causal and the subtle, so that therapists who are in contact with the causal can move into the subtle as necessary.

I thought I would see what Ken Wilber had to say about love, and here is the passage. It comes after a long discussion of spirituality in its various aspects:

No, it seems that we are part and parcel of a single and all-encompassing evolutionary current that is itself Spirit-in-action, the mode and manner of Spirit's creation. The same currents that run through our human blood run through swirling galaxies and colossal solar systems, crash through the great oceans and course through the cosmos, move the mightiest of mountains as well as our own moral aspirations – one and same current moves throughout the All, and drives the entire Kosmos in its every lasting gesture, an extraordinary morphogenetic field that exerts a pull and pressure which refuses to surrender until you remember who and what you are, and that you were carried to this realization by that single current of an all-pervading Love, and here 'there came fulfilment in a flash of light, and vigor failed the lofty fantasy, but now my will and my desires were moved like a wheel revolving evenly, by the Love that moves the sun and other stars.'

(Wilber 2000a: 153)

The quotation which Wilber uses at the end, of course, comes from the final canto of Dante's *Paradiso*. It seems that love has quite a big part to play in this whole business (the Sufis talk about heart), and this is perhaps why some therapists do not distinguish between the subtle and the causal. Amy Mindell, for example, is a wonderful therapist at the subtle level, but continually speaks as if she is working at the causal level. It is possible to assume that she does not make the distinction because to her the matter is obvious. It is the same spirit in both.

However, I have come across two examples of actually working at the causal level. The first one comes from a book on Jung and Buddhism. It would not be proper to feature such a long quote without permission, so here is the reference: Shore (2000), page 41 from 'More concretely' to page 42 '... like to have tea' followed by page 37, 'Boundless in expanse ... none other than the empty sea'.

In this example, the Zen professor Hisamatsu first interviews in a very direct way a young man dying of cancer, and then speaks to him about the paradoxical nature of the sea: 'Bearing all yet grasping none/Grasping none yet bearing all'. This speaks to me very clearly of the causal level in action.

The second example is to be found in Epstein (1988). He recalls visiting Ram Dass with various problems in mind. Even as he entered the room he realized that this was going to be unlike any therapeutic encounter he had experienced before. After the briefest of hellos, Ram Dass began to gaze at him unceasingly, looking straight into his eyes, but at the same time looking past him, 'he seemed filled with love but also completely uninterested in me, or at least in who I thought I was. He did not respond to any of my smiles, nods or grimaces, or to any of my attempts to engage or avoid him. He simply waited, gazing at me with unnerving intensity'. Epstein says that he felt perplexed. He tried to explain what he wanted, 'But he [Dass] seemed remarkably unmoved by my words and just continued moving his head ever so slightly back and forth while occasionally making a soft sound like, "Ahhhh"' (Epstein 1988: 76–77). Epstein recalls that he eventually settled into an uneasy silence, and felt he had entered the realm of Freudian unconscious. But this did not seem to interest Ram Dass:

> He seemed infinitely patient and subtly encouraging, as if beckoning to me from afar. 'What was this man doing?' I wondered to myself. 'How should I react?' But no matter what I tried, Ram Dass did not budge. Finally, out of desperation and unable to think of anything else to think about, I began to return his gaze. This was suddenly very different. Finding myself in a place beyond words, I actually felt a connection with him and sensed a moment of mutual recognition. And then all of a sudden, I realized the answer to my question. Ram Dass was not doing anything, which is why my attempts to figure out what he wanted were not moving him. He was simply being. I was going through all kinds of internal gyrations, but he was simply being. Although I was mobilized to feel done to, that was not what was happening. I was being given room to be and out of that experience discovering that we could be together.
>
> (Epstein 1988: 77–78)

Soon after, the session ended, with Epstein feeling very moved by the experience.

In both of these examples I am convinced that the therapist was in a causal state of consciousness, and that therefore this must be possible. I have experimented in workshops not only with demonstrating this myself, but also with inviting the participants to try it themselves. The results have been encouraging and have again confirmed my belief that this kind of work can be done. In the list that follows, I have given an account of what it might be like for a Christian mystic to remain at this level of consciousness for some time.

1 *Clear perception.* Here there is no ego inflation; humility is prevalent; people look for and rely on people who are further ahead than they are to help them avoid self-deception.

2 *Self-oblivious delight in the divine.* There is no hyperintrospection or over self-consciousness; no looking for kicks, trips, trouble and experiences; contact with the divine is frequent; we are made participators in the divine nature without changing our human nature into the divine.

3 *Vitality.* The wisely receptive mystic responds to the superactive vitality within, and does not succumb to quietism. There is no need to avoid the world, but there may be a need to engage with it.

4 *Open to the world.* Real mystics always remember the world of people and events outside of themselves. Mystical experience is not a conversation with the divine but life lived on its deepest level. They don't imagine they can do without a teacher or support group; they do not succumb to privation and pride.

5 *Surrender of the body-person.* This is inspired by love and may involve a constructive asceticism or celibacy, but it does not involve fakirism: people at this level do not believe that they must annihilate a nature which is evil or rebellious, nor do they go in for a psychological fakirism which blunts and dulls the spirit.

6 *Love for the whole of creation.* The true causal mystic, who possesses all in the All, loves the whole of creation. There is no disdain or contempt for the world. There is no fear, because nothing is alien. Love is one of the key aspects of the causal. Compassion at this stage is steady and unwavering.

7 *No seduction by psychophysical phenomena.* The somatic marvels which accompany subtle mystical experience do not express the essence of causal mysticism; they are only accidental and secondary and must neither be sought after nor clung to, should they occur. They are all essentialy limited images.

8 *Commitment to growth.* There can always be further growth, leading to greater heights or deeper dimensions. It is important not to get fixed on one point: this can lead to fanaticism. The fanatic forgets the end and multiplies the means.

9 *Step by step.* In humility the causal mystic proceeds through

the discipline in order; there is no attempt to skip steps and leap on towards the end; the slowness of the growth process is respected.

10   *Imperfections*. Finally, mystics, because they remain in continuity with physical-biological-psychological life, are susceptible as the rest of us to both neuroses and psychoses. People assume that to be spiritually inclined is to transcend the neurotic traps of life, but this is not true.

Groupwork

One of the most interesting questions in the field of training is the place of groupwork.

Instrumental

The first thing to notice is that while in theory groupwork is eminently suitable for training from an instrumental point of view, it is much less popular and well developed among the people one might think most identified with the instrumental approach.

Both on grounds of cost and efficiency, groupwork might have been made for the instrumental approach. It is obviously a very economical place for learning the skills of human interaction. And Tim Lacey (2004) has argued that cognitive-behavioural therapy could and should use groupwork more than it does at present. He also argues that such groupwork should always have two facilitators.

Scott and Stradling (1988) show how groupwork can be done in the field of cognitive-behavioural therapy, but they do not say much about training. A fuller account, though only in one subfield of instrumental work, is to be found in Dryden and Neenan (2002). In Chapter 1, Dryden suggests that a number of techniques are used in their form of group therapy, such as:

- ABC framework analysis;
- disputing of specific and core irrational beliefs;
- homework assignments;
- correcting cognitive distortions;
- skill training and role-play methods;
- advice giving and problem-solving.

The same methods are used in training, both in the training of rational emotive behaviours therapy (REBT) practitioners and in the training of group therapists.

However, in Chapter 2 of Dryden and Neenan (2002), Albert Ellis puts forward a slightly different set of operations, from which it can be seen that he is even more precise and formal:

- active disputing;
- rational coping self-statements;
- cost-benefit analysis;
- modelling;
- cognitive homework;
- psychoeducational techniques;
- proselytizing;
- recording therapy sessions;
- reframing;
- forceful coping self-statements;
- rational emotive imagery;
- role-playing;
- reverse role-play;
- forceful taped disputing;
- use of humour;
- relationship methods;
- encouragement;
- encounter exercises;
- *in vivo* desensitization;
- avoiding running away from obnoxious events;
- use of reinforcement;
- use of penalties;
- skill training;
- relapse prevention.

It can be seen how well ordered all these categories are. First of all we get the cognitive techniques, then the emotional techniques and finally the behavioural techniques. These groups must be pretty busy places at times. When we read the words 'encounter exercises' it must be understood that this does not mean anything like the unstructured nature of an encounter group: these exercises are more like what used to be called a 'mini-lab' – in other words a series of exercises designed to bring out various issues set by the facilitator.

In Dryden and Neenan's book there is a chapter on women's groups, written by Kristene Doyle. Are women's groups any different from the other groups? Again there is a list of exercises which are given to the group:

- role-play;
- *in vivo* disputation;
- honest feedback from group members;
- general topics for discussion.

It looks as if these groups are somewhat more unstructured than the standard ones, but the emphasis is still on the rational solution of common problems.

In Chapter 9, Michael Neenan contributes on the use of REBT groups in training. Trainees are taught that 'REBTers do not attack their clients or their beliefs or attempt to brainwash them. You want to engage clients in the disputing process, not alienate them from it' (p.196). The tutor has to model the correct way of doing things, because 'therapist modelling provides a stimulus for trainees to explore for themselves "the veracity of the teachings" and be thereafter less inclined to follow unproductive group norms' (p.198). There is therefore quite a demanding role for the therapist in this kind of group.

It seems clear that groups, in this instrumental way of working, are highly disciplined with clear aims and purposes, and provide an exercise and an example for everything.

Authentic

The most common type of group to be found on training courses is the experiential training group, often called a personal growth group. 'Personal growth' is a term coming from humanistic psychology (Rowan 2001a). This approach includes person-centred therapy, Gestalt therapy, psychodrama, bioenergetics, focusing, experiential therapy, existential analysis and some of the feminist methods (Ernst & Goodison 1981). In this context, growth strictly means development in terms of the Maslow (1987) theory of a hierarchy of needs. This says that we all start off with physiological needs. When these are satisfied, we move on to safety needs, involving basic trust. When these are satisfied, we can move on to the higher levels as we grow up – for example, learning our roles so as to be good conformists. As Kohlberg (1981) showed through his research, we can then continue growing, moving from the conventional to the postconventional forms of consciousness. Psychodynamic therapists used to avoid the term 'personal growth' but in recent years many of them have adopted it. Of course they do not mean by it what Maslow meant, but something more like working through their issues: though of course Jung independently pursued the idea under the heading of 'individuation': 'The process of individuation is a circumambulation of the self as the centre of the personality which thereby becomes unified' (Samuels *et al.* 1986: 76). This means working through the hang-ups of the persona and the distractions of the Shadow and other archetypes.

Groupwork is particularly good for moving across what I have called 'the great gap'. This is the gap between Levels 4 and 5 of Table 5.1. This gap is between needing esteem from others and look-ing to them to see how they expect us to behave, and moving on to giving esteem to ourselves and being open to discovering what each of us can be. Crossing the great gap begins when the group gives us a forum for questioning our customary assumptions and our usual roles. Being real is central in personal growth groups. Being real simply means not hiding behind our roles and the expectations we have adopted without noticing: our unaware 'shoulds'. In personal growth groups we say what we mean and mean what we say. We see out of our own eyes, rather than out of the eyes of others. We take full responsibility for what we say and do. Learning how to do this is often harder than we at first thought it would be, and groupwork is ideally suited to help in this. It works by confronting us with the task, and supporting us in carrying it out. This combination of support and confrontation is crucial to groupwork, as Peter Smith's (1973) classic work has shown.

There are really two main kinds of personal growth groups, in terms of the people who go to them. Firstly there are groups which people go to entirely off their own initiative, for their own satisfaction. We are not concerned with that here. Secondly there are the personal growth groups which are part of a course in counselling or psycho-therapy. Here the person is required to go to the group to enhance the personal development that is expected to take place on such a course. It would not be right, the reasoning goes, to try to counsel other people if one had done no work on oneself. Some of the blocks to being oneself can be worked through in individual therapy, but there are some which cannot. For example, if someone talks too much, this is never going to come out as a problem in individual therapy, but it will emerge straight away in a group. These groups are

Table 5.1 Maslow's Hierarchy of Needs and Some Collateral Research

Level	Maslow	Kohlberg	Loevinger	Piaget	Alderfer	Wilber
6	**Self-actualization** Being that self which I truly am Being all I have it in me to be Fully functioning person Authentic Creative	**Individual principles** True personal conscience Universal principles fully internalized Genuinely autonomous Selfishness B	**Autonomous: integrated** Flexible and creative Internal conflicts are faced and recognized Tolerance for ambiguity Respect for autonomy	**Dialectical operations** (Klaus Riegel 1984) Beyond formal logic Integration of contradictions	**Growth**	**Centaur 2** Vision-logic Body-mind integration Peak experiences Existential self
5	**Esteem 2** Goals founded on self-evaluated standards Self-confidence	**Social contract** Utilitarian law-making Principles of general welfare Long-term goals	**Conscientious** Bound by self-imposed rules Differentiated thinking Self-aware	**Formal operations** Substage 2: thinking about thinking Forethought, speculation	**Growth**	**Centaur 1** Ecological imagination Awareness of awareness Relative autonomy
	THE	GREAT		GAP		
4	**Esteem 1** Respect from others Social status Recognition	**Law and order** Authority maintenance Fixed social rules Find duty and do it	**Conformist 2** Seeking general rules of social conformity Justifying conformity	**Formal operations** Substage 1: capacity for hypothetico-deductive thinking	**Relatedness**	**Mental ego** Full rationality Syllogistic logic Science/mathematics

3	**Love & belongingness** Wish for affection Need for acceptance Need for tenderness	**Personal concordance** Good-boy morality Seeking social approval Liking to be liked	**Conformist I** Going along with the crowd Anxiety about rejection Need for support	**Concrete operations** Ability to take role of other	**Relatedness**	**Mythic-membership** Dependent on roles Norm-dominated
2	**Effectance** Mastery Imposed control Blame and retaliation Domination	**Instrumental hedonism** Naive egocentrism Horse-trading approach Profit-and-loss calculation Selfishness A	**Self-protective** Wary and exploitative People are means to ends Competitive stance Fear of being caught	**Preoperational** Mastery Incapable of seriation	**Existence**	**Magical** Primary process thinking High credulity
1	**Safety** Defence against danger Fight or flight Fear: world is a scary place	**Obedience/ punishment** Deference to superior power Rules are external and eternal Musts and shoulds	**Impulsive** Domination by immediate cue, body feelings No reflection	**Sensoriphysical**	**Existence**	**Body ego** Archaic level of thought

Source: After David Wright (1973), omitting lowest level of Maslow (physiological) and Loevinger (pre-social, symbiotic).

often a humbling experience, and demonstrate convincingly to people that they are not as ready to become counsellors as they had first thought. In all cases those attending are not called 'patients' but rather 'participants' or 'group members'.

The people who lead such groups are counsellors or psychotherapists who have taken specific training in groupwork, and are experienced at working in this way. They are usually in supervision, but in privately-run groups there is no guarantee of this. If this is a concern, it is easy enough to ask about it.

The general point to be made about personal growth groups is that there is no assumption made that people are sick or inferior or defective in any way. As can be seen very easily in the Maslow model, it is more a question of following a developmental path a bit further than most people bother to do. The journey begins with the permission and encouragement to be real. Then quite a number of specific approaches are mobilized in the search for further help in crossing the great gap.

Jacob Moreno (see Karp *et al.* 1998) was one of the pioneers of this direction. Through the method of psychodrama which he developed Moreno showed how people could be helped to be more creative and spontaneous then they had been before. In psychodrama people can re-enact scenes from their past with the help of other group members. Each member takes different roles; for example, that of a father, or mother, or a previous teacher. The member then acts as if they were that figure. Group members can also see themselves acted out by others. Each member can then change their current responses to others in their daily lives, or see other possibilities of getting out of old and apparently impossible situations.

Carl Rogers (see Kirschenbaum & Henderson 1990) was another pioneer, insisting that a growth group had to be person-centred in the sense of helping people to find who they really are instead of having fixed aims for them. People in person-centred groups are encouraged to give up the masks they generally use to get by in social interactions. Instead, each member is enabled and supported in expressing directly and genuinely the feelings that arise for them in the group. Rogers' emphasis on genuineness, empathy and acceptance has influenced many other approaches to counselling and to psychotherapy. A useful summary chart is given in Zimring (2001: 92) (see Table 5.2).

A third name that must be mentioned is that of Fritz Perls (see Clarkson & Mackewn 1993). Perls developed Gestalt therapy and emphasized awareness and personal presence. He insisted on paying

Table 5.2 Differences in functioning in the two self-states

Maslow Chart Levels 3–4 ('Me')	Maslow Chart Levels 5–6 ('I')
Socially defined self	Personally defined self
Behaviour guided by incorporated social standards	Goals set by own values
Morality defined by society	Morality based on personal values
Agenda for what has to be done set by society	Agenda set by self
Enables problem solution according to social standards	New, creative solutions
Repository of social knowledge and expectations	Contains self-knowledge
Provides social viewpoint in line with assimilated social values, attitudes and interactions	Reacts creatively to 'me'.
Passive recipient or reactive self	Proactive
Concerned with past and future	Experiencing the present
Focus on others	Focus on self
Lives in roles	Acts from present personal values
Negative feelings and distress occur as a result of judgement of others	Distress occurs as a result of not meeting own goals

Source: Zimring (2001:92).

attention to the how (rather than the why) and the now (rather than the past or future). Perls encouraged paying attention to unfinished cycles of making contact with people, and to the splits we create to disrupt such cycles. An example can be to apologize whenever the cycle would call for expressing anger. In this case the cycle of contact is disrupted by splitting the expression of anger from the expression of appreciation. Perls also developed ways of enabling group members to intensify the aspects they split; for example, expressing appreciation more intensely and then expressing anger more loudly. By shuttling between the two extremes, a new resolution emerges. Perls' contribution was basic to the theory of paradoxical change (Beisser 1972) that has been adopted in many other areas of counselling and of psychotherapy.

We do need help to begin crossing the gap. Up until the great gap, society gives a great deal of support and help in ascending the Maslovian hierarchy of needs. It may even sometimes feel like being carried up an escalator. But at the point where the great gap begins, society ceases to encourage us, and we have to carry on by ourselves, under our own steam. We have to become more autonomous in order to progress at all. That is where these types of growth group come in. In this sense there is a sort of paradox about growth groups: we join them to become more autonomous, yet we have to be a little bit autonomous in order to take the risk of joining such a group.

A range of types

Shaffer and Galinsky (1989) offer the best account of the range of groups that have been developed over the years. They describe: the social work group (support groups, educational groups, groups for empowerment and even self-help groups); the psychoanalytic therapy group (the group-analytic group from Foulkes, the Tavistock group, the group-dynamic group, the Wolf and Schwartz type group, the Whitaker and Lieberman group and so on); the existential-experiential group (Hora, Mullen and Berger are specifically mentioned); psychodrama (the powerful and widely influential group developed by Moreno); the Gestalt therapy workshop (owing to Fritz Perls); cognitive-behavioural therapy in groups (desensitization, imagery work, assertiveness training, many techniques from Albert Ellis, Meichenbaums's work and so on); T-groups and the laboratory method (the most unstructured of all the groups mentioned here, stimulating research which led to the generally accepted sequence of stages in a group); the encounter group (Rogers, Schutz and so forth – perhaps the most flexible of all the group approaches, in the hands of a well-trained and experienced facilitator); the theme-centred interactional method (from Ruth Cohn); and the self-help group (well described in the wonderful book by Ernst & Goodison 1981). In each case they give a general introduction and historical background, an illustration of a typical session, key concepts and special techniques, and the role of the facilitator.

Any of these groups can be used for personal growth, although this is not always the case. In practice the two main approaches in this country are the person-centred group developed by Carl Rogers in the USA, and naturalized into the UK by people like Brian Thorne, Dave Mearns and Tony Merry, and the group-analytic group developed by Sigmund Heinrich Foulkes in Britain. The person-centred group is most similar to the encounter group or the existential-experiential group as described by Shaffer and Galinsky, and comes from the humanistic camp. The group-analytic group is most similar to the psychoanalytic group as described by Shaffer and Galinsky, and is often described as a psychodynamic group. There are other types of group on offer in some locations, such as psychodrama groups, which are in most cases excellent now, because the training has become quite rigorous in recent years. Gestalt groups are also now mostly run by well-trained people, and are a very good source for use in training. Tavistock groups are not so good for personal growth, and are of more use to people working in organizations who want to deal with their fantasies about authority figures.

We must not forget the self-help group. People who want to embark on a programme of self-development often find in this a way of doing the work they need to do without spending large sums of money. Sheila Ernst and Lucy Goodison (1981) have written an excellent text on this, which gives a great deal of information about starting up and running such a group. Co-counselling (Evison & Horobin 1988) is a way of working in a one-to-one way, though groups are also used. A brief training course is involved, but after that the procedure is free. The women's movement developed a variety of consciousness-raising groups. The men's movement has included various forms of groups where men explore how to change and develop new gender identities and gender roles (Rowan 1997).

Aiming at the whole person

Personal growth groups, in the sense of groups that did not assume any pathology, started in the 1960s as part of what was called the growth movement. They often took place in growth centres such as the Esalen Institute in California or the Open Centre in London, both of which still exist. The idea was that all the techniques used in psychotherapy, and new ones too, could also be used simply for the benefit of ordinary people with no particular illnesses or defects. They could then develop further, and leave behind their compulsions, unconsidered assumptions and unexamined values, and ascend the Maslovian ladder. They could grow to become what Carl Rogers used to call 'a fully-functioning person', or 'that self which I truly am' – what Maslow called the self-actualized person. Nowadays the number of growth centres has diminished, but the approach is more widespread than ever, forming part of virtually every course in counselling and psychotherapy which aims at authenticity. Counsellors and psychotherapists, more than most, need to be whole persons, as authenticity demands, and as Jung (1966) pointed out long ago.

Some key issues

Generally speaking, psychodynamic groups have lower horizons and more restricted aims. They are more oriented toward adjustment and coping, and therefore come more under the instrumental rubric. But some of them, with a more eclectic approach, do seem a bit more ambitious. As far as personal growth in the psychodynamic group is concerned, one of the best discussions is to be found in the chapter by Wolf and Kutash (1986). They go into the interesting question, for example, of how things can go wrong in such groups.

Some of the important issues which arise in groups are trust, safety and confrontation.

Trust

Trust influences learning, because we have to trust a communication to some degree before we can even hear it, never mind learn from it. Trust influences cooperation, because it is hard to cooperate with someone if we do not trust them. Trust influences getting along with others, establishing friendships and inspiring the confidence of one's peers.

Trust is just as important in a group as it is in individual therapy, but it is actually harder to achieve. It is important in both cases because we cannot open up to another person if we do not trust them. Risking (very necessary in a good group) and trusting go hand in hand.

In a group, if no one takes any risks, stagnation can easily result. But mistrust can get in the way of risking anything. However, there is a paradox here. There is no way of proving that anyone is trustworthy: so we are always going to have to go beyond the evidence if we are going to get anywhere at all. It there is no way of ever proving finally that a person or group is trustworthy, we may as well take a risk and find out that way. So in order to engender trust, we have to act as if we trust even if we do not trust. We have to risk if we are going to create trust. Then a two-way interaction can start up between trust and cooperation, and the whole group can come alive.

Trusting behaviour influences risk-taking. This is the basic point. To test whether someone is trustworthy involves taking some kind of risk. This testing goes on more at the beginning of a relationship than later on, but it can be renewed at any point where trust wavers. Perceived trustworthiness makes everything easier. Reliance on the words or actions of another is never total, nor should it be, because that way lies disappointment and disillusion. But openness is certainly to be aimed at: partly because it is one of the goals of groupwork in terms of personal growth. This means the owning of behaviour, and taking responsibility for our own actions or, in other words, authenticity. Less important in the end are our expectations of what others will do. The door to cooperation can only be opened from our side. We cannot expect someone else to do it for us.

Safety

Often at the beginning of a group people are a little scared of what might happen in the group. The customary reassurance about confidentiality and no violence in the group does not go very far to allay their fears. But really the best answer to this is given by Starhawk (1987: 145), when she says: 'Safety in a group is not a matter of niceness or politeness . . . But a group can establish safety by assuring that risks are shared, that boundaries are clear, and that power structures and hidden agendas are brought out into the open. We cannot eliminate risks, but we can face them with solidarity'. It is part of the role of the group facilitator to hold the boundaries of the group, and to ensure that important issues are not ignored or glossed over.

Confrontation

Confrontation (sometimes also called challenging) has to be well handled if it is to be fruitful. It is best done in the spirit of accurate empathy, really trying to get into the other person's shoes before speaking. It should be tentative rather than dogmatic. It should be done with care, meaning that there should be some real involvement with the other person. It should be done with attention to your own motivation: is it really for the other person's benefit, or for your own benefit? Use real or authentic communication so that the message comes from your own self and your own experience, not from some pseudo objectivity (Egan 1976). One handy slogan that emphasizes real communication and how to achieve it is: 'Use giraffe language, not jackal language'. Giraffe language is always a description of what is happening inside you: it is a kind of owning up. The giraffe is the animal with the biggest heart in the jungle. Jackal language attacks the other person by labelling, by blaming, by questioning, by preaching – all those types of communication which distance us from the other person and make them defensive.

Also important in a group is the way in which you respond to confrontation: try not to be defensive. Let in the communication, and make sure you understand it – ask questions if necessary to clarify what is being said, and listen to the answers.

Answers to questions

All these types of group have been well researched, and the interested reader can find the key references in Shaffer and Galinsky (1989). There is also some good material in Chapter 9 of Brammer *et al.* (1993), that goes into considerable detail and gives many further references to follow up.

Questions have been raised about the value of groups like these in counselling training, as for example by Irving and Williams (1996). Are they really necessary to good training? But good replies to the worries about this have come from Lyons (1997) and Mearns (1997). If the group can have the effect of enabling people to understand themselves better, and understand how they come across to other people better, and interact with other people more effectively, it can obviously help them to be better counsellors or psychotherapists. It seems that the personal growth group as a required part of training is not on its way out just yet.

Questions have also been raised about the politics of such groups. In fact, some of these groups have been very political (see Ernst and Goodison 1981) and have worked well in raising issues concerning feminism, sexuality, race and religious experience. Such issues are by no means ruled out in personal growth.

The future

This is a healthy and burgeoning field, and it is to be expected that such groups will continue for many years to come. Personal growth groups are grounded in a long tradition of philosophers concerned with existentialism. James Bugental (1981), who is both humanistic and existential, is one of the classic writers on the subject, particularly on authenticity: the drive to be real and fully present while being with people. In fact, there is a new interest in existentialism and phenomenology in universities at the moment (van Deurzen-Smith 1997), and personal growth groups are oriented very much towards the values of such approaches. As already mentioned, one of the key concepts in existentialism is authenticity, and this is also one of the key values in humanistic psychology.

Although it is not talked about so much in psychodynamic therapy, authenticity is in fact cultivated in that field by the use of countertransference. Getting in touch with one's own countertransference enables one to be self-aware in just the same sense as that used by people who talk about genuineness and self-actualization. Winnicott talked often about the real self, as distinguished from the false self, and of course the real self is an authentic self. Paula Heimann, in a brief paper (1950), was the first person to make waves about this issue sufficient to alert the psychoanalytic community to the importance of recognizing countertransferance as a valuable and even necessary part of being a good therapist. People then remembered that Jung had raised this question as far back as 1933.

Genuineness and authenticity are still not talked about much in academic psychology, but in a personal growth group these values are often highly cherished. People express such values in the phrase, 'Say what you mean and mean what you say' – an expression that is all about authenticity, and one which is a major aim of personal growth groups. The experience of being authentic, fully alive and present, is close to the end of the path leading to self-actualization. As I said at the beginning, it is about seeing through your own eyes, instead of seeing the world through the eyes of other people. In a postmodern climate, it is salutary to remember that truth is still important, no matter how difficult it may be to reach it. To get in touch with our own inner truth is also important, and there is a great deal of research available to say that this task is a feasible one. We can know ourselves and we can relate to others.

The transpersonal

The great pioneer in the field of groupwork in the transpersonal field was Roberto Assagioli. His follower, Piero Ferrucci (1982), wrote one of the best books on this, full of useful exercises suitable for initiating people into transpersonal work. In this field, mental imagery is used a great deal, and in a group such images can be brought into the room and worked with very thoroughly. Martha

Crampton (1969) was one of the first people to write about this, and is quoted in Diana Whitmore's (1991) excellent book on psychosynthesis.

Another technique which was pioneered in psychosynthesis was working with subpersonalities (Rowan 1990), and this is eminently suited to groupwork, where a variety of exercises can be used very fruitfully. Transpersonal training groups tend to be quite formal, rather than open-ended and free-form. They are often designed to bring out some issue that needs to be dealt with in training.

One of the most important resources in transpersonal groupwork, particularly as used in training, is the guided fantasy.

Guided fantasy

This is one of the prime areas where the transpersonal approach has dominated and led the field. So where did guided fantasy come from? Fortunately the story here is quite clear. After a number of pioneers had concentrated on imagery as very important for exploring certain psychological areas, an engineer named Desoille developed quite a sophisticated way of working, using scenes for people to imagine, which were calculated to take them up or down into relevant areas of the psyche for self-development. He called this the 'waking dream' method.

He suggested to people, without putting them into a hypnotic trance, that they imagine a scene. These scenes were carefully planned beforehand, but mostly involved ascents and descents. The ascent put the person in touch with their spiritual nature, and the descent put them in touch with their personal unconscious. In both cases archetypes (as defined by Jung) could be evoked, and were regarded by Desoille as most important. This work was developed during the 1930s.

Of course the basic approach can be used more spontaneously, taking off from a dream or fantasy which emerges from the client. The client experiences his or her personal conflicts as having an impersonal and collective background: 'The motivational (libidinal) conflict is not resolved by being transferred upon the therapist, as in psychoanalysis, rather, the patient uncovers, in himself, the basic roots of the conflict' (Assagioli 1965: 310).

Quite independently, in the 1940s and 1950s, Hanscarl Leuner was developing a system which he called 'guided affective imagery', based on some of the same sources which had inspired Desoille. In the 1960s many people took this up and Leuner renamed it 'symboldrama'.

Symboldrama uses a series of well worked out scenes, and invites the client to enter a scene. There is no need to induce a hypnotic state nor even a particularly deep state of relaxation. Leuner says that simply asking the client to sit back and imagine a flower is sufficient as a check to see whether the person is capable of symboldrama. The type of flower reported can then be a good indication of whether it is wise to proceed with this approach: a black rose, a flower that quickly wilts, a flower made of steel, a flower that develops menacing teeth, might all be indications not to use this technique for a while.

There is a sequence of scenes, and the first one is the meadow. The instructions are given like this:

> Now please try to imagine a meadow. Imagining is not difficult. Simply any meadow. If something else appears before your eyes, that's all right, too. Everything that comes along is fine. (Pause) Wait calmly and patiently until something appears before your eyes, perhaps a meadow or something else too. (Pause) And when an image appears, please talk about it. (Pause) But even if this should cause difficulties, tell me that, too, so that I can perhaps help. (Pause) You can also nod your head as a first sign that you have something in view.
>
> (Leuner 1984: 31)

Then the person is asked to explore the meadow and speak about anything that appears. This running commentary can be interrupted by the therapist if the client gets into difficulties of any kind. In one session the client was climbing a mountain, and met a huge boulder blocking the path. The therapist proposed that a bulldozer was now removing the boulder, enabling the journey to continue. This would not always be done, but it does show the range of interventions which are possible.

Mary Watkins enters an important caution at this point, by highlighting some of the possible drawbacks of the therapist introducing helpful symbols in this way:

> Desoille felt that the introduction of new symbols to the person's unconscious liberated him from 'vicious circles'. These 'vicious circles' may, however, be that person's means of getting in touch with his psyche. It is true that they may stand in the

way of certain lines of growth, but are these preferred lines the choice of the therapist or of the patient? In my opinion, directivity should not seek certain ends which are not the patient's.

(Watkins 1976: 63)

What the therapist can always do, however, is to act as if the situation were real, and ask appropriate questions, as for example, 'What colour is it? What does it do next? What else can you see?' So in a sense the therapist is right there in the scene with the client, 'in the picture' at the same time, not leading but facilitating.

Besides the meadow, other scenes include: climbing up a mountain; following the course of a stream (either from the source to the sea, or from the estuary to the source); visiting a house; the edge of the woods (these first five form the basic level for Leuner, and can be carried out with most people); an ideal person of the same sex; a cow; an elephant or bull; a lion; (for men) a rose bush; (for women) being offered a lift in a car (these form the intermediate level, and should only be used by an experienced therapist, according to Leuner); pool of water in a swamp; waiting for a figure to emerge from a cave; eruption of a volcano; and an old picture book (these last items are described as advanced, and are not so often used).

Assagioli did not discover these methods until the 1960s, but they immediately became a part of psychosynthesis, so much so that when they were introduced into encounter groups and other types of growth group in the 1960s and early 1970s they were almost always introduced as something out of psychosynthesis. It is clear in the book by Ferucci (1982) that guided fantasy (as psychosynthesis preferred to call it) can be used in a masterly and very flexible way in this discipline.

Ira Progoff has also worked in this area, and has suggested a guided fantasy of 'the road of life' (1975). This too has been taken up in psychosynthesis, and the client is encouraged to come to a crossroads and explore travelling in each direction to discover its implications.

Recently a fantasy has been used of a sphere with many concentric layers, each representing a different level of the client's personality, until the central Self is reached (Whitmore 1991: 124).

In some training courses, guided fantasy is used a great deal, because it is a good way of giving the trainee experiences which can then be explored with clients at a later date. It is important to dintinguish, however, between guided fantasy and pathworking.

Pathworking is superficially similar to guided fantasy in that it takes the person on a journey of some kind to meet some significant symbolic experience. The difference is that pathworking is not a form of therapy, and therefore it often tells the person what to think or feel. In therapeutic work one would never say: 'In the meadow you feel great peace. As you listen to the splashing of the little fountain, you feel more and more relaxed.' The emotions have to come from the client, not from the therapist.

DIALECTICAL INTERPOLATION 5: WE ARE AND ARE NOT CONCERNED WITH CURE

Some forms of therapy are more concerned with cure or adjustment – that is, with getting the person back to being as healthy as before. Other forms are more concerned with growth – that is, with helping the person to move on in their psychological development. This is often phrased as adjustment versus self-actualization. In reality, all therapists have to be able to handle the former, and many do just that. But if the therapist also has an eye to the question of growth, it is possible to help the client in that area as well. This requires the therapist to have done his or her own growthwork first.

If we assume, as we have been doing, that there are three quite different things all called therapy, we have to know how this turns out in each case.

Instrumental therapy is dedicated to cure. The client comes for the removal of symptoms which may be intensely painful or even disabling. Much crisis work is like this. In a case of bereavement, for example, it may be just a question of listening and being present on the part of the therapist. There may in such cases be no need for any technique or any specific approach at all. In any case there is usually a pretty clear focus for the work, and one might call it focused therapy. It is relatively easy for therapist and client to agree on what is wrong and how to go about making it right again. We are talking about restoration to normality. Most therapists have to do some of this work, and counsellors in particular are often faced with the need to do it, because they are often in front-line positions. In all situations where there is an external constraint on the number of sessions allowed, we have to speak of this form of therapy. And obviously if research is being done, such as for example the CORE system, the question of cure, of efficacy, will rise to the surface and have to be dealt with.

Authentic therapy is dedicated to emancipation. The client comes in either with similar symptoms (but soon reveals that more is involved), or more commonly with much vaguer complaints. Phrases like, 'My life is not working', or 'I just can't make sense of it all', or 'I should be happy but I'm not' indicate that there is no specific symptom to aim at. Such people are more in need of personal growth than any kind of cure. The task here is to open up the way for the client to move on to the next stage in their psychospiritual development. We could call this unfocused therapy. Some authentic therapists refuse to get involved with things like the CORE system, on the grounds that it falsifies all that they are trying to do. Sometimes a refusal to get involved with research may be much less justified, because not all research is statistically organized.

Transpersonal therapy is also not very much concerned with cure. June Singer (1972) speaks movingly about the time when her supervisor told her to stop worrying about whether the client was getting better or not. Transpersonal therapy is more concerned with helping the client move on in his or her psychospiritual journey. In doing so, it typically uses imagery and intuition more than either of the other two approaches. In recent times, there has been a tendency to expand the scope of the transpersonal approach by using more far-reaching but less predictable forms.

If this simple division were only better understood, many of the current arguments would be cut short. The demands of insurance companies, Employee Assistance Program employers, NHS Trusts and accountants in general for specific results would be seen to apply only to instrumental therapy. In authentic therapy there are no specific results, because there is no clear aim. In fact, the very same move from 'Esteem from others' to 'Esteem from self' (in the Maslow system for example) could mean (for one client) becoming more involved with others, more open, more compassionate, more loving or (for another) becoming less worried about the opinions of others, and more authentic and autonomous. In transpersonal therapy there is really no question of trying to produce a result at all: it is more about learning how to let go of all results.

Instrumental therapy involves horizontal translation – we move from one position to a better one at the same level. In this case there is no need to question the status quo. Authentic therapy, and still more transpersonal therapy, may involve vertical transformation, where our whole idea of who we are and what we are about may change quite radically. Our ideas about the world may also change, often becoming more challenging and less dominated by received ideas.

Looked at in this light, the old argument about short-term versus long-term therapy looks quite different. Short-term work is often very much indicated for instrumental therapy but it is seldom much use for authentic therapy. Transpersonal therapy is much more variable, because it relies so much on where the client is – it is more like midwifery than like surgery. If the person is ripe and ready enough, short-term work is sufficient.

It can happen, of course, that someone comes for instrumental therapy, but it then turns out that the problems are much older, much more deep-seated than was apparent at first. It will then become long-term work, but will not necessarily turn into any other type of therapy. A person who is damaged deeply and early may require long-term work, not because they have moved over into personal growth, but because there is so much work to be done at a deep level if anything at all is going to change. And a person who thinks they are coming for a long-term stint may find everything resolved in short order, simply because they are so ready to move on – ripeness is all.

The paradox here is that cure is and is not important. To let go of either horn of this dilemma is to risk failing to do what is most important for the client.

Chapter 6

Written work

The academic and the experiential

In the vast majority of training, and even more usually since universities have started to validate courses, we are trying to run two horses in the same harness – the academic and the experiential. Often people come in paying lip-service to the importance of the academic, but when faced with the excitement and deep involvement offered by the experiential work, they lose interest in the academic side and regard it as irrelevant or even handicapping. But it is not necessary for this to happen. The academic side has a fascination of its own. If it is taught well, it can be inspiring and enlivening. Usually the people who do the teaching of the academic work have been through their own therapy, and often they are currently engaged in the practice of psychotherapy or counselling. They really know what they are talking about at a deep level, and may use examples from their own experience and their own practice.

But the point really of the academic side, from a human point of view, is that having the language and the concepts derived from theory makes it easier to converse with, negotiate with or convince people from other disciplines. By writing essays and getting feedback on them, the student becomes able to feel more confident of their ability to speak to doctors, psychiatrists, social workers and other professionals with whom they may have to have dealings.

Another advantage is that it enables the practitioner to get away from the trap of 'flying by the seat of the pants' – having a cavalier disregard for theory. Once one gets into the habit of having such a cavalier disregard, one may be seduced into a similar disregard for ethics. A suitable self-discipline works well in both cases.

Instrumental

At the instrumental level, essays are seen as possibly the main thing on the course. Since therapy is all about getting it right, essays are seen as an important demonstration that one is doing so. Of course there are the basic differences between men and women which Belenky and her co-workers (1986) discovered. Men find it easier to adopt the critical stance valued in academia (and courses today are more and more dominated by academic values), while women tend to prefer a more positive approach, delving more deeply into one person or theory rather than comparing two or more. However, at this level there is not much resistance to toeing the line and producing essays according to the prescribed form. The whole emphasis is on playing one's role well, and this is just one part of it. A useful book here is Bor and Watts (1999), which has many helpful hints on how to write essays and tackle other written work.

At the level of dissertations there is again no problem. The student will peruse carefully the literature on dissertation writing, and will produce a dissertation with all the correct bits and pieces.

When it comes to case studies and process reports, the emphasis will be on following the conventional guidelines, perhaps using such helpful books as Papadopoulos *et al.* (2003), which covers a broad spectrum of approaches.

Authentic

At the authentic level a problem tends to appear relating to the experiential aspects of the course. The parts of the course which are devoted to experiential learning (exercises, group experiences, workshops, own therapy and so forth) are so much more rewarding personally that it becomes hard to see the value of essay writing. So there tends to be a sort of rebellious undercurrent here. It sometimes shows itself in a reluctance to do proper referencing. Someone who is otherwise quite up to scratch will suddenly produce references which are in the form of numbers, or footnotes, or long descriptions in brackets – anything but the standard Harvard referencing which is required. At this level, however, there is no problem about being critical, because the paradoxical style of thinking is beginning to appear, which sees another side to everything. If the tutor says that character styles are important, a student at this level will be seeking out all the references which critique the idea of character styles, and this will make for a good essay.

At the dissertation level, there are likely to be real problems. It is very common for students to take on subjects which are much too large, and then be unable to let go of that original concept. Precisely because the student is moving into authentic consciousness, they will be personally very involved with the subject matter they are discussing, and reluctant to omit material which they feel to be relevant or essential. There may have to be a protracted wrestling with the tutor or supervisor in order to get the length right.

Here the formulaic books are less helpful. They certainly make clear what the basic requirements are, but they do not offer much help when it comes to authentic writing.

Transpersonal

At the transpersonal level, the temptation is to turn the essay into an aesthetic exercise, and it may be illustrated with pictures or cartoons, embellished with poems or long quotations, broken up into sections with headings in different fonts, and so forth. Referencing may be quite eccentric. The bibliography tends to be either very limited, because of the tendency to go deep rather than wide, or very wide-ranging, because of the need to bring in sources from here, there and everywhere: some relevant, some not so obviously relevant. The word count may be eccentric in some way. There is no resistance to writing essays, but they may get too personal or too lacking in a real point or purpose.

Dissertations are even bigger traps for all these errors. A dissertation at this level may be highly original and groundbreaking, but the difficulty of presenting it in the required form may be excruciating. Negotiations with the supervisor may be even more demanding than those at the earlier levels.

But because of the creativity normally found at this level, a proposal may be invented that breaks the mould in some way. The 'dissertation' now takes the form of a play, or a set of poems, or a video recording – something requiring the same dedication and discipline as a dissertation, but in quite a novel form. This will be more difficult to mark than the ordinary version, but may be more stimulating all round.

DIALECTICAL INTERPOLATION 6: WE CAN AND CANNOT TAKE OUR OWN CULTURE FOR GRANTED

In earlier years, a therapist could assume that the client would come from the same country. There could be differences of age (some therapists will not take clients below or above certain ages), gender (some clients have strong views on what gender of therapist they need to see), social class (a potent source of misunderstandings) and so forth, but, broadly, client and therapist would share the same cultural background, and could take for granted a great deal of common ground. But today this is not so. Laungani (1999) lays out very clearly four differences which can appear when a western therapist meets an non-western client:

1   *Individualism and communalism.* Our western culture tends to assume that people should be responsible for themselves, and should not depend too much on other people. Moving from other support to self-support is reckoned to be a good thing, and autonomy is regularly put on the list of aims for psychotherapy. As we grow up, we should be more independent, leave home and strike out on our own. But many other cultures are much more family-oriented, and regard too much independence as harmful to the family structure. Resistance to parents is not only harmful but morally reprehensible. Identity in some cultures is ascribed rather than achieved – the person's whole being is given rather than having to be achieved. The sense of belonging, regarded in western society as something to grow out of, may be regarded elsewhere as primary, and as a source of strength. The client may even talk about 'we' where a western client would use the word 'I'. Meeting a client with this view may be profoundly disconcerting for a therapist, and training can help in reducing the number of assumptions being made.

2   *Cognitivism and emotionalism.* In western society, the idea of self-control is very important. This usually means not being at the mercy of one's feelings, as the phrase has it. Feelings are private things, not to be displayed to all and sundry. In many other cultures, however, it is regarded as inhuman to hold back feelings, and much more appropriate to show them in public. British people, in particular, are noted for not wanting to make a scene. Someone brought up like this, faced with a client from

another culture who believes in expressing feelings in public for all to see, is going to be wrong-footed or perhaps even shocked by a display of grief or anger. The question of time is also significant. In a western culture, time is regarded as linear and limited. In other cultures, time may be seen as circular and unlimited.

3   *Free will and determinism.* Part of western culture is to believe in free will. 'We are our choices', as the existential statement has it. Whatever happened to us in the past, it is our responsibility as to what we do in the present. But in some other cultures, determinism is regarded as much more important and relevant. The weight of our previous actions (and particularly moral actions), whether in this life or another one, is still with us in this view of the matter. This means that the question of responsibility is much more complex, and the therapist who takes it for granted may be quite put out by a contrary view being expressed.

4   *Materialism and spiritualism.* In western society we do have a place for religion, but for the most part we tend to act as if materialism were true. We certainly find it unusual and slightly embarrassing when ideas of the supernatural are mentioned. And so when a client talks about spirits, or taking advice from a religious authority, the therapist may be quite unable to relate to such things in an optimal way.

Obviously the degree of difference, and the extent to which these considerations will cause problems, will differ depending on the maturity of the therapist and the acculturation of the client, but they are going to hover in the background in any case, and need to be given due attention.

It is a question of respect, as much as anything else. It has often been remarked that the therapist is wiser to adopt a position of one-down, rather than one-up. Ultimately, of course, therapist and client are on the same level of humanity, but on the way to that, various differences are bound to manifest themselves. If the therapist persistently adopts the role of learner rather than teacher, this puts fewer obstacles in the way than any other choice. However, the therapist generally has a better set of maps of the psyche than does the client. If this is not the case, the therapist is going to be wrong-footed too often.

Of course this is not all there is to be said about the question of cultural differences, but perhaps it will indicate that there is a vast area here which is ignored at our peril. People from other cultures often feel a sort of automatic rejection from Europeans, and it is important that a therapist should genuinely have emerged from such a set of prejudices, which can get in the way to a great degree if they are not dealt with in training.

We also have to remember the whole anti-discriminatory movement which has now become so important. Books like Lago and Smith (2003) can be very helpful here, pointing up the importance, and the difficulties, of doing justice to this question. There are challenges here which mean that we cannot take for granted any of our standard responses to cultural difference.

The paradox is that if we forget our own culture we become a rootless thing, but if we take it for granted we become a danger to others. Holding both sides of this paradox is very important for any therapist.

Chapter 7

Ethics

Instrumental

Most of the existing work in ethics is produced by, and is most relevant to, the instrumental level. The emphasis on correctness fits very well here, and the basis of the ethical research boards which exist in universities is clearly instrumental. All the emphasis here is on getting it right, and being precise about what is allowed and what is not.

The basic principles are laid out well in the document issued by the BACP in 2002 (pp. 2–4). This states that there are six ethical principles which should be observed by practitioners:

- *fidelity*: honouring the trust placed in him or her;
- *autonomy*: respect for the client's right to be self-governing;
- *beneficence*: commitment to promoting the client's well-being;
- *non-maleficence*: commitment to avoiding harm to the client;
- *justice*: the fair and impartial treatment of all clients and the provision of adequate services;
- *self-respect*: fostering the practitioner's self-knowledge and care for self.

This agrees with many other ethical lists, and does not seem to be controversial. But of course at the instrumental level we are not satisfied with this, and want to go into some specific areas and spell out the requirements for each of them. And so in the same document we get 42 detailed points which follow from the general principles mentioned, all of which are carefully described.

One of these points deals with the question of dual relationships. The statement here is broadly framed, and goes like this (pp. 5–6):

Dual relationships arise when the practitioner has two or more kinds of relationship concurrently with a client, for example client and trainee, acquaintance and client, colleague and supervisee. The existence of a dual relationship with a client is seldom neutral and can have a powerful beneficial or detrimental impact that may not always be easily foreseeable. For these reasons practitioners are required to consider the implications of entering into dual relationships with clients, to avoid entering into relationships that are likely to be detrimental to clients, and to be readily accountable to clients and colleagues for any dual relationships that occur.

The clearest example of such a relationship is when therapist and client have sex. This sets up a dynamic which all the research to date has confirmed to be harmful to the client, and so is against the requirement of non-maleficence.

This all sounds quite bland and obvious, but it conceals two very important difficulties. One is that the psychoanalytic tradition, now most often referred to as the psychodynamic orientation, has a much stronger aversion to dual relationships than any other approach. This applies not only to sexual relations, but to any dual relationship at all. The reason for this is that the reliance on transference, which is such a feature of the analytic approach, makes it imperative to isolate and keep intact the exclusive therapist-client close relationship. To see one's therapist in a sauna, for example, might considerably affect the transference. To meet one's therapist as a waiter serving a customer might do the same. To work for one's therapist as a house painter would again be likely to harm the transference. To employ one's therapist as a consultant to one's firm – same problem again. And because of the prestige of psychoanalysis in the whole field of therapy, these views have had a huge influence on other fields and other trainings. However, the book by Lazarus and Zur (2002) has shown that this is a narrow view which ignores the facts of life in small communities, military camps, university campuses and many specialized communities. In such situations, dual relationships are the rule rather than the exception, and do no harm at all. Lazarus and Zur make an important distinction between boundary crossing and boundary violation. Boundary crossing is not normally a problem: in a local community a client may well be your window cleaner or your carpenter. Boundary violation occurs when there is some form of exploitation involved. If I as a therapist get the carpenter to do work for me for nothing because I am his therapist, that is exploitation, and ethically forbidden.

A second difficulty has to do with the increasingly litigious atmosphere in the whole field of therapy in recent years. Lawyers have been able to say that since sexual relations between therapist and client are clearly condemned by all parties, any other relationship might lead to this. And if this is accepted, then even something like saying 'Thanks' for a Christmas card might be suspect. This is the 'slippery slope' argument, which has been used successfully in litigation as an indication that the therapist has been at fault. At the instrumental level, this is taken as a very strict prohibition. Again, the Lazarus and Zur book throws quite a different light on all this, and has some strong criticisms of the legal profession.

For a therapist, some of the usual injunctions hardly make sense. For example, non-maleficence in most contexts involves not upsetting people. But in therapy it is common and I would say normal to upset people by asking them to pay attention to their problems. Clients often cry, and it is usual to provide a box of tissues for people to use when this happens, because it is so common. Yet in other contexts this would be ethically unacceptable. And even in therapeutic circles, the actions of some therapists in forcefully challenging clients is seen by some observers as unacceptable. Jeffrey Masson (1988) has been forceful in criticizing therapists like Rosen, for example, and indeed the courts took a similar view in that case.

Similarly, in most contexts it is regarded as unethical to deceive people. But family therapists, and some other therapists too, do deceive clients on a regular basis, telling them that certain actions will be positive for them when they are actually negative. And clients may respond in kind – it is quite common to hear clients saying that they would never tell their therapists about some of their actions. One therapist told me rather ruefully, 'We start by deceiving them, and then they start deceiving us.' Richard House and Nick Totton have produced a hard-hitting critique of ethical pretensions in the helping professions in which they say: 'Didactic codes of ethics can have the effect of simply redistributing abusive behaviour to less visible parts of the work rather than removing it' (1997: 325).

What is common to all therapists at this level is that they have to be aware of their ethical position, and be capable of defending it. I sometimes advise therapists to act with a client in such a way that if a reporter from a tabloid newspaper were sitting in the corner watching, he or she would find nothing worth writing about.

A particular problem arises when cases come to court through some complaint or other litigation. Terrill Gibson (2000: 180) makes the point well:

> Therapy is not designed for a courtroom. This may be hard to explain to an eager client whose own attorney tries to convince her or him of the benefits of opening confessional records to a judicial process. There, a barrister can instantly turn the most benign information into hurtful weapons that wound in unexpected and permanent ways.

It is sad but true that supervisors very often have to guide therapists to warn their clients away from taking a complaint to the ultimate sanction of the courts. There is a good discussion of these issues in Bond (1993).

Authentic

At the authentic level all this changes. Because there is supposed to be a genuine meeting between therapist and client, such that the personhood of the one is involved with whole personhood of the other, there is no emphasis on transference. Transference is just something which happens occasionally, and when it happens it can be dealt with directly. To meet the client socially or in an employment capacity is no big deal. This is not to deny transference, of course, and those psychodynamic therapists who are authentic take it just as seriously as any other psychodynamic therapists. The difference is that the real person is taken just as seriously. Petruska Clarkson (2003) has well argued that the person-to-person or dialogic relationship is always present even if not attended to, and there is nothing to stop a psychodynamic therapist from understanding this, and paying more attention to it.

On the other hand, ethical questions become much more intimate. It is no longer sufficient to quote the six principles and hope that that will take care of things. It is no longer appropriate to quote the 42 points, as if they will take care of the thing adequately. We experience ethical attitudes as a real part of ourselves. The authentic approach is about the subjectivity and intersubjectivity of human phenomena and human relations. Accordingly, it includes hermeneutics and phenomenology, and truly understands the importance of reflexivity. Ethical interests run right through this approach, because it involves treating the other person like oneself. Whatever values one holds for oneself one does not deny to the other. We have to treat the other as fully human, not as a set of variables for us to measure or a set of transferences to interpret.

Reflexivity is not a word often found in books on psychotherapy, but at the authentic level it is extremely important. Personal investments in the process of therapy are not only recognized but become a subject of attention. There is a kind of humility about this. The authentic therapist will admit to mistakes when they occur, and not hide behind the role. There is a political aspect, too. Patti Lather challenges us 'to develop a kind of self reflexivity that will enable us to look closely at our own practice in terms of how we contribute to dominance in spite of our liberatory intentions.'(1991: 50). The ethical demand here is to throw on ourselves the same pitiless light we direct onto the client, and to accept that we are subject to the same pressures, the same social demands, that apply to the client.

Phenomenology has deep roots, and continually questions the way in which we take for granted the categories of the everyday world (Valle 1998). There are also now new forms of phenomenology such as existential-phenomenological research and hermeneutical-phenomenological studies (von Eckartsberg 1998). One of the most noted exponents of existential phenomenology in this country is of course Ernesto Spinelli, who says:

> As *authentic* beings, we recognize our individuality. Further, we recognize that this individuality is not a static quality but is, rather, a set of (possibly infinite) potentialities. As such, while in the authentic mode, we maintain an independence of thought and action, and subsequently feel 'in charge' of the way our life is experienced. Rather than reacting as victims to the vicissitudes of being, we, as authentic beings, acknowledge our role in determining our actions, thought and beliefs, and thereby experience a stronger and fuller sense of integration, acceptance, 'openness' and 'aliveness' to the potentialities of being-in-the-world.
>
> (1989: 109)

This seems to me a fine statement of the authentic view in therapy, and it shows how important the existential-phenomenological approach is if we want to understand authenticity in therapy.

Hermeneutics also has its place and needs to be understood but it

is not often found in the index of a psychotherapy text: 'A herme-
neuticist sees his culture and self as the product of a tradition that he
is both perpetuating and changing through the act of interpretation
. . . Observer and observed are both embedded in historical contexts
through which any interpretations must be conducted' (Bentz &
Shapiro 1998: 109–10). There is a full discussion of hermeneutics in
Chapter 10 of Reason and Rowan (1981).

One of the ways in which hermeneutics comes into therapy is
through the concept of countertransference. By being in touch with
our countertransference we can be in touch not only with the client
at a very deep level, but also in touch with the social context in which
all therapy takes place. Andrew Samuels (1993) has been one of the
foremost writers to contend for this view.

Take this statement from David Berg and Kenwyn Smith (1988: 25).
They say that for them good work of any kind with human beings
entails:

1   direct involvement with and/or observation of human beings or
    social systems;
2   commitment to a process of self-scrutiny by the researcher as he
    or she conducts the research;
3   willingness to change theory or method in response to the
    research experience *during* the research itself;
4   description of social systems that is dense or thick and favours
    depth over breadth in any single undertaking; and
5   participation in the social system being studied, under the
    assumption that much of the information of interest is only
    accessible to or reportable by its members.

This is a good statement of the authentic position in the ethics of
research, which also applies in an analogical way with the ethics of
therapy. In item 3 above, for example, we only have to substitute the
word 'therapy' for the word 'research' to make perfect sense.

In this arena feminists have been very active, and have helped to
shape this way of looking at the world. Feminists have been very
influential in introducing critiques which have made a real difference
to the world of therapy: 'The women's movement has brought forth
a scholarship that emphasizes identification, trust, empathy and
non-exploitative relationships' (Punch 1994: 89). They have paid
particular attention to the Self-Other relationship, and indeed to the
hyphen which connects Self and Other (Fine 1994: 70–82). This

raises profound ethical questions, which Laura Brown has spelt out in some detail (1997: 51–67). On the other hand:

> By contrast, critical psychology generally views the individual and society as so fundamentally intertwined that they cannot be separated from one another in any way that makes sense. Individuals and the social world they inhabit are one and the same thing, two ways of looking at the same phenomenon. The problem then becomes explaining this reality, not in terms of a *relationship* between two separate phenomena, but in terms of some sort of totality or whole.
>
> (Nightingale & Neilands 1997: 73)

We start really to come up against social issues. Most of the previous ethical concerns were about individuals. Now we are also concerned about the effect of our work on a whole organization or community. Our social vision, our social philosophy, come into play. We have to be careful about the side-effects of our actions, the unintended consequences of our therapeutic efforts.

If we deepen our authenticity, and insist on the other participants relating to us in an authentic fashion, we take another step on the ethical path. All the previous issues become intensified. We might say at this stage:

1   Therapists recognize that all therapy carries with it the ideological assumptions of the therapist, reflective of his or her time in history and position of power within a culture and subcultures.
2   An honest evaluation is made of how these assumptions affect all phases of the therapeutic inquiry, including the choice of areas to explore and the methods and theory employed.
3   As a result of this analysis, balancing points of view are considered and employed. Where balance is not completely feasible, therapists disclose their assumptions, as well as aspects of the procedures and conclusions that favour the view of any one group, culture or subculture over another.
4   When the therapy uses the experience of past therapy, each successive involvement is more balanced in empowering the silenced voices of society and thereby attempts to rectify the imbalances of past therapy and more fully explicate and understand the phenomenon being studied.

5   Taking seriously the power of knowledge in culture, therapists
     work individually and collaboratively to balance the hierarchical
     structures inherent in therapy and to create better structures
     for the benefit of all people (adapted from Anderson & Braud
     1998: 248).

We are now talking about power much more, and bring up to
awareness many matters which were dormant before. We are also
talking about the self of the therapist as an issue. What are the
unspoken assumptions of the therapist, and can the therapist become
much more aware of these? What are the needs of the therapist for
emotional support when getting so close to other people? With
reflexivity coming to the fore so much more, the therapist may need a
support group, a supervisor or some form of co-counselling in order
to survive.

It is fair to say that this approach to therapy asks more from the
therapist than did the earlier types. Only at this level is the therapist
aware that there are alternative frames, that perceptions, including
one's own, are always framed by assumptions, and that such assumptions can be tested and transformed. So awareness is not only deeper,
but wider too.

Transpersonal

At the transpersonal level, the distance between therapist and client
diminishes once again, and it is hard for transference to creep in
anywhere. By working through the authentic level (and it is hard to
obtain a genuine transpersonal experience without having done this)
one has dealt with one's Shadow material and made the unconscious
conscious. That is what happens at the authentic level. Now one
is free to inhabit the client's world completely. The ultimate dual
relationship has already happened: the client is not just a client, but
also a friend, a colleague, a customer, a brother or sister, a parent, a
child, everything. It would still be unwise and inappropriate to have
a sexual relationship with the client – both because it is unethical
at this level, and also because of the reactions of the outside world.
The injunctions to the therapist change again at this level, as the
Buddhist version has it:

1   Become aware of your personal addictions or addictive needs
     with regard to your work as a therapist.

2   Become aware of how you define and construct the client as 'Other'.
3   Through the practice of compassion and right conduct, pay attention to the suffering of sentient beings in the world, and ask yourself what kind of inquiry and action would diminish that suffering.
4   By following the Eightfold Path of Buddhism, focused on rightness of thought and action, and increasing your own mindfulness and non-attachment to things and desires, increase your capacity to experience ecstasy, particularly in relation to both the object and the process of inquiry (adapted from Bentz & Shapiro 1998: 52–3).

It is of course not necessary to be a Buddhist to appreciate the importance of ecstasy. In this approach, intuition becomes important as a basic way of knowing, not just an erratic source of hunches. It takes its place alongside propositional knowledge, practical knowledge and experiential knowledge as one of the big four in the theory of knowledge. At this level of consciousness, intuition becomes normal rather than abnormal, regular rather than chancy, dependable rather than capricious. We can cultivate intuition, value intuition, work with intuition every day.

So we now have to pay ethical attention to the spiritual level in human beings, not to everyday life. If we ignore that, we are leaving out something quite crucial. If a whole person includes body, feelings, intellect, soul and spirit, we have to do justice to that whole person in all their glory. Otherwise we are are selling the person short, depriving them of their birthright.

Because of the opening up which the transpersonal approach offers, we are able to survey the whole field and make new decisions as to what is fitting and suitable for a given piece of work, without being necessarily limited to just one outlook, just one point of view. This is not a question of looking into one's toolbox and choosing the right tool. It is a case of going into a place of not-knowing, and waiting.

We have to take into account all the ethical principles we have encountered so far, and determine how to apply them in a given situation. This is the highest and most demanding ethical position of all, and requires most attention from the therapist. We have to know how to think and act appropriately in each therapeutic setting, taking care of the participants, ourselves and the wider society in all its ramifications, and paying attention to the spiritual implications of what we are doing.

It must be acknowledged that the power imbalance between therapist and client remains, despite the use of democratizing practices and the efforts of the therapist to disown and shrug off the role of expert. It is the therapist who is firmly positioned by the client as knowledgeable, who sets the process in motion, who decides on the initial questions to ask, which frameworks to use, which prospective clients to take on. In the final analysis it is the therapist's version of reality that is given public visibility. It is perhaps not possible to achieve complete mutuality and equality. As always, we simply have to do the best we can, and leave the rest to the highest or deepest we know. Not everything can be controlled as we might wish.

Suicide threats

But what if the client threatens suicide? The practitioner at the instrumental level will see any tendency to countenance such a thing as maleficence, because it means harm to the client, and will therefore do everything to prevent it happening. Such a practitioner will see nothing amiss about calling in the health services or even the police to prevent such an occurrence. There is a good discussion of this question in Bond (1993), including the legal issues involved.

At the authentic level, the practitioner will see this as an existential choice, and will go no further than helping the client face and deal with such a choice. The existential respect for autonomy will lead the practitioner to avoid any attempt to control the client. And the existential respect for death will encourage the practitioner to enable the client to explore in deep detail all the feelings and assumptions which may make it difficult for him or her to understand what death means.

At the transpersonal level, the practitioner will in most cases not regard death as final, and will therefore feel much easier about enabling the client to deal with the matter in a completely unpressured way. If death is not the end, then it will be just as important to explore the beliefs and feelings associated with what happens after death. Perhaps the therapist will encourage the client to go into a past-life experience where death was experienced in some fashion. Not every transpersonal therapist will necessarily work with past lives, and there is no particular expectation that this will be so. Every effort will be made to explore all the ramifications of what death means to the person.

DIALECTICAL INTERPOLATION 7: EMPATHY IS AND IS NOT A SKILL

When we speak about empathy we mostly refer to the version put forward by Carl Rogers. Here are some of the things he and other authors have said about it.

> The third condition we may call empathic understanding. When the therapist is sensing the feelings and personal meanings which the client is experiencing in each moment, when he can perceive these from 'inside', as they seem to the client, and when he can successfully communicate something of that understanding to the client, then this third condition is fulfilled . . . When the therapist can grasp the moment-to-moment experiencing which occurs in the inner world of the client as the client sees it and feels it, without losing the separateness of his own identity in this empathic process, then change is likely to occur.
>
> (Rogers 1961: 62–3)

> The fourth condition for therapy is that the therapist is experiencing an accurate, empathic understanding of the client's world as seen from the inside. To sense the client's private world as if it were your own, but without ever losing the 'as if' quality – this is empathy, and this seems essential to therapy. To sense the client's anger, fear or confusion as if it were your own, yet without your own anger, fear or confusion getting bound up in it, is the condition we are endeavouring to describe.
>
> (Rogers 1961: 284)

> One of its implications is that the techniques of the various therapies are relatively unimportant except to the extent that they serve as channels for fulfilling one of the conditions. In client-centred therapy, for example, the technique of 'reflecting feelings' has been described and commented on. In terms of the theory here being presented, this technique is by no means an essential condition of therapy. To the extent, however, that it provides a channel by which the therapist communicates a sensitive empathy and an unconditional positive regard, then it may serve as a technical channel by which the essential conditions of therapy are fulfilled.
>
> (Kirschenbaum & Henderson 1990: 233)

Rogers wrote extensively about empathy and often suggested that of the three 'core conditions' it is the most trainable . . . Rogers wrote of empathy: 'It involves being sensitive, moment to moment, to the changing felt meanings which flow in this other person, to the fear or rage or tenderness or confusion or whatever, that he/she is experiencing. It means temporarily living in his/her life, moving about in it delicately without making judgements, sensing meanings of which he/she is scarcely aware, but not trying to uncover feelings of which the person is totally unaware, since this would be too threatening. It includes communicating your sensings of his/her world as you look with fresh and unfrightened eyes at elements of which the individual is fearful. It means frequently checking with him/her as to the accuracy of your sensings, and being guided by the responses you receive. You are a confident companion to the person in his/her inner world' (Rogers 1980: 142). No therapist can be the 'confident companion' of which Rogers speaks in this moving passage unless he or she is secure enough in his or her own identity to enter the other's world without fear of getting lost in what may turn out to be bizarre or even frightening terrain.

(Thorne 1992: 38–9)

[Empathy] is one of the most potent aspects of therapy because it releases, it confirms, it brings even the most frightened client into the human race. If a person can be understood, he or she belongs (Thorne 1986: 129).

But in the fulness of time, researchers wanted to pin down empathy more precisely so that it could be researched more easily. Also their research results could then be used in training, where it was convenient to be able to measure empathy. Students could then be rated on their mastery of this skill. Two of the most assiduous researchers were Truax and Carkhuff. Here is the scale they produced to measure empathy.

- *Level 1*: the verbal and behavioural expressions of the helper either do not attend to or detract significantly from the verbal and behavioural expressions of the helpee in that they communicate significantly less of the helpee's feelings than the helper has communicated.
- *Level 2*: while the helper responds to the expressed feelings of the

helpee, he does so in such a way that he subtracts noticeable affect from the communications of the helpee.

- *Level 3*: the expressions of the helper in response to the expressions of the helpee are essentially interchangeable with those of the helpee in that they express essentially the same affect and meaning.
- *Level 4*: the responses of the helper add noticeably to the expressions of the helpee in such a way as to express feelings a level deeper than the helpee was able to express himself.
- *Level 5*: the helper's responses add significantly to the feeling and meaning of the expressions of the helpee in such a way as to accurately express feelings levels below what the helpee himself was able to express or in the event of ongoing deep self-exploration on the helpee's part, to be fully with him in his deepest moments (Carkhuff 1969: 174–5).

It can be seen here very clearly that the attempt is a strong one, and in fact it has been taken up in training courses, which have produced scales to be filled in for trainees.

But is this a good idea? Whether it is working in a job, or a question of finding a job, or whether it is getting other people to interweave their tasks with yours, communication is essential. And it is one of the areas where managers are often weakest. They tend to think that if they say something clearly, the other person will understand and act accordingly. They often do not appreciate that communication is a two-way thing. You cannot know whether you have communicated unless you get some feedback confirming it. Counsellors understand this, and often get called in to run courses on counselling skills or other communication skills.

Communication is sometimes reduced to 'communication skills' which can be taught on a short course – in fact the courses seem to get shorter and shorter – but this is to turn it into something mechanical, which it cannot be. It is something human, and depends for its success on human qualities. Counsellors understand this, too, but it is often hard for them to get the message across to the people involved. What I want to argue here is that we should give up the idea of teaching communication skills, except to people who already have the requisite human qualities.

What do we mean by human qualities? One of the essentials for good communication is to be genuinely present. As Alvin Mahrer (1978: 591) puts it rather convincingly:

The intensely experiencing person is with you: he does not merely talk about being with you or tell you about it. He is irritated at you, rather than talking with you about his irritation. He shares with you – instead of telling you about sharing, or explaining how important sharing is, or lapsing romantic about the notion of sharing.

This quality of being genuinely present is not easy to achieve. As Mahrer is telling us, it can only be done by someone who is open to intense experiencing. It cannot be done by defensive people, who are not in touch with their inner experiencing, and shut down on any suspicion of intensity. Carl Rogers called it genuineness, and said that it was one of the most important qualities for a therapist to possess, particularly when working with the most difficult clients. Ronnie Laing called it presence, and remarked on how central a quality it was for any therapist, no matter what school they might come from.

Let us look at another human quality. Openness is a very important key to communication. It is a synergistic question: if I am open that makes it easier for you to be open, and if you are open that makes it easier for me to be open. And if we are open, communication flows easily instead of meeting with blocks and misunderstandings. One of the discoveries of modern management theory is that openness and trust are necessary to good communication. We now talk about management *with* people rather than managing *over* people. We distinguish between healthy and unhealthy organizations, saying that in a healthy organization conflicts are brought out and dealt with openly and are not ignored. This is true in all human relationships. This quality of openness is all about being non-defensive. Being defensive keeps the other person out, at a distance; it does not let them in. It has been argued that openness is the secret of self-actualization. It is the opposite of aiming at safety and self-protection. Maslow used to say that at every moment we had the choice between safety and growth.

A third discovery is the value of honesty. The late Will Schutz spelt out in great detail the importance of telling the truth. He said: 'Individual empowerment is enhanced through learning and examining the truth, through increasing self-awareness, and through recognising the ability of each of us to choose our own life. This aim is accomplished while supporting the humanness of us all' (1984: 3). This comes hard to many managers, who have been socialized into hierarchical patterns. Such a manager wants control, and does not feel easy until it is achieved: yet the implication of all the work which has been done on communication is that the attempt to control people always reduces the extent and accuracy of any communication. People just do not like being treated as impersonal things, to be controlled like things. Communication is only possible between equals, and if one person tries to control another, that necessary sense of equality is lost. One of the joys of genuine human development is dropping the need to control, the need to defend one's ego, the need to be right. And this enables us to see the value of constant learning. At every moment we have the choice between the path of learning and the path of protection which conserves all our existing beliefs and values.

However, presence, openness, constant learning and a commitment to truth are only four of the interpersonal qualities that are needed, either at work or in getting work, or in negotiating about work. We neglect interpersonal qualities at our peril. One of the less obvious things about counselling is that it offers a demonstration, live, week by week, of good interpersonal qualities. The client gets angry at the counsellor, the counsellor responds in a non-defensive fashion: what an excellent example of the quality of openness. The client gets into an area the counsellor has never been into or dealt with, and the counsellor learns how to get into and deal with that area: what an excellent example of commitment to constant learning. The client ignores and rejects the counsellor, but the counsellor refuses to be destroyed: what a good example of the quality of presence. The client gets confused and goes off in all directions, but the counsellor gently brings him or her back to the point at issue: what a good example of the quality of gentle leadership.

If, of course, the counsellor does not have such human qualities, no such examples can be given, but it is hoped that any decent training explores such matters. It is also to be hoped that training in counselling would include enough personal work to ensure the graduate is opened up to intense experiencing as part of the process. In my experience most of the people on a good training course do consider it a form of initiation into deeper experience, and act accordingly. Any training which omitted therapy for the counsellor would be unlikely to cover all the areas necessary to achieve this. We cannot develop qualities such as these without opening ourselves up in the presence of another person. Groupwork, too, is essential in my opinion, because it is only in a group that all our interpersonal peculiarities can come out, be recognized and worked on. Gradually we can come to be less defensive of our precious egos, and less determined to hang on to our personal put-downs. We can work on and lose our self-defeating stories about how we are and how we came to be that way. This is a long process, not a short one.

What I am trying to say is that what counsellors do best is counselling. When asked to run a quick course on communication skills they would be better advised to offer straight counselling instead. The skills are in applying the qualities mentioned, and others too, such as empathy for an obvious example, so that the client, or the employee, can receive them and get the benefit of them. But we can only teach the skills of applying them if they are there to start with. If they have not yet been developed, trying to apply them can only be a kind of false performance. We are not trying to train human impersonators – that would be a dangerous and unworthy thing to do.

This is really the same point that Dave Mearns has been urging since about 1990. He has been saying that if we want to do person-centred counselling, we have to be person-centred people. To the extent that we are not, we are kidding ourselves and kidding the client (Mearns & Thorne 2000). We are putting on a performance rather than being person-centred, which means having the human qualities which are required. Let us then be clear about the difference between skills and qualities.

Coming back now to empathy, recent work has been moving into the area of making more distinctions about the various activities which can be included under the heading of empathy. Let us look at five of these:

1   *Empathic understanding responses.* These are simple reflections that are intended to communicate understanding of clients' experiences. They may also be symbolic representations of clients' implicit experiences that they themselves have not quite stated fully. These responses begin to fill out the canvas on which clients' life experiences will be drawn. Thus they also begin to help clients see aspects of their experience freshly and in new ways.

2   *Empathic affirmation responses.* These responses are meant to confirm and corroborate a client's sense of self and situation. They convey a sense that the therapist is right beside the client and sees and understands how good or bad things seem to be right now. At these moments therapists are not pushing clients

to explore their experience but are rather standing together with them, confronting things as they truly are.

3   *Empathic evocation.* With these responses therapists are trying to concretely evoke and heighten clients' experiences of events so that their impact and significance become clear. By heightening clients' access to their inner experiences therapists can help clients to better differentiate their emotional reactions and obtain clearer views of their situations. To do this therapists try to use fresh, connotative language that will throw clients' experiences into sharp relief.

4   *Empathic exploration.* These types of response have a probing, tentative quality to help clients explore the peripheries and margins of their experience. These responses are attempts to have clients go further into the tunnel of their experience, to unpack and illuminate aspects of it of which they are unaware and that might give them a somewhat different view. It is in this way that therapists help to reveal what is unspoken and assumed by clients. Here clients are being asked to go beyond that which they have represented and to peer into other corners of their experience to see if something has been missed, or could be rendered more fully, and to re-evaluate and confirm their perspective and construction of reality.

5   *Empathic conjecture.* These responses are attempts by the therapist to tease out the implicit meanings of what the client is saying. Here the therapist is attentive to the nuances of the client's experience. Usually this requires that therapists be attentive and highly sensitive to the language their clients are using as well as their non-verbal behaviour as they try to amplify and develop what the client is saying. Empathic conjecture is when therapists try to distil the personal meaning of events for their clients (Watson *et al.* 1998: 70–3).

These seem to me to be very useful distinctions, showing how empathy is deeper and wider than we thought before. But let us look at just one more issue before we leave. This is: what is the difference between empathy and love?

An example of the difference between love and empathy occurred when a husband looked at his wife quietly reading across the room, felt overwhelmed with love for her, and rushed over to hug her. This triggered a loud and irate response in the woman, because her experience in that moment was not of being loved by him, but of having him suddenly and violently break into her peaceful contemplation – leading to an argument with hurt feelings on both sides. Here the man was not acting empathically towards her, but responding only to the excitement of his own loving feelings. The unique experience of the woman in that moment was unseen, and so transgressed.

Much the same can happen when caregivers express their love and care for the child, or their excitement over the achievements of the child – the emphasis may be on their love and care, upon their excitement, rather than on the unique experience of the child. Without empathy, love and affection will not be directed at the person, but at some aspect of the person or, worse, at one's own fantasy of the person.

(Firman & Gila 1997: 95)

This seems a point well worth making.

Chapter 8

Research

Research awareness

The first step is to emphasize research awareness as a part of every module taught on any training course. This means that the tutor will refer as appropriate to the research which informed the material being presented. In many cases there is no formal research, because the theory being presented emerged from clinical material rather than formal research. Nevertheless, it did come from somewhere, and tutors will normally make clear what that source was, and when it was. Knowing these sources enables the student to be suitably critical, and not to take too much for granted. In the cases where formal research was carried out, the place and date can be stated and references given. The point is that students are always entitled to ask the question, 'How do we know this?'

Social effects

Not only are we interested in where some piece of information comes from, we are also interested in where it is going. What is its relevance? How has this theory or conclusion been received? How has it been used? How widespread is its influence? What is its place in the world? In an integrative course these are important questions, and they can be specified by doing a little research.

Research methods

One of the most interesting things that has been happening in the world of research is the move from the dominance of quantitative methods (methods which rely on numbers and statistics for their basis) towards the increased acceptance of qualitative methods – methods which avoid numbers and statistics and rely instead on greater depth. The instrumental mind finds this hard to accept, because in a way it goes against the grain, but even the most instrumental viewpoint has to admit that qualitative methods are much more effective if we want to get real understanding of what is going on and what really motivates people. A good account of what is involved here is to be found in the work of Arne Collen (1998), who uses a concept of levels which is very similar to the levels being urged in the current volume.

Philosophy

There is also a different philosophy behind the newer methods. The philosophy behind quantitative research is positivism, or sometimes post-positivism. This brings with it an emphasis on objectivism – the belief that objectivity is always the best thing or the only thing to aim at. In the world of therapy, however, we have found that a disciplined subjectivity is what we need if we are to avoid the many traps of the medical model. And it is this disciplined subjectivity which is needed and valued in qualitative research. Instead of taking on the impossible task of remaining totally outside what we are studying, we admit that we are involved, and we take the risk of influencing the phenomena in front of us.

Being research aware means that we must be acutely aware of the dangers of reification.

Reification

Reification is that process by which we take a theoretical concept and turn it into a real thing. Put at its most general, it is treating things of one type as if they were things of another. Treating an idea as a real thing is just one example of this.

For example, Kohut criticizes the reification inherent in Freud's tripartite model, especially the reification of the ego by Hartmann and the ego psychologists. They wrote as if there actually was such a thing as the ego, and therefore there could be no questioning of such a concept, and so no room for Kohut's idea of a self (see Siegel 1996).

Reification is similar to Whitehead's notion of 'misplaced concreteness', which is the way in which we can take something as abstract as the schizoid position, and start to treat it as if it were a real thing. If someone said that there might be no such thing as a schizoid position, anyone who thought it was a real thing would be unable to hear that, or accept it.

Talking about things, or ourselves and others as though we were things, keeps out any emotional responses or other genuine involvement, as Perls used to say. If we take something like depression as a real thing, rather than as a way of describing certain processes in certain contexts, we fall into the trap of objectivism.

Objectivism, like scientism, or positivism, assumes that there is a truth out there that is independent of anyone's subjective opinions. This is now a discredited view, and we now realize much better how truth is constructed in social contexts. We talk about *a* truth rather than *the* truth. Someone told me that in one of the psychosynthesis institutes they used a blackboard which had printed in one corner, 'This is not the truth'.

Putting all this together, we see that concepts such as the ego, the unconscious, the oral personality, the masochistic posture and so forth come in the realm of theory. They are concepts which may or may not be useful in certain contexts. They do not represent the truth.

It is therefore very important when teaching about such concepts not to leave students with the impression that they represent real things out there in the world for all to see, like tables and chairs. This is a bitter pill for the instrumental outlook to swallow, but swallow it they must, if they are to do good research. Reification is not just a quirk to be accepted with a shrug – it is a serious philosophical mistake and just has to be corrected.

Research is complicated

There is a paradox inherent in the idea of research: on the one hand there is a plethora of different research traditions, each with its own history and its own rules; and on the other hand there is just one basic form of research. It is important to do justice to both, if we are to get interested in research. If we just notice the multitude of methods, we may throw up our hands and declare the whole thing impossible; if we just notice the one basic form, we may oversimplify and not do justice to that which we study. Let us therefore look at both. We have to understand that there are many approaches to research. However, they group rather naturally into four main styles.

The first is the positivist and empiricist style, which comprises the following:

- quantitative research
- quasi-experimental research
- positivism/postpositivism
- experimental research
- empirical positivism

These are the styles of research with which we are most familiar. They all assume that human beings are material objects to be studied from a suitable distance, and that the best way to treat them is to reduce them to variables. The difference between observer and observed is taken for granted and not examined in any way. Postpositivism is not so rigid but is basically little different, just a little more flexible.

The advice is not to get involved with this type of research unless you are prepared to feel alienated, and unless you have a good grasp of statistical method. You will have to reduce whatever you are studying to a set of variables which can be counted. That which cannot be counted does not exist for this approach. On the other hand, this is the best approach if you want hard data, which can be used to beat someone over the head. Yet even here there is a paradox: administrators often want the hardest statistics to prove their point, yet when they get the figures they generally ignore them, and are actually much more influenced by the juicy quotes which are also often included. Don't be fooled by the demand for objectivity: the people who commission research generally want it to demonstrate what they already believe.

And there is even a further point to notice, which is that scientists who set the pattern for this kind of approach – hard scientists studying things rather than people – do not actually follow many of their own precepts, as Ian Mitroff (1974) showed years ago in a fascinating but little-read book.

The second style is the same sort of thing, but less alienated. The researcher is more involved with the other participants, and more personally present. The following come within this rubric:

- field studies
- symbolic interactionism
- qualitative (little q) studies

- causal-comparative studies
- correlational studies

These are styles of research which expose the researcher to the real world, where the people being researched are allowed to use their own language and their own perceptions of the world. But the researcher is still separate, and only contacts the others in order to extract information from them. It is the researcher who holds the entire responsibility for the research plan, the research execution and the research communication. Kidder and Fine (1987, 1997) use the terms 'big Q' and 'little q' to distinguish qualitative research which fully distinguishes itself from quantitative research, as against qualitative research which still falls within the general rules of quantitative research.

Third comes a style of research which occupies a rather uncomfortable space, and is more pretentious than the previous style, claiming to be developing theory and not just taking it for granted. Here we encounter:

- grounded theory
- discourse analysis
- multi-method eclecticism
- textual analysis
- hermeneutic studies

These are styles of research which occupy an uneasy middle ground, often trying to get closer to the other participants, but not being quite sure what their own role is. There is a much greater openness here to genuine discovery, and much less prejudgement as to the outcome, but it is limited and a bit half-hearted in most cases. Denzin and Lincoln (2000: 15) say this is the realm of 'blurred genres'.

Two books by Clifford Geertz, *The Interpretation of Cultures* (1973) and *Local Knowledge* (1983), defined the beginning and end of this moment. In these two works, Geertz argued that the old functional, positivist, behavioural, totalizing approaches to the human disciplines were giving way to a more pluralistic, interpretive, open-ended perspective. This new perspective took cultural representations and their meanings as its point of departure. Calling for 'thick description' of particular events rituals, and customs, Geertz suggested that all anthropological writings were interpretations of interpretations. The observer had no privileged voice in the interpretations that were written. The central task of theory was to make sense out of a local situation.

Geertz went on to propose that the boundaries between the social sciences and the humanities had become blurred. Social scientists were now turning to the humanities for models, theories and methods of analysis (semiotics, hermeneutics). A form of genre dispersion was occurring: documentaries that read like fiction (Mailer), parables posing as ethnographies (Castaneda), theoretical treatises that look like travelogues (Levi-Strauss). At the same time, many new approaches were emerging: poststructuralism (Barthes), neo-positivism (Philips), neo-Marxism (Althusser), micro-macro descriptivism (Geertz), ritual theories of drama and culture (V. Turner), deconstructionism (Derrida) and ethnomethodology (Garfinkel). The golden age of the social sciences was over, and a new age of blurred, interpretive genres was upon us. The essay as an art form was replacing the scientific article. At issue now is the author's presence in the interpretive text, or how the researcher can speak with authority in an age when there are no longer any firm rules concerning the text, its standards of evaluation and its subject matter (Geertz 1988: 9). Much of this information is taken from Denzin and Lincoln (2000) in the Introduction to their great *Handbook*.

The fourth style is the most recent, and the most complex. Doubtless in the future it will split into a number of separated forms, but for the moment such research seems most at home in such journals as *Qualitative Inquiry*.

- phenomenological research
- organic studies
- cooperative ecological inquiry
- action research/developmental action inquiry
- interpretive/constructivist approaches
- feminist research
- heuristic studies
- qualitative (Big Q) studies
- emancipatory approaches
- transformative approaches

These are the most interesting styles of research which have emerged, and what they have in common is an openness to involving other people much more, and on more different levels. There is a social awareness which means much more attention being paid to the social context within which the research takes place, and to the social results of the research process. It is here that we find transpersonal research approaches, described by Braud and Anderson (1998), and mindfulness research, described by Bentz and Shapiro (1998). A good summary of all this is to be found in Mertens (1998).

Research is simple

In spite of all this complication, there is only one basic form which research always takes. The differences arise out of the way in which this single form is used. The form can be seen in Figure 8.1.

If we look at a representation of the basic standard research cycle, we can see that it has a very definite form, with some unavoidable stages within it (Rowan 2001b). We normally start over on the left-hand side, just being. We are working happily away in our field, when some disturbance arises. It may be negative, in that we have to solve some problem in order to survive; or it may be positive, in that we see an opportunity and take it. There are many possibilities as to why we should need to take action, but when we do so, the first thing we do is to get more information. This is the phase I have called thinking. During this stage we are taking in material and processing it, in order to find whether there is some answer already, so that we do not need to do research. We survey the literature, we make

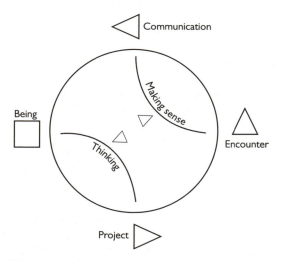

Figure 8.1 The research cycle

telephone calls, we pick people's brains, we keep our antennae out, we lay ourselves open to receiving ideas and information. During this process, we become clearer as to what our research question really is.

At a certain point, when we are sure that we do have a question but do not have an answer, we start inventing a project. Projects are very important: Sartre once said that people are known by their projects. A project is a plan of action, a statement that if we do this, we shall get the answers we need. We may revise the project, scrap the project and start again, amend the project in the light of advice from experienced people in the field, and so on. The project may be invented by one person, or be the result of much consultation with a number of people, but it has to be a plan of some kind.

But at a certain point, we need to abandon planning and actually get out into the field and do something. Here comes the encounter with reality, the test of all our planning and plotting. We open ourselves up to the possibility of disconfirmation. We lay ourselves open to the possibility of learning something, genuinely and for ourselves. And there is a paradox here: the more planning we have done, the more spontaneous we can be in responding to the needs of the new situation as it presents itself.

Again, at a certain point the involvement has to stop. We have to stand back and assess where we have got to, bring all the results together and make sense of them. Some of this is done by contemplation and soaking ourselves in the data, and some is done by thinking and analysing and systematizing the results obtained. We may do it on our own, or a part of a research group, or with the participants in the research itself.

Eventually we arrive at something communicable, and we put it out in some form. We write or co-write a report, we go on television, we speak to journalists, we go on chat shows, whatever seems to be appropriate and possible. This is the stage of communication. And when we have delivered ourselves of all we have to say, we go back to being again, in our field, as before but not as before. Once more around the spiral.

Now that we have this general schema for what research is, we can use it in an interesting way. Suppose we represent alienation by a dotted line, and non-alienation by a solid line. And suppose that we represent the researcher by the circle, and the people whose experience is being studied by a line making some sort of contact with the circle. Then pure basic research, quantitative empirical research, would look like Figure 8.2. The circle represents the researcher being alienated and role-bound, and the line represents the subject meeting the researcher, only at a tangent, at the point of encounter, or in other words only during the experiment or observation or survey. We can show another style of research in Figure 8.3. Here the solidity of the lines means that neither the researcher nor the subject is alienated, but the two only meet even now at one point on the cycle. The researcher is genuinely open to the subject, and is setting or making

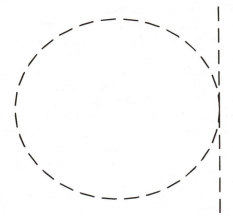

Figure 8.2 Quantitative empirical research

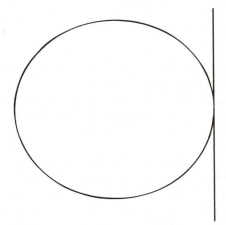

Figure 8.3 Non-alienated research

use of a situation in which the subject is genuinely open to the researcher, but is not otherwise involving the subject in the whole research process.

It is also possible to show the extent of the involvement between researcher and subject. Figure 8.4 illustrates research in which there is a greater degree of participation. Here the dashed line indicates that the degree of alienation varies, depending on the people involved and the social context. But the crucial difference is that the research subjects are also involved in the project stage and the communication stage. This means that they are involved in planning the research, and also involved in the final interpretation of what the research outcomes mean. We can now show more authentic types of research which both decrease the amount of alienation and involve the subjects at more points on the cycle (see Figure 8.5). This is the kind of more humanistic research which is represented in many of the examples in this book, where all are authentically engaged on most points of the research cycle. In some cases the being and thinking points are also involved, particularly if the researchers engage in more than one inquiry cycle. This model is useful because it can be used to sketch out a research project at the planning stage, or as a means of checking the quality of interaction.

From an **instrumental** point of view, research is not only desirable but necessary. There is a strong tendency at this level to think that what that means is that large-scale empirical surveys and deep laboratory experiments are primary. Anything less that that is not really scientific. Most of the research performed in the field of psychotherapy is done from this point of view. But what has happened

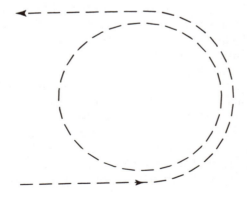

Figure 8.4 Participative research

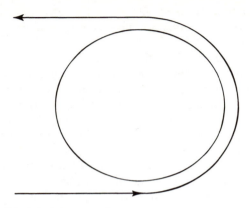

Figure 8.5 Fully authentic research

is that the researchers have got further and further away from the practitioners. It is remarkable how useless to the practitioner most of the research has been.

However, this is beginning to change. The journal *Counselling and Psychotherapy Research* started up with the expressed intention of publishing research which was of relevance and benefit to the practitioner, and this is a real breakthrough in the field. The journal makes it clear that any training must foster a respect for research evidence, and an openness to anything that can be clinically effective. If the editors can be convinced that suitably conducted case study research can be rigorous and objective, they will move towards more case studies. And indeed, Malcolm Robertson has argued that 'recent methodological advances make the application of single-case research more rigorous and empirically grounded' (Robertson 1995: 24). He has specifically quoted E. E. Jones (1993) as offering an informative discussion of these methodological advances.

From an **authentic** point of view, research is treated with more suspicion, because so often it embodies a treatment of the human being which seems to reduce him or her to the level of a machine, or a collection of variables which can be measured and perhaps manipulated. But qualitative research of the reflexive kind is highly regarded and much more readily accepted. Such research is not necessarily generalizable, but as Carl Rogers often used to point out, what is most personal is often most general as well.

Reflexivity

Reflexivity is in fact one of the most important ideas to come out of the field of qualitative research. It means that we take seriously the idea that whatever applies to the participants in our research may also apply to ourselves. In other words, the term refers to 'that which turns back upon, or takes account of, itself or the person's self' (Holland 1999: 464). In all the interpretative forms of research, this turning back upon oneself or the subject of study is central to the effort.

Russell Walsh (2003) has been writing recently about reflexivity in a way which builds upon the work of Holland, and puts forward four types of reflexivity: personal, interpersonal, methodological and contextual. These four perspectives seem very useful, and we may stay with them for a moment.

Personal reflexivity is based on the kind of openness which we have seen is so characteristic of the authentic stage. It exposes the assumptions, reactions, and unconscious expectations which constitute our research awareness (Finlay 1998). This goes further than the frequent practice of keeping a research diary (Tedlock 2000). As has been remarked by Ellis and Bochner (2000), feminism has been a powerful influence on the incorporation of the researcher's own self into the research narrative. Feminists have argued that the proper place for the author is in the text, if research is not to degenerate into an alienated performance where the people being studied become things to be used.

Interpersonal reflexivity emphasizes the relationships which are set up in research. It points to the way in which such relationships are subject to powerful ethical demands. Not only can the researchers dominate and control those being studied, but also the way in which they themselves can be dominated and controlled needs to be looked at. Petruska Clarkson (2003) has a sensitive examination of what she calls 'the vengeance of the victim' in the therapeutic relationship, and something similar can also happen in research.

Methodological reflexivity refers to the place of theory in research. It entails a critical examination of all the basic philosophical assumptions on which the research endeavour is based. As can be seen in the Introduction to the *Handbook of Action Research* (Reason & Bradbury 2001), the whole field of research has been re-examined in recent years, and its philosophical basis has been completely dismantled and reconstituted. This radical examination of basic theory has been much needed, and is still not understood by many researchers plodding on in the old grooves.

Finally, contextual reflexivity, as Walsh (2003: 61) says, 'recognizes research as an historically situated activity. As such it can include both a cultural analysis of the phenomenon studied and a local analysis of the research project itself'. This has been developed especially at Duquesne University, where phenomenological methods are encouraged. Walsh suggests that the four approaches to reflexivity belong together and may be integrated, thus offering a powerful and solid approach to research.

Maslow and authenticity

If we want to get another angle on an authentic approach to research we cannot do better, in my opinion, than to go back to the classic written by Abraham Maslow (1969), who arranges his book into ten sections, each one dealing with a dilemma which faces everyone trying to work on research with human beings. In most cases he resolves this dilemma by grasping both sides of it.

1   *Humanism vs. mechanism.* Science is often seen as mechanistic and dehumanized. Maslow sees his work as about the rehumanization of science. But he conceives this to be not a divisive effort to oppose one 'wrong' view with another 'right' view, nor to cast out anything. He tells us that his conception of science and of psychology in general is *inclusive* of mechanistic science. He believes mechanistic science (which in psychology takes the form of behaviourism, of cognitive science and of the empirical approach generally) to be not incorrect but rather too narrow and limited to serve as a *general* or comprehensive philosophy (Maslow 1969: 5).

2   *Holism vs. reductionism.* If we want to do psychology, in the sense of learning about people, we have often in practice to approach one person at a time. What is the state of mind in which this is best done? This is one of my favourite quotes from Maslow:

> Any clinician knows that in getting to know another person it is best to keep your brain out of the way, to look and listen totally, to be completely absorbed, receptive, passive, patient and waiting rather than eager, quick and impatient. It does

not help to start measuring, questioning, calculating or testing out theories, categorizing or classifying. If your brain is too busy, you won't hear or see well. Freud's term 'free-floating attention' describes well this noninterfering, global, receptive, waiting kind of cognizing another person.

(Maslow 1969:10–11)

If we adopt this approach, Maslow says, we have a chance of being able to describe the person holistically rather than reductively. In other words, we can see the *whole* person, rather than some selected and split-off aspect of the person. But this depends crucially on the *relationship* between the knower and the known. We have to approach the person as a person: 'This is different from the model way in which we approach physical objects, i.e. manipulating them, poking at them, to see what happens, taking them apart, etc. If you do this to human beings, you *won't* get to know them. They won't *want* you to know them. They won't *let* you know them' (Maslow 1969: 13). My own view is that this is a basic point which has to be taken on board by anyone studying people.

3   *I-thou vs. I-it.* Maslow was way ahead of his time in recognizing the importance of Martin Buber's distinction between two ways of approaching another person. It is only today that this idea is being taken up by many other people as important for research. Maslow never mentions Merleau-Ponty, but the thinking is clearly related to phenomenological ideas (Valle 1998).

4   *Courage vs. fear.* Most research and most knowledge, Maslow says, come from deficiency motivation. That is, it is based on fear and is carried out to allay anxiety; it is basically defensive. Maslow enumerates 21 cognitive pathologies which emanate from this basic stance (Maslow 1969: 26–9). There is a very good discussion of fear in Griffin (1998), as it relates to research, showing once again how Maslow got there first.

5   *Science and sacralization.* Science is notorious for the way in which it seems to oppose religion and also such emotions as reverence, mystery, wonder and awe. Maslow suggests that deficiency-oriented science has a need to desacralize as a defence. The question Maslow wants to ask is whether it is in the intrinsic nature of science or knowledge that it must desacralize, must strip away values in a way that Maslow calls 'countervaluing', or not? On the contrary, says Maslow, and in this he is close to the

recent thinking of Ken Wilber (1998), who in his book *The Marriage of Sense and Soul* is making some very similar points. (See also Bentz & Shapiro 1998; Braud & Anderson 1998.)

6   *Experiential knowledge vs. spectator knowledge.* The world of experience can be described with two languages, a subjective (first person) one and an objective (third person) one. 'In his presence I feel small' is first person, while 'He's trying to dominate me' is third person (von Eckartsberg 1998). This question of first-person knowledge is now being explored in detail in the *Journal of Consciousness Studies.* Mitroff and Kilmann (1978) speak of 'authenticity' in relation to the kind of scientist we are now considering. If we want to know more about how to do the other kind of science (the experiental kind) we can go to Taoism and learn about receptivity.

> To be able to listen – really, wholly, passively, self-effacingly listen – without presupposing, classifying, improving, controverting, evaluating, approving or disapproving, without dueling with what is being said, without rehearsing the rebuttal in advance, without free-associating to portions of what is being said so that succeeding portions are not heard at all – such listening is rare.
>
> (Maslow 1969: 96)

But if we can do it, says Maslow, these are the moments when we are closest to reality. Contemplation is something which is hard to learn, but it can be learned, and it is an essential moment in the scientific process as Maslow sees it. And again recent thinkers such as Anderson and Braud (1998) agree with him.

7   *The comprehensive vs. the simple.* Scientific work has two directions, poles or goals: one is towards simplicity and condensation, the other towards total comprehensiveness and inclusiveness. Both of these are necessary, but we should distrust simplicity as we seek it. We should also not value simplicity and elegance to the exclusion of richness and experiential truth.

8   *Suchness vs. abstraction.* There are two different kinds of meaning, which are complementary rather than mutually exclusive. Maslow calls one 'abstractness meaning' (classifications) and the other 'suchness meaning', having to do with the experiential realm. One tends to reduce things to some unified explanation; the other experiences something in its own right and in its own nature. There may be two kinds of scientists: the cool, who go

most for abstraction and explanation, and the warm, who go for suchness and understanding. But great scientists integrate both.

9 *Values and value-free science.* If we say that science can tell us nothing about why, only about how; if we say that science cannot help us to choose between good and evil, we are saying that science is only an instrument, only a technology, to be used equally either by good men or by villains. But Maslow believes that science can discover the values by which people should live.

10 *Maturity vs. immaturity.* Science is incredibly 'masculine', in the sense of idealizing the stereotyped image of the male. Maslow sees this as a sign of immaturity, much more to do with the adolescent boy who desperately wants to be accepted as a man, rather than with the mature man, who may have many 'feminine' traits.

It can easily be seen in these ten points how the authentic consciousness comes through again and again. It also does so in the work of Alvin Mahrer (1978). The connection I want to make with the next section is that if we are sceptical about the either/or, as Maslow clearly is throughout his writings, we have to find models which enable us to reconcile apparent oppositions.

My own opinion is that all these people are very much in line with the contribution of feminism to this kind of thinking. I think of Ann Oakley (1981) and Janet Finch (1981) as having been some of the first in the field, with their contributions on the problems connected with the interviewing of women. I might add that more recently there has been a very interesting book edited by Erica Burman (1990) which makes a definite connection between feminism and new paradigm research. It appears that in the last few years, feminist research has taken up these new ideas and found them to be more relevant to their concerns. For example, Jan Burns says:

> Furthermore, as new paradigm research becomes more acceptable women must fight for the acknowledgement that feminist psychology deserves in this development. As Reason and Rowan point out, many women have been doing new paradigm research for a long time with little recognition and credibility. Only now that it has been given a different name and taken under the more credible umbrella of new paradigm research has it become acceptable. Thus, feminist psychology should be recognized

as not only participating in, but as being one of the leading influences of, this changing paradigm within the social sciences.

(1990: 161)

Some feminists go further than this, in outlining a specifically feminist approach. For example, Maria Mies (1983) has set out specific criteria for feminist research. She agrees with the view of Sue Wilkinson (1986: 2) that 'A female perspective is to be regarded as central to the research, not as an additional or comparative viewpoint'. It is interesting to note that the Reason and Hawkins, (1988) research was about gender, and that the Meade (1993) approach is clearly from a masculine standpoint. There seems to be something here about gender taking us to the cutting edge of research in some way. Perhaps race is another site where this sort of thing is going to happen, as Gill Aitken (1996) suggests. An important point made by Wilkinson is that feminist research entails a critical evaluation of the research process itself – one of the main tenets of all these new approaches. Ann Phoenix (1990), however, makes the point that there is no unitary feminist methodology to which all feminists have to subscribe.

The transpersonal angle

From a transpersonal point of view, research has to be conducted with a spiritual awareness. This is often called transformational research. It is a form of research which goes beyond being non-alienating and thinks in terms of genuine transformation – not so much *involving* the people being studied, but more like *being* the people studied. The barrier between researcher and subject, which has been eroded a good deal in collaborative research, disappears altogether at times. In terms of our earlier analysis, we are now talking about Column 3 Table 1 (see pp. 6–7).

This approach says that we are essentially spiritual beings in a spiritual universe, that humans ultimately seek meaning within their activities, and that creative living is necessary for both psychological and spiritual growth (May 1991). Mythology and storytelling are valued and worked with, and there is some emphasis on ecological vision and planetary consciousness (Gomes & Kanner 1995).

Just to say something about Column 4, at this level we cannot do research, because our interests have changed so much away from any kind of instrumentality. So I am proposing to ignore Column 4 in this particular context, although I think it is true that work at the level of Column 3 is much helped if the people involved have an experience and an appreciation of the nourishment which can be obtained from their own involvement in meditation and other activities which belong in Column 4.

Case example

So with this much as background and context, let us now look at an example of this approach in action. John Heron carried out a piece of research on altered states of consciousness (Tart 1990) which brings out the way in which these things work out in practice. One of the first points which Heron makes is that the researchers must share in the experience. He says: 'It makes sense for ASC researchers to be involved in the altered states they are studying, if they want to generate appropriate categories of understanding and methods of inquiry. It is unsound to map an unknown country by never visiting it yourself, and by trying to make sense of the reports of others who have visited it' (Heron 1988: 182). This means that the research becomes at the same time a training in entry into and use of altered states. Here we get the theme of initiation (Whiteman 1986). The researchers need to be initiated into the quality and depth of the altered states they wish to study. This point is also made by Sheila McClelland: 'there was a sense that we could only learn, develop and hone these skills by launching into action. Paradoxically, the skills needed to start out are precisely those which engagement in the inquiry actually develop' (1993: 114).

The case research was carried out in a five-day workshop with 20 participants located at the CAER centre in Cornwall. The altered state it was decided by the group to study was that where we are at one and the same time in everyday physical reality and aware of and paying attention to another non-physical reality, a subtle energy world of presences and powers that is somehow within and around the physical world.

The first round used ritual as the method of getting in touch with non-ordinary reality. As a result of this ritual, three people obtained what seemed to them to be instructions for how to proceed further. These seeming instructions were then used for the second round. We must hurry past the intriguing details of all this, which is a pity, because they have much to say about the concepts of alignment and attunement which we shall be talking about later on. In the third round, everyone practised noticing extrasensory impressions at the very edge of the ordinary physical visual field. In the fourth round, the group first found the spot in the garden where the birds flocked (this was one of the instructions from round one) and then filed into the *fogou* – an underground cave used in prehistoric times for religious ceremonies. Some strong impressions and impacts came from these activities.

Out of all these experiences five things came: streaming of energy in and out of the energy field of the physical body; visions of faces and symbolic objects; a felt sense of presences, and of their energies and activities, in the other reality within certain areas of physical space; a sense of the numinous, the holy; and emotional uplift.

The group then got worried as to the status of these experiences. Were they genuine altered states of consciousness, putting the participants in touch with non-ordinary reality, or were they, on the other hand, evidence of a massive consensus collusion which had created a set of shared illusions? It seemed important to have some way of telling which was which.

There were two more rounds which introduced more material again, and tremendous energy and involvement was released, but let us stop there with this account. John Heron says: 'One of the major difficulties with ASC research is that there is a tendency to come not quite fully back from an altered state, and so to fall short of sufficient critical discrimination, in an ordinary state, about what was really going on' (1988: 192). Yet one of the most interesting findings of this research was that there were six criteria which, when taken all together, could in principle distinguish between true and false impressions.

1   *Agreement*. Two or more persons have the same or similar impressions of the other reality.
2   *Heterogeneity*. Very different sorts of impressions of the other reality, which occur both simultaneously and serially, in the same person and in several persons, are compatible.
3   *Synchronicity*. Impressions of the other reality occur simultaneously to two or more persons, and are meaningful to them in the same or a similar way.
4   *Spontaneity*. Impressions of the other reality often come unexpected and unbidden; are often surprising in their content; and the recipient did not want or intend to produce them in the way in which they occurred.

5   *Independence.* Impressions of the other reality have a life of their own and are not amenable to manipulation or interference.
6   *Spatial reference.* Impressions of the other reality have reference to locations in a subtle and inwardly extensive space that is somehow *within* physical space.

You might like to consider whether these criteria could validate the existence of UFO abductions, extra-sensory perception, angelic presences, mystical experiences and so forth. Such experiences have of course been studied much more in recent years, as for example in the work of Stanislav and Christina Grof (1990).

Heron makes the point that although the research was transformational, and although the content was at least partly within the subtle realm, and although the participants did manage and control a good deal of the research process, it fell short of the full promise of transformational research in two respects. One was that the five-day format was set by John Heron, without any kind of consultation with the prospective participants, and the other was that it was John Heron who wrote up the report, all by himself. Hence though it was in large measure non-alienating research, there were still elements of alienation involved in it.

One of the most striking things about research done in a non-alienating way is the amount of energy released. This is why it seems fitting to call it a high-energy type of research. What is more, energy seems to be released as each point on the cycle is left behind. This seems to have to do with the much higher degree of involvement and commitment required of the investigator. The researcher is in touch at several levels, not just the one level favoured at the mechanistic end of the continuum.

If we now ask the question as to what is the difference between transformative research and collaborative research, we can perhaps express it as shown in Figure 8.6 Here the distinction between researcher and subject has disappeared altogether. But is this possible? It is certainly rare – I have not been able to find any fully realized examples. Some certainly come close; think of Freud's own self-analysis as revealed in his book *The Interpretation of Dreams.* Here the researcher and the subject went round the cycle many times, and real discoveries were made in this way. But perhaps it is too easy if the researcher and the subject are the same person: how about if they are different people?

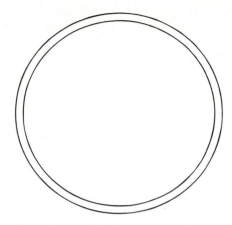

Figure 8.6 Transformational research

Storytelling as research

One interesting approach to research which follows these lines is storytelling as inquiry, as used by Peter Reason and Peter Hawkins. They investigated male-female relations in a mixed group by asking each participant to write a story involving a male/female interaction. Then instead of discussing or analysing the stories, other participants replied to the stories by telling another story of their own. These responses took the form of replies, echoes, recreations and reflections.

A reply is 'my reaction to your story': an expressive way of giving shape to the feelings and ideas arising while listening to the story. An echo is 'your theme in my story': here the listeners make a sharing response, of telling their own stories on the same theme. A re-creation is 'your story as re-created by me': here the listeners take the story and reshape it into another form, finding their own way of telling the tale. This could be a poem, a fairy tale, or some other kind of story. It may stay at the same level as the original, or move toward the mythic or archetypal level. A reflection is 'my story about your story': essentially the reflection involves standing further back, pondering on the story and its meaning.

What they found was that instead of simply obtaining data on male-female relationships and interactions, they were moving towards the deeper meanings of these things. They say:

Once we begin to inquire into the origins of meaning we begin to enter the paradoxical realms of transpersonal and spiritual knowing. In a holistic view of knowing, matter, mind and spirit interpenetrate: we have moved beyond the unreformed materialism of orthodox inquiry, and we need now to integrate a knowing from spirit (psyche, soul) with our existential human inquiry. A science of persons is inadequate without a knowing from soul.

(Reason & Hawkins 1988: 97)

This was a short workshop, only extending over two days, but it seems that the promise is there of something which could be used very effectively in various forms of heuristic and hermeneutic research, where the emphasis is on exploring meaning rather than obtaining generalizable results. The work of Michael Meade (1993) is not formal research, but could easily be turned in this direction, and I personally find it quite inspiring.

Some themes

Let us now try to draw together some of the threads, and make some general points about a transformational approach. Themes which I think emerge from all the data and need to be thought about are nine in number. In terms of our original four-column chart, this is now all about Column 3. Let us look at them one by one.

1   The first is balance. This means balancing the active with the receptive, the intellectual with the emotional, the body with the soul, the tough with the tender, and doing justice both to the male and the female. This is not a one-sided and partial approach – it embraces opposites in what is for some a confusing and paradoxical way. This is very much the thinking found in The *Tao Te Ching*, which is so characteristic of the transpersonal approach. A good critical edition comes from Ellen Cheng (1989).

2   One of the typical concepts is 'alignment'. Transformational research requires vision. A clear and timely vision catalyses alignment. Alignment is a condition in which people operate as if they were part of an integrated whole. It is exemplified in that level of teamwork which characterizes exceptional sports teams, theatre ensembles and chamber orchestras. When a high degree of it develops among members of a team committed to a shared

vision, individuals' sense of relationship and even their concept of self may shift. In a team of people committed to research, it channels high energy and creates excitement and drive, as we saw earlier, in connection with the Heron and the Reason and Hawkins research.

3   Another idea is 'attunement', defined as a resonance or harmony among the parts of the system, and between the parts and the whole. As the concept of alignment speaks to us of *will*, so that of attunement calls up the mysterious operations of *love* in organizations: the sense of empathy, understanding, caring, nurturance and mutual support. Attunement is quiet and soft, receptive to the subtle energies which bind us to one another and to nature. There is a good description of this and the previous concept in a pioneering piece by Roger Harrison (1984) in the context of management generally. Doing transformational research can stir up powerful emotions, and mutual support is crucial in such a case. Anyone doing this type of research (e.g. Traylen 1994) needs to look to their own emotional competence and the way in which it is to be supported.

4   Another concept is 'empowerment'. This word had been used before, mainly by humanistic people in the sense of self-actualization – that is, self-empowerment. But the new twist here is the emphasis on mutual empowerment. Where there is empowerment, 'people at all levels feel directly responsible for results, are continually learning and developing their skills, feel the trust to share their best ideas, and work together in teams that contain not one, but many, leaders.' (Jaffe & Scott 1993: 140). This has particular implications for women in eroding the invisible barriers that tend to keep them in mundane organizational roles. With mutual empowerment people suppport each other rather than trying to put each other down. This again makes us think of the connection with feminism.

5   We talk about intuition freely in this work, and encourage the development of intuition quite consciously and deliberately. But it is important to realize that intuition is a form of knowledge which is distinct from propositional knowledge, practical knowledge and experiential knowledge. New paradigm research pointed out that propositional knowledge is not enough, and that it is also not enough to add practical knowledge: experiential knowledge is important too. But transformational research adds that intuitive knowledge is necessary in addition to these as

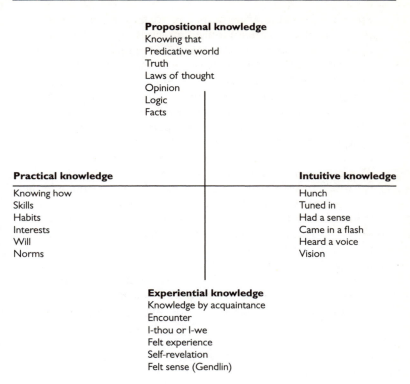

Propositional knowledge
Knowing that
Predicative world
Truth
Laws of thought
Opinion
Logic
Facts

Practical knowledge
Knowing how
Skills
Habits
Interests
Will
Norms

Intuitive knowledge
Hunch
Tuned in
Had a sense
Came in a flash
Heard a voice
Vision

Experiential knowledge
Knowledge by acquaintance
Encounter
I-thou or I-we
Felt experience
Self-revelation
Felt sense (Gendlin)

Figure 8.7 Intuition as a form of knowledge

an essential condition (see Figure 8.7). We can see how similar these ideas are to the conventional Jungian layout of the four functions, and there are some interesting thoughts we might pursue along these lines.

6   An important phrase to remember is 'co-creation'. This goes beyond the familiar notions of competition and cooperation, and speaks of a way of being which enables new ideas and new ways of working to emerge out of personal experience. 'Co-creation combines the best of competition and cooperation with a balance between goal and process orientation' (Joba *et al.* 1993: 55). In research terms we come across many examples of this in the books we have looked at in this chapter.

7   Another thought is summed up in the phrase 'planetary consciousness'. Everything done in the research is related to this higher (or deeper) purpose. If we find on reflection that there is

no longer joy in the struggle, that we are burning ourselves out in the effort, that we are no longer energized by what we do, then that may be a signal that it is time to move on to a new vision of what we are doing. Perhaps we have lost touch with our purpose on this planet. And perhaps the direction of effort needs to change to reflect what is happening. This gives us a much more ecological consciousness in what we do – we become conscious of the side-effects of our actions. Transpersonal ecology (Fox 1995) is now an important discipline, and research has to take it into account. This represents a change in our horizons.

8   This approach says that we are essentially spiritual beings in a spiritual universe, that humans ultimately seek meaning in their lives, and that creativity is necessary for both psychological and spiritual growth. It represents a transpersonal approach to research, insisting on its place in a much wider context of time and place. This involves transformative changes in the funda-mental nature of the research effort: it is about giving research a new kind of vision and mission. As Peter Reason and Peter Hawkins say: 'We need to find a way to acknowledge both the independent meaning-making of the authentically autonomous human being and the universal patterns to which we all belong' (1988: 97).

9   A transformative approach to research goes beyond Aristotelian logic (A is A, A is not not-A, nothing can be A and not-A at the same time), and starts to be interested in dialectical logic, pro-cess logic, many-valued logic, fuzzy logic and so forth – all sorts of variations which show that Aristotelian logic is a choice, not an inevitable law of thought. (The Boolean logic which underlies most computer programs is based on the Aristotelian model.)

When we are working from the transpersonal position of Column 3, it makes sense to say that A is never simply A, and that if it were it could never change. It is only because A is not simply A that it has within it the potentiality for change. And it is research which can often reveal the potential for change lying within a given situ-ation. Perhaps not every researcher realizes that they are denying Aristotelian logic every time they work for real change, but this is one of the many instances of where we are working transpersonally without even realizing it.

Conclusion

Research can be exciting stuff, which changes the consciousness and the lives of those taking part. If we let it move into the transpersonal ranges, it can be an inspiring source of movement into a new world.

Counselling psychology, with its emphasis on the importance of scientific research, has a big part to play in developing the styles of research which can go beyond the crippling paradigms of the past. We can be involved in a radical questioning of science, and can take on board the expanded notions of science spelt out in this chapter and in such key texts as Mitroff and Kilmann (1978), which shows so well how limited most accounts of science are.

It was of course Ian Mitroff (1974) who showed that the 'storybook image of science' given in so many psychology textbooks bore very little resemblance to the actual work of researchers in the hard sciences. He produced a list of 11 'conventional norms' and their corresponding 'counter-norms' in science, and showed by careful research that it was the counter-norms which were used in practice by hard scientists. Thus, for example, conventional norm No. 1 was 'faith in rationality': the corresponding counter-norm was 'faith in rationality and non-rationality'. Conventional norm No. 2 was 'emotional neutrality as an instrumental condition for the achievement of rationality'; the corresponding counter-norm was 'emotional commitment as an instrumental condition for the achievement of rationality'. This was not even an attempt at improving notions of science: it was simply an account of what went on as distinguished from what was going on.

Similarly in psychology it is important to distinguish between what we do and what the texts say we are supposed to be doing. We shall then find that what we are doing is far from the ideals laid out in the texts, and quite possibly nearer to the ideas we have been encountering in this chapter. The aim here has been to lay out a coherent picture of the third revolution in research methodology: but it may turn out to be a picture of what is actually going on today in the field of therapy, as distinguished from what is supposed to be going on.

DIALECTICAL INTERPOLATION 8: WE MUST BELIEVE AND DISBELIEVE THE CLIENT

Particularly in the case of sexual abuse, but also in the case of all sorts of statements about how adults were treated as children, the question of belief arises. When someone comes to a counsellor or therapist, they sometimes want the therapist to believe that what they are saying is true; the therapist may have doubts about this. Sometimes the client doubts it themselves, and the therapist then may want to encourage them to take more seriously their own reality. Sometimes the therapist wants to introduce the possibility that some of it is fantasy. This is a very tricky area.

I think there is a paradox at the heart of all this. It is that the therapist has to be the most gullible of people, and also the most suspicious of people. Let us explore both sides of the paradox.

Empathy, which is more or less approved of by all schools of therapy, means that the therapist has to enter into the world of the client. The therapist has to open up to learning what this world is like, and be able to move about in it without making too many mistakes. This means acceptance of the client's reality. We have to take seriously the client's way of seeing the world, and really enter into it.

Some people even think the therapist can go further than this, and actually share in the client's world. Several therapists have recently suggested that the therapist can actually *become* the client at times, can identify completely with the client, and can even sometimes know the inner world of the client better than the client does, because of fewer defences against it. The therapist can share the same imaginal world as the client – something that is between them rather than belonging to either of them separately. We saw in the Introduction that this phenomenon has been given several names – 'linking' is one of them.

In either case, whether through empathy or linking, the therapist is opening up to the world of the client in such a way as to be completely gullible – to be swallowing the client's story hook, line and sinker. It is not even believing the client's story, it is sharing in the client's experience of that story, and even sometimes becoming part of that story. And the better the therapist, the better this can be managed. Whatever the client says in that intimate relationship, that is the truth for now.

The other side of the paradox is that the therapist has a trained sensibility, a disciplined subjectivity. The therapist has an internal gyroscope, so to speak, which is quite independent of anything the client says. This is partly to do with therapist's grasp of theory, partly to do with their own self-knowledge obtained through the necessary work on themselves, and partly to do with the therapist's access to supervision. The concept of the 'inner supervisor' is relevant here, too.

The therapist is trained to look for discrepancies in the client's story and discrepancies between the client's words and body language. The therapist is sensitive to overstatement, overelaboration, exaggeration, drama, one-sidedness, games, passivity, bias, avoidance, overcontrol, transference distortions, prejudice, misinformation, blame, self-blame and so forth. All these things can be confronted, and confrontation is one of the skills of the therapist, as we saw in Chapters 3 and 5.

Confrontation has to be done carefully, and with love, and at the right time, if it is to be therapeutic. It has to be done in the spirit of accurate empathy, tentatively, with respect, and perhaps using successive approximation. There has to be a relationship of trust between therapist and client if it is to work well. But the fact that there can be such a thing at all must mean that the therapist has an independent position. Part of the virtue of the therapist is not to be a part of the client's system, but to stand outside it. There has to be a fulcrum outside the client's system if the therapist is to be able to apply any kind of therapeutic pressure at all. So the therapist cannot accept everything the client says as the truth.

How can this paradox be resolved? Because it certainly is resolved, every day. I think the most elegant resolution is to say that the client's story is *a* truth, rather than *the* truth. It is the truth for today. It is the best sense the client can make at the moment. It is as far as the client has got at the moment. It is never the whole truth, and it is quite doubtful whether the whole truth is anywhere to be had. Certainly the therapist doesn't have it.

What the therapist does have is a longer perspective than the client. Experience tells us that the client often goes through several phases in understanding their own story, particularly when it comes to childhood. It is therefore wise to hold off any action based on such understanding until we are all convinced that there are no more phases to come. Therapists who encourage the client to act on the first truth they come across are doing the client a disservice. They are not being good therapists. Someone once said that planned procrastination is something worth learning, and this is one area where it might be useful. Ripeness is all.

Chapter 9

Dangerous omissions

Therapist resistance: a common problem?

One of the things which can happen in counselling is that the therapist can actually get in the way of the client. This may happen in various ways, but the way I want to draw attention to here is that it is hard for a therapist to deal with something in the client which the therapist has not yet dealt with in his or her own therapy.

A good example of this is to be found in Malan (1979) where in Chapter 15 he deals with a case history where there are clear signs of umbilical affect – in other words, the patient is remembering life in the womb, and traumatic experiences which happened there. It is all about tubes and starvation and all the rest of the phenomena which Lake (1980) has described so well. But because Malan himself has never been into this area in his own therapy, and because there is no place for this in his own theory, he is compelled to falsify it. He says that the experiences link firmly with '*feeding at the breast*' (his italics), and that 'any reference to an umbilical cord cannot be anything other than psychological anachronism' (1979: 164–70)!

This is a particularly vivid example of an issue which recurs again and again in psychotherapy. Some therapists are psychologically open, and can and do learn from their clients; some do not.

In the past this has mainly been true about early experience. The experience of birth, for example, is crucially important for many clients, and the traumas resulting from it affect their lives in many ways, as Grof (1985) more than anyone else has spelled out in detail. But most therapists of all persuasions have never been into this experience in their own work on themselves; and so when the client brings it up, he or she gets pretty short shrift. Such a client may then fall into the hands of the rebirthers, which as Albery (1985) makes clear, is not a good idea.

But now we can see that the same is true at the other end of the scale. Not only have most therapists not been through their own (probably psychotic) material in the womb and the birth process, but also they have not been through their own (probably mystical) material at the transpersonal level of development. And so they are going to falsify this, too. If a client brings up such material, he or she is going to be diverted into a channel which the counsellor is more familiar with.

But there is more to it than that. Not only do therapists have the problem of blindness to those matters they did not cover in their training or their own therapy, they also have the problem of narcissism.

There is plenty of literature about resistance in clients and patients, and this is something that we are all familiar with, even though some therapeutic schools say that there is no such thing. But I want to look at something which is less often talked about, which is resistance in therapists. Of course there is a good deal in the literature about resistance among therapists in training. The classic work on supervision by Ekstein and Wallerstein (1972) talks about blind spots, deaf spots and dumb spots among trainees. Dumb spots are those areas where the student lacks the required knowledge and skill in dealing with the client. This is most likely to happen when the trainee is faced with clients who are very different, whether they be poor and disadvantaged, or whether they be other oppressed groups, or indeed if they come from a higher social class. The trainee just does not know enough about what it is to be like the client. But it can happen in other ways too, and is relatively easy to deal with. The trainee just needs more training.

Blind spots are those places where the trainee's own psycho-dynamics gets in the way of appreciating what is going on in the client. All the phenomena of countertransference can come in here. This is harder to deal with, because the trainee may be quite unaware of what is the problem, and the supervisor may be saying something quite new and unfamiliar.

Deaf spots are those where the therapist not only cannot hear the client, but cannot hear the supervisor either. These are likely to involve particularly defensive reactions based on guilt, anxiety or otherwise unpleasant and disruptive feelings. Difficulties with authority figures may come into the picture.

What I want to suggest here is that there is another problem, which is better defined by existentialist writers, which I call 'therapist resistance', which is often due to the therapist's narcissism. Existentialist writers are much concerned with what they call 'presence', and regard this as a central requirement for any therapist. The essence of therapist resistance, it seems to me, is that the therapist ceases to be genuinely present for the client, and is off on some pursuit of his or her own. I want to emphasize that this is not about countertransference, and not about projective identification either. It is simply that the therapist has lost touch with the client, in most cases because they have one agenda and the client another. It is a question of the therapist's ego being more important than anything the client might need. And this is not just about trainees: well trained and seasoned therapists may fall into this trap. Some interesting examples of this are to be found in a striking paper by David Winter (1997) entitled 'Everybody has still won but what about the booby prizes?'

Let us first of all recognize two kinds of resistance in the client. The first comes from the client's inner conflicts and hidden issues – things which the client has not worked out yet and which are getting in the way of progress. The second comes from actual mistakes made by the therapist, which get up the client's nose or make the client feel demeaned or not listened to. This latter kind generally causes more trouble, because the therapist's training may have emphasized the first kind of resistance, and not alerted him or her to the possibility of the second.

Faced with a resistant client, the therapist has several choices. One is to vary the approach in such a way that the client's needs are better met, and the resistance diminishes or disappears. Another is to work with the resistance by bringing it to the surface in some way, so that it can be brought out and transformed. A third choice is to insist on persevering with the original approach, the one which possibly provoked the resistance in the first place. Winter calls this third response the 'heroic' reaction, and it seems to me from what he says that it is mainly male therapists who take this course.

From an instrumental point of view, this is simply an error in technique, which can easily be put right. From an authentic point of view, it may be due to deep-seated faults in the therapist, probably connected with basic narcissism. From a transpersonal point of view, it may be due to losing touch with the higher source of wisdom, however conceived.

One therapist (Salter 1949) suggested that resistant clients 'should be chased from the office with a broomstick'. He goes on to say 'I explain to them that my appointment book is like a life raft. There is room for only a limited number of people, and I do not intend to waste my time trying to convince any of the bobbing heads around me to get on board. There are others drowning who are only too happy to cooperate in their rescue'. This seems to represent a classic way of refusing to learn from the patient. Actually the phrase about 'cooperating in their rescue' is quite suspect in my book. The therapist is not a rescuer, and only trouble results from trying to be one.

Winter's next example is Albert Ellis, a prime exponent of the instrumental approach, who suggests that resistance may be due to 'the therapist's engaging in . . . therapy in a namby-pamby, passive way instead of vigorously getting after clients' (Ellis 1980). He called resistant clients DCs, or difficult customers, and accused them of generally 'not listening to others or to their therapists' (Ellis 1983). What the therapist should do is to 'do violence to' the client's 'resistant thoughts' and 'search out and destroy . . . these phony ideas' (Grieger 1989). It would be hard, in my view, to find a more dogmatic statement in the literature. And it indicates a therapist who is quite resistant to using any of the other approaches to resistance, or indeed admitting that there is anything they can do other than to oppose the opponent.

Winter goes on to talk about a therapist from the school of Aaron Beck, another therapist in the instrumental tradition, who gives details of a session where the client admitted that she only filled in her daily homework chart once a week, just before coming to the session, instead of daily as the assignment demanded. The therapist pursues her on this, and 60 per cent of her 247 interventions are about this issue. It seems clear that the client found it a fairly meaningless exercise, but the therapist would not accept this. Here is another way in which the therapist can be as resistant as the client. (These details were not reported by the therapist but extracted from a transcript of the session.)

Winter's example from psychoanalysis is where a patient was being treated for sexual problems, and the analyst came to the conclusion that 'a significant part of his motivation for homosexuality was the danger of the incestuous wish for a castrating and intrusive woman' (Blatt & Ehrlich 1982: 83). The report goes on to say that this patient was 'unable to curtail the homosexuality' despite being provided with insight into the relationship between his homosexual activity and feelings of loss. In the ninth month of his analysis, the patient showed his resistance by getting up from the couch and announcing that he was leaving because the analyst didn't care about him. The analyst responded 'in a somewhat authoritative manner' by telling the patient to return to the couch and continue his associations (p. 80). This he did, and continued with the analysis for two more years. But 'in the third year of the analysis, the patient abruptly terminated the analysis'. The analyst regarded this as resistance, but the patient regarded it as successfully emerging from a bad experience. My own view is certainly that the therapist here was so convinced of his own rightness that no other possibility even occurred to him: a characteristic example of psychoanalysis sometimes turning into an instrumental approach. This is therapist resistance in all its glory.

Winter also quotes the research on encounter group leaders by Lieberman *et al.*. They described one such leader who said to a quiet group member, 'I get so fuckin' tired of having to push you and find out what you're like. Do you want us to be all like you? How long do you want us to go? Twenty-four hours without saying anything?' He then hurled his cup of coffee across the room and and slapped the group member's face (Lieberman *et al.* 1973: 43). Of course this was in the early seventies, when such behaviour was more common, but it certainly demonstrates an inability to really hear or appreciate a more subtle form of action which did not fit the desired model. It seems to be this lack of fit with the therapist's model which causes the most trouble. It also shows how the authentic approach may have its weaknesses too, if the therapist's narcissism comes into the picture.

David Kennard, and colleagues (1993) carried out a research study on the interventions of therapists in group analysis: 'The group analysts were presented with vignettes of situations which might arise in therapy groups, often involving what might be regarded as resistance, and asked how they would intervene if they were the therapist' (Winter 1997: 7). What they found was that on occasion the response would be an interpretation which was more witty than therapeutic, and which could be regarded as self-indulgent. In such cases the therapists' comments on such interventions 'indicated no acceptance of the possibility that clients might genuinely fail to understand their interventions or that these might be too far removed from clients' own constructions of the group experience to be of any value' (Winter 1997: 7). One therapist later commented that he enjoyed making one of these interpretations 'so I get out of the trap of working hard and getting nowhere and becoming irritated and fed up'. I feel that this shows a complete lack of the ability to listen to one's internal supervisor, and that therapist resistance was definitely present. The instrumental seems present here.

Hans Strupp (1989), on the basis of many years of researching the therapeutic process, states that interpretations, when used with resistant clients, 'often have a blaming or pejorative quality and are experienced as such by the patient' (p. 722). He concludes that he sees 'little room for the large array of traditional analytic interpretations. A frequent consequence of these abstract, highly inferential pronouncements may be to antagonize the patient, diminish his or her self-esteem, and merely teach a vocabulary of jargon that may become a weapon to be turned against the therapist' (p. 723). It takes someone who has as much stature and experience as Strupp to say something like this and be believed, but of course it is extremely important. If any therapist puts himself into the position of being infallible, it is clearly a form of resistance. Daniel Wile (1984) makes a similar point in a paper in which he argues that classical psychoanalytic theory 'inevitably leads to pejorative and accusatory interpretations' (p. 355) which may result in negative therapeutic reactions. I am not sure about that, but certainly any interpretation or other intervention which is persisted with in the face of the client's rejection of them can do real harm to the relationship. Winter quotes Striand's account of a client who considered that she had been harmed by her psychotherapist, 'If I disagreed with him about his interpretation of what was happening with me, he very often would not even deal with it, not even entertain the notion that my interpretation might be valid. As he said – "Do you want to listen to me? I'm the therapist. If you don't want to listen to me then I can't help you" ' (Striano 1988: 68; Winter 1997: 8). This is a good example of what I mean by therapist resistance, the therapist's ego defences in full bloom. It is also an example of turning a potentially authentic approach into an instrumental one.

Hugh Gee (1998: 16) gives an interesting example when an experienced therapist in supervision described an interaction with a client.

> She was feeling a bit fed up with her patient. She went on to describe how the patient had arrived at a session and having sat in silence for some time he then reported that he had no feelings and no thoughts at all. The supervisee had then asked the patient a number of questions, 'why do you think you are in this state?', and 'what do you think lies behind this state?'

These are clearly persecutory questions, coming from the therapist's anger at the silence of the patient. The patient's resistance is matched by the equivalent resistance of the therapist, who had clearly departed from the rubrics of good practice. Hugh Gee sums this up very neatly by saying that 'When resistances in the patient are matched by a similar resistance in the therapist, a vicious circle is introduced' (1998: 31).

One example which actually became a whole book is reported by Anna Sands (2000). She and her therapist engaged in an unprofitable and agonizing dance, in which her suffering steadily increased. Of course we cannot be sure of what actually happened. Even if the therapist's story had been available, it would still be just another story. But it certainly appears as if the therapist's resistance came into the picture. Much clearer is the account by Ellen Plasil (1985), where the therapist was clearly not only resistant but completely out of order and sexually exploitative. This has been commented on by Carl Goldberg (2001), a long-time researcher in this area, who believes that such behaviour is on the increase. He says:

> I believe that the psychotherapy crisis today has primarily to do with the high incidence of practitioners who inflict harm on their clients because they are even more emotionally unstable than their clients. Many of them may try to help their clients but cannot; still others wreak damage because they disdainfully prey upon their clients' vulnerabilities for their own personal gain. No small number of these toxic practitioners are highly prestigious members of the psychotherapy profession . . .
>
> (p. 107)

He gives details of a case which is too long to quote here, but is almost unbelievable in its hostility and damage to the client.

There are some interesting examples in the book edited by Rosemary Dinnage (1988), and it is very clear from this book how powerful the resistance of the therapist can be. One therapist intimidated the patient; and she fought with him for 11 years. Another therapist would suddenly make a put-down remark and never seemed to help in any way; she stayed with her client for 3 years, three times a week. A third therapist saw the patient five times a week for 3 years; the patient eventually came to the conclusion that the therapist was afraid of her. She was a very difficult patient, and the analyst eventually referred her to someone who could handle her much better, but it would have been better to have arrived at this conclusion sooner. Another patient had an analyst, again five times a week, who started to have a drink problem, but would never admit it or even mention it.

It seems very clear to me that therapist resistance is a very real and not particularly uncommon problem. Certainly the well-known book by Jeffrey Masson (1990) has plenty of warnings about this.

One of the best books on this whole area is the text by Dave Mearns and Windy Dryden (1990) which not only contains many more examples, but also some interesting and valuable research on success and failure in therapy.

Male consciousness

Now I would like to raise the question as to whether there is more therapist resistance among men than there is among women. Although there do not seem to be any well-researched statistics on this, it is obvious at once that most of the examples I have found so far do involve male therapists. There are of course also many examples of resistant female therapists, and I do not want to make any kind of a case that this is an exclusively male preserve. Nevertheless, there are good reasons to suppose that this is a greater problem area for men than it is for women. Let us look at one or two examples.

The first is the well-known fact, checkable from virtually every training programme on offer, that most of the people who come forward for training as therapists are women. It is largely a women's profession although, as in other professions, the most eminent and prominent and best-paid exponents are men. This immediately tells us that men have some kind of difficulty with the demands of being a therapist. And the most obvious of these, noted many times in the area of being a client, is that men tend to steer clear of the realm of emotions, and of empathy. Hence this is something they have to learn. Mostly this is learned through the experiential part of their training, whether it be in one-to-one therapy or in experiential exercises or in an experiential training group. And of course this is the hardest part to control or to measure: some people get a lot out of their own therapy experiences, and some do not. I met one therapist who had been through 12 years of training, largely experiential in nature, and who still had great difficulty in communicating on an emotional level.

The second is the equally well-known fact that men are brought up to suppress emotions, just as women are brought up to express them. Every book examining male psychology tells us this. Perhaps the clearest analysis comes from Bob Connell (1995), who has given us the concept of 'hegemonic masculinity' – a kind of masculinity which is culturally dominant and comprises a set of rules for how men should be. The big compendium edited by Ronald Levant and William Pollack (1995) is full of research telling us this in field after field, and the journal *Men and Masculinities* brings us more information, quarter by quarter, confirming that this is still the case. Men tend to think that emotions weaken them. Even Warren Farrell (1990), who is much concerned to set the record straight on male psychology in opposition to feminism, does not deny this, but simply puts a more favourable construction on it. He points out, for example (p. 294), that in a road accident it is very valuable to suppress emotions until the emergency is dealt with and the necessary action has been taken. However, in the role of therapist a man has to be in touch with his feelings if he is to be any good at all. And this is just more difficult for men than it is for women, in general and on average. It can of course be done, as I can testify!

One of the things which has to be done in therapy is to get the client to own up to his or her feelings and inner conflicts. We have only to remember Freud's original statement that the therapist can only move the patient to the limit of the therapist's own resistances. If the therapist has difficulty getting in touch with his own inner world, he is thereby less able to help the client to do the same. If the therapist is warding off some of his inner experience, he is going to have difficulty encouraging the client to encounter that same material. This is one of the most characteristic, authentic insights. And it means that the therapist may actually get in the way of the client reaching into some of the more difficult regions of his or her experience. There are some interesting examples of this quoted in the Mearns and Dryden (1990) book already mentioned.

And I could think of an example of this from my own work in therapy. It concerns a teacher, a man in his forties, who met a most beautiful girl who worked at the same school, and who he saw every day. They started going out together, and he started to fall in love with her. She sometimes stayed at his flat, but more often he stayed at hers.

She came from a different culture. He invited her to meet his brother, but she did not invite him to meet hers. He was afraid of being found out because that might affect his position in the school;

she was afraid of that, too, but was also afraid of the reaction of her friends and relatives if it were known that she was seeing a white man. As he grew closer and closer to her, he became more and more agonized and conflicted. Emotionally and sexually she meant more to him than anyone he had ever met before.

He was quite a heavy drinker, and tended to visit the pub every night; she did not like pubs. He was quite a heavy smoker, and smoked many cigarettes in the course of a day; she did not smoke. He liked to spend the weekend with his brother. She did not like the brother very much. He agreed that these things got in the way of the relationship, but he was not prepared to change his habits in any way.

They had great rows, which they made up affectionately and explosively. The strain grew. They went on a week's holiday together, and this led to further stress rather than resolving anything.

I came to the conclusion that unless he cracked, he would lose the opportunity to achieve greater happiness than he had ever had before. In his previous relationships, he had always been in charge, it seemed to him. But here he was not in charge at all. It was disconcerting. He agreed that nothing very terrible would happen if his school did find out. It could be handled. But he still would not let go, would not move.

In an attempt to get through to him, I told him the story of the Skeleton Woman (Estes 1992) who is caught by a fisherman and taken home by him. As he sleeps, a tear comes from his eye. She drinks it and revives. She reaches into his body and takes out his heart and bangs on both sides of it, and it makes a sound like a great drum. She sings, and as she sings her flesh fills out, her hair comes back, and her eyes, and her breasts, and her sex. She drums his clothes off and slips into the bed with him, and returns his heart to his body, and that is how they awaken, wrapped one around the other. Then she and the fisherman go off together.

He could not see the point of this story. I became more and more frustrated. I felt I knew the answer, but he was so obtuse that he would not see it. He needed to learn how to trust, how to give in. I became so sure that this was the answer that I became quite boring to him. He could not take it. He felt that he had nothing more to gain from me, and left the therapy.

I thought at the time that the hard-earned lesson here was that I must not take things to heart – not let insights involving the client have such an effect on me that I would take them on as my own. I thought that the moral of it was that *authenticity is not enough*. But now I see that it is deeper than that. I had actually broken the unity which we needed for the therapy to work. I had allowed my ego to break free and assume an independence which was isolating.

The circle of healing

I now think that the moral of all this is that the therapist is only efficacious and positive to the extent that he or she abandons the notion that they are a separate ego. It is better to think in terms of a team, or an alliance, or a dual unity, or an interpenetrating mix-up – anything rather than a separate ego. There must be some kind of awareness that there is not only the dreadful danger of thinking that I am right – there is the even worse danger of thinking that I am separate. Although this is quite expressible in authentic terms, it is really a transpersonal insight.

Of course I am separate, in the sense that at the end of the hour, the client goes one way and I go another. But during that hour, we both form part of a greater whole; and if we do not, terrible things can happen.

Of course I am a separate person, with a separate history, a separate home and a separate bank account; but during that hour I am linked inextricably with the other. As soon as that link is broken, the therapy ceases to work. And what is most likely to break that link is my ego.

As soon as I think that it is *me* doing it, as soon as I think it is *my* responsibility to put things right, as soon as I think that the client is wrong, I step outside the healing circle.

Perhaps that is a good way of putting it. In good therapy, a healing circle is created. As soon as the therapist steps outside that circle and wants to be right in contrast to the client, a destructive form of interaction is set up. It is in that situation that therapist resistance can enter in most readily. It is not countertransference, because very little of it is below the level of ordinary consciousness: it is available for inspection at any time, and the client is just as likely to notice it as the therapist. The transpersonal insight is that one has to go to another level in order to understand all this to the full.

It seems clear from all this that therapists are often subject to several different kinds of emotional blocking, and find it hard to meet their clients where they really are. And the most worrying of these kinds of blocking is what we may call therapist resistance or narcissism: the way in which the therapist's own personal sense of a separate ego can get in the way of the work. Of course I am not saying that there should be a kind of symbiosis between therapist and client: the aim is for both of them to be able to be genuinely present, both in the consulting room and outside it.

Psychosis

We are getting more sophisticated now in the extent to which we can distinguish between psychotic or neurotic material and mystical material. No longer can we be content with romantic statements such as 'The schizophrenic and the mystic are both in the same sea: it is just that the schizophrenic is drowning and the mystic is swimming'. Rather, we say with Lukoff (1985) that it is possible to distinguish seven possible diagnoses, ranging from the psychotic at one end to the mystical at the other. We ask basic questions such as: is the person suffering from a standard psychiatric complaint? Is there overlap with mystical experiences? Is a positive outcome likely? Is there a low risk of damage or danger? If the answer to all these is yes, the person is suffering from mystical experience with psychotic features, and needs to be treated by transpersonal psychotherapy and not committed to a hospital. If the answers to any of these questions is no, other things are suggested. We cannot go into the details here, but we can start to be very specific about what is going on in any individual case. David Lukoff now has a website where such things are discussed in more detail.

Now obviously this has very big implications for the future training of counsellors. Training courses are going to have to cover the birth and pre-birth material at one end, and the spiritual material at the other end; or as Wilber (1986) puts it, the pre-personal and the transpersonal. It is not hard to do this at an intellectual level, but the rest of the person needs to be involved too, in individual and group therapy. And of course this raises immense problems as to how the teachers are to be taught or retaught.

Pre- and perinatal experience

It seems clear that there is such a thing as pre- and perinatal experience. Let us just present some of the evidence for that. Some people still do not believe that people can remember their own birth, but this is because they have not read the research by people like David Chamberlain (1998), a highly respected psychologist who has written very helpfully about these matters. Similarly some people still do not believe that the foetus has personal experiences in the womb, but this is because they have not read the research by Alessandra Piontelli (2002), which uses camera evidence to show that twins react to one another in the womb in ways that feature later in the conscious interactions of the same individuals as infants and children. Some people still do not believe that the effects of the birth experience can affect later life, but this is because they have not read the research by Stanislav Grof (1980) or Frank Lake (1980) which shows with a wealth of detail how there are four different stages in the birth process, and how traumas at any of these stages produce observable effects in adult life.

What tends to happen is that some very early event causes panic. This panic gives rise to a form of defence. This defence works sufficiently well at the time, and the person gets by for the moment. When the next emergency arises, panic is again dealt with by the same defence which worked before. But this defence then becomes part of the character structure of the person, and they are stuck with it. It gets to be too good. It protects all too effectively, cutting the person off from their real experience.

Because of the emphasis of much of this work on early trauma, people sometimes think it is going to put all one's problems down to one trauma, happening just once in one's life. But of course traumas are seldom as dramatic as this. The commonest causes of mental distress are simply the common experiences of childhood – all the ways in which our child needs are unmet or frustrated. This is not necessarily a single trauma, in the sense of a one-off event – that is much too simplistic a view. Rather would we say with Michael Balint (1968) that the trauma may come from a situation of some duration, where the same painful lack of 'fit' between needs and supplies is continued.

Historically, this approach is close to early Freud, the early work of Reich (who placed great importance on the body being directly involved in therapy) and Arthur Janov (1983). But all of these adopted a medical model of mental illness, which primal integration rejects. As Thomas Szasz (1961) pointed out long ago, neurosis is only a metaphorical sickness, not a disease in the true sense of the word.

As soon as one gets down into the early roots of mental distress, deep and strong feelings come up, because the emotions of early life are less inhibited, less qualified and less differentiated than they later become. In other words, they are cruder and clearer. And so the whole question of the importance of catharsis in psychotherapy arises. Catharsis means the expression of strong emotions. It makes sense to say that catharsis has two related but separate components: one is cognitive, (the thinking function) and relatively intellectual – the recall of forgotten material; the second is emotional and physical – the discharge of feelings in deep sobbing, strong laughter or angry yelling. But in the kind of work we are interested in here, it seems better to be more specific, and to say that catharsis is the vigorous expression of feelings about experiences which had been previously unavailable to consciousness (Nichols & Zax 1977). This lays more emphasis upon the necessity for the emergence of unconscious material.

Much of the thinking behind object relations theory in psychoanalysis (Gomez 1997) is compatible with this. The internal objects of Melanie Klein (Hinshelwood 1989) are very much the product of very early experience, and since the idea was proposed a vast amount of work has been published about it.

Most of the trainings available today ignore pre- and perinatal experience, and they should not. Anyone who believes in the unconscious and has not read the book on it by Grof (1979) can have only a very limited notion of what riches are to be found there.

Transpersonal psychology

It is surprising how many courses have no place for transpersonal work. It is not necessary to say much about that here, because all through this book I have tried to remedy that omission: but it is worthwhile to note that it is a real problem. It may be hard to see how such an important area of human experience could be left out, but left out it certainly is in most cases.

The reasons for this are perhaps not far to seek. Ever since the Enlightenment, it has been fashionable in academic circles to dismiss spiritual matters as old hat – as simply part of a medieval worldview which we have now left behind. But this is of course to confuse religious observances and prejudices with authentic personal experience within the spiritual realm.

Possibly the best corrective for this view is the book by Ken Wilber (2000c) on integrating science and religion. He makes an unanswerable case, it seems to me, for allowing the transpersonal into the realm of ordinary discourse, as a legitimate part of human experience, today and for the future. The old idea that science could somehow take over everything no longer seems to hold water, not because there is something wrong with science, but simply because it leaves out some very important aspects of human experience which should not be ignored. We are more than just three–dimensional creatures crawling about the surface of the earth. We are infinite and extraordinary too, and to leave this out is to leave out too much. There is a part of me which was never born and will never die.

DIALECTICAL INTERPOLATION 9: INTEGRATIVE PSYCHOTHERAPY IS AND IS NOT INTEGRATIVE

On the one hand integrative psychotherapy does try to create a new integration, a new shape, which can be just as formal and just as well worked out as any previous form of therapy. Bill Swartley's structure (Rowan 1998a: Ch. 6) covers the four great realms of sensing, feeling, thinking and intuiting, and uses these to form a structure within which all the well-known forms of therapy can take their places. Petruska Clarkson's structures (2003) of the five relationships and the seven levels cover the process and the content of therapeutic consciousness. These are just examples of the many kinds of integration which can be formalized.

On the other hand it questions the whole idea of new shapes and new forms, and wants to stay with incompleteness and not-knowing. James Hillman continually comes back to the idea that formalism is a mistake, and that the living interaction is always unique. Ernesto Spinelli likewise denies all attempts to make new structures to improve on the old one, holding instead to the view that we have to stay with the unique experience of each client and therapist interaction. Arnold Mindell, as we saw earlier, has found a way to integrate all sorts of different approaches into his own unique method, more by letting go than by adding things on.

What are we to do about this? Do we have to choose, as Mahrer (1989a) suggests, between competing views of integration, or is it more a question of somehow integrating them all? I argued in Chapter 2 that some things cannot be integrated, so the latter solution seems not to be available.

However, perhaps we can get further by admitting that there is a paradox here. Perhaps we can only solve the paradox by going beyond its assumptions. If we cease to regard psychotherapy as the meeting of two people for the mental improvement of one of them, but instead regard it as the nodal point of a process which involves the I, the We and the It, such a new view might enable us to see some light. The I is the subjective process which involves the client most particularly; the We is the therapeutic pair, and also the communal and social-emotional context in which the work can thrive; the It is first of all the individual behavioural and neurological structures involved, but secondly the fixed social structures within which all therapy takes place.

From this point of view, integration is a much broader and more inclusive approach, which does justice to all four of the quadrants described by Ken Wilber. If we can do this, and it is something I am still exploring, something much more adequate than any of the existing approaches may be within our grasp.

Chapter 10

The body in therapy

The final important issue we need to address is the question of how the body is treated in therapy. If we say that there are three levels on which we can experience and deal with the body, it makes sense to start with Level 1. This belongs to the state of consciousness we have been calling the mental ego or the instrumental.

Level 1

If we think of the way in which the body is generally known at this level it is evident at once that the stereotype is a very clear one:

1   The body is not the mind. At least since Descartes, dualism has reigned. At the instrumental level we think of the body as something which belongs to us, and which has a will of its own. The body is something like a child, or an animal, for which we are responsible. Saint Francis called it 'brother ass'.

2   The mind is or ought to be in charge of the body. Going back to Plato and Aristotle, the rational faculties are assumed to be superior to everything else about a person. The body is the horse and the mind is the rider, in the popular image. As Freud put it, the ego should be in charge, not the id or the superego. We should be fully conscious, not sunk in the unconscious or the preconscious. As Albert Ellis put it, we should be rational and not irrational.

3   The body has needs, instincts, desires, lusts and appetites which can be very demanding. The mind has to attend to these so that they are satisfied in ways which do not offend society. We see the body much as Freud saw the id, much as Ellis saw the irrational.

The implication of this, of course, is that we leave the body to experts. We hand it over to the medical profession, we call in our personal trainer, we go to the physiotherapist, the chiropractor, the osteopath, the homeopath, the acupuncturist, the expert at the gym, the nutritionist, the dietician, the health psychologist – the list is endless. I am not saying, of course, that all health psychologists think in terms of Level 1: it is clear that many of them do not.

This view of the body is so well known and so ubiquitous that there seems no need to labour the point. Ken Wilber, in his discussion of the mental ego level of psychospiritual development, has explained it very well. The reason why Wilber will be so useful to us in this discussion is that he has described three levels of such development (Wilber 1996) which correspond to three ways of seeing the body. As we know, the next in order after the mental ego is what he calls the centaur level, and it is to this that we must now turn.

Level 2

Wilber tells us that the centaur level is about body-mind unity. Instead of the dualism of the previous level, we have a monistic view. One of the pioneers of this new way of looking at the body was Wilhelm Reich, and we may lead into it by considering his approach. Most people know that Reich was originally a student of Ferenczi, and later led Freud's seminar group on resistance. What Reich said was that a natural energy normally flowed through the body. This energy could be blocked at various points, usually where the segments of the body (he distinguished seven) joined on to one another. These blocks might have been set up originally as defences to some forbidden impulse or some painful trauma, and might be maintained as part of the person's character structure. By working on these blocks and releasing the energy, the person might be made more healthy and happy.

> Bodywork, involving the client's body and their awareness of their body as part of the therapy, was a crucial contribution by Reich to modern psychotherapy. This can include awareness held by the therapist, enhancing the client's awareness of their body, actually changing posture or using bioenergetic exercises (Lowen & Lowen 1977), Reichian massage by the therapist on

> the client's body and encouraging the client to use their body in
> movement, voice work and emotional expression.
>
> (West 1994: 139)

If removing fixedness in this way is important, this makes it sound as if fixedness of character, which we usually admire, were highly suspect, and Reich actually said that character is neurosis. In other words, we are responding to the world and acting in it either in an appropriate way, which stays in close contact with reality, or in a more rigid or floppy or otherwise inappropriate way. To the extent that it is the latter, Reich would see the undue rigidity or floppiness as neurosis, and would seek to undo the blocks responsible. Reich was a very interesting character himself, and biographies of him have been written by David Boadella (1985) and Myron Sharaf (1983).

This view of the person as a body-mind unity is very useful to the therapist, and of course the field of body psychotherapy has burgeoned, particularly in Europe. One of the main approaches within the humanistic and integrative section of the UKCP is bodywork, and two or three of the training organizations within it are devoted mainly to such work. This comprises a number of approaches: bioenergetics, vegetotherapy, biosynthesis, biodynamic psychology, neo-Reichian work, Radix education, Hakomi therapy, Hellerwork, Rolfing, postural integration, Tragering, Feldenkrais method, bio-release, Alexander technique and so on.

David Boadella has developed a particular approach within the field, called biosynthesis, and has written about it many times (e.g. Boadella 1988). He also edits the prime journal in the field, *Energy & Character*. He delivered the main speech at the First Congress of the World Council of Psychotherapy in Vienna (Boadella 1997a). He also submitted a position paper to the Subcommittee for Scientific Validation within the World Council for Psychotherapy in Rome, which sets out in detail the scientific claims of bodywork in general and biosynthesis in particular (Boadella 1997b). There is a whole somatopsychic tradition in Europe, and regular conferences are held in the area.

This general approach has been adapted and extended in a number of ways by humanistic practitioners. One of the main schools where this has been done is in bioenergetics, led by Alexander Lowen (1976), who came to the UK a number of times. Bioenergetics lays particular emphasis on grounding, and has many exercises concerned with making better contact with our legs and feet and what they mean to us.

Stress positions are used to stir up valuable material which may be connected to the person's energy blocks (Lowen & Lowen 1977).

Both Reich and Lowen think it worthwhile to say that certain patterns of blockages, certain systems of holding energy back, are very common. They draw attention to the existence of certain character types – the schizoid, the masochistic, and so on – and go into much detail as to the way of standing, the body posture and attitude, the type of breathing, the cognitive and affective patterns and contents and so on, which belong to each type. One can actually do a 'body reading' which amounts to a character reading, simply by getting the person to stand up and move about, so that one can see how the body is set in particular patterns of action (Kurtz & Prestera 1977). This gives some very clear ideas how to work with such a person in therapy.

One of the methods of working is to touch the body itself. The touch may be very light, as in Gerda Boyesen's biodynamic massage (Southwell 1988), or may involve pressure on tense parts, as in Lowen's bioenergetics, or may involve deep restructuring of the muscles, as in Rolfing or postural integration (Painter 1986). This means that therapists in the area of bodywork must know the body very well, and many of them take massage qualifications, both because of the excellent education it gives on the whole body, and because of the legal requirements in certain countries. So in much bodywork some of the clothing is removed to give access to the muscles and also to enable the therapist to see any changes in colour of the skin as therapy progresses – these may be very important (Whitfield 1988). Not all body therapists use massage tables, but it is quite common for them to do so.

Because of this emphasis on the body, and the possible sexual implications of this, it is particularly important for body therapists to have gone through their own therapy in this way. They can then work through sexual and other feelings which may arise in them when in contact with another person's skin, before ever meeting a client (Emerson & Shorr-Kon 1994). Good supervision is also particularly important in this form of therapy, and very often the therapist will have a supervisor who will help in resolving any distress which occurs as a result of the therapist making any mistakes in this sensitive area. The supervisor can also keep an eye open for any infringement of the rather stringent ethical requirements of this discipline. It is extremely important that no one does this kind of work without adequate training and supervision.

For a wide-ranging rundown on a whole host of approaches to the body it is worth looking at Nicholas Albery's (1983) book. One of the problems with the body therapies is that they seem to lead to a proliferation of individual practitioners each with a method about which he or she is completely dogmatic. For some reason, this seems to be much more the case in the body therapies than in any of the other approaches. It is quite a relief to come across someone like Boadella, who has a lot of knowledge and quite wide-ranging sympathies. He now lives and works in Switzerland.

Anyone who goes in for bodywork should be aware that it can get into very deep material quite quickly. If the client is ready for that, having done a good deal of more conventional therapy already, and feeling a bit impatient with it, this may be fine. But it is in any case important for any client to make sure that the therapist is a well trained and well practised person, who has worked on themselves for at least five years. It is also important to check that the therapist is in supervision. Most good body practitioners recognize the need for supervision in their work. This is, of course, desirable for all therapists and compulsory for members of the Association of Humanistic Psychology Practitioners, and also for the other practitioners who are recognized by the UKCP, and to be found on their National Register.

The body therapy techniques developed by Reich and Lowen and their followers, and described above, involve much stressful and often painful work, such as hitting, kicking, screaming, intense breathing, stress-inducing positions and movements, and deep pressure applied to tight musculature, referred to as one's body armour. The need for this is well described by Stanley Keleman (1985), one of the people who has done most to make explicit the underlying emotional structures in the body.

In contrast to this approach is the bodywork developed by a few German women, including Elsa Gindler, Magda Proskauer, Marion Rosen, Ilse Middendorf, and Doris Breyer (Moss 1981). Their work promotes mind/body awareness and integration using such techniques as movement, touch, natural breathing, sensory awareness and voicework. These are much less stressful and painful practices, as Kogan (1980) and Rush (1973) also make clear.

All these methods of bodywork emphasize therapeutic regression, catharsis and integration. Catharsis is well understood in bodywork:

Reich therefore laboured, not so much to produce catharsis, as to reduce the defensiveness that prevents it. Furthermore, he helped his patients to learn about their armouring, so that defences could be less readily reconstituted after therapy. Catharsis combined with insight into the nature of defences helps patients to counteract repression long after therapy is over.

(Nichols & Zax 1977: 114)

In recent years there has been less emphasis on catharsis among most therapists, because of the dangers which Alice Miller (1985) pointed out of the psychotherapist becoming unconsciously abusive. But of all the approaches to psychotherapy, it is bodywork which uses catharsis the most, for example by encouraging loud sounds:

> Often the person isn't immediately in touch with the feeling that is being held in. If we persuade them to make a sound, it will start as a flat, toneless 'Aaaaa', then begin to take on emotional colouring . . . it may become a yell of anger, a scream of fear, a cry of pain or grief . . . the whole sense of stuck tension in the body suddenly turns over. The energy has peaked in this act of ex-pression and re-membering – the bodymind has become whole again. As the storm passes there will generally be a sense of release, relaxation and spaciousness.
>
> (Totton & Edmondson 1988: 96)

Sometimes direct touch is used to produce the same kind of result. The therapist may press on tense muscles, for example. This usually hurts, and provokes strong reactions which release the held emotions. Groupwork is used a good deal. The therapist gets involved very directly at times, encouraging the client to shout at him or her, or even lash out at a cushion held in front of the therapist. There is a good discussion of all this in Totton and Edmondson (1988). There is typically a good deal of risk-taking in a bodywork group, and the group leader has to be well trained and experienced to handle these very direct interactions.

But it is possible to work with the body without touching it. An interesting version of this is to be found in the work of David Grove (Grove & Panzer 1989). He will take a bodily sensation such as tightness in the chest and work with it on a metaphorical level. Here is an example:

Client: I have a tightness in my chest.
Therapist: And you have a tightness in your chest. And when you have tightness in your chest, that's tightness like what?
Client: Like a rock.
Therapist: And a rock. And when it's like a rock, what kind of rock is that rock?
Client: A hard rock.
Therapist: And a hard rock. And when it is a hard rock is there anything else about that hard rock?
Client: Nothing can break it.

(Tompkins & Lawley 1997)

The therapist then continues to explore the symbol of the hard rock by asking further questions, until some kind of transformation takes place. This is a surprisingly effective way of working, and works simply by taking the bodily sensation seriously and working very directly with it, taking it where it needs to go. The repetition of words which may have been noticed above has to do with Grove's view that the child within the client must not be left out, and such language is inclusive of the child mind.

The work of Arnold Mindell also proceeds without necessarily touching the body, but just following the promptings of the physical sensations experienced by the client. His excellent and very helpful book *Working with the Dreaming Body* (Mindell 1985) is packed with examples of how he works on this level. His wife Amy is also now doing interesting work which moves into Level 3 (Mindell 1995).

Of course, not all the work at this level is bodywork. The same emphasis on body-mind unity is to be found in existentialism: 'I am not just a body or a combination of body and soul. I am rather this process of embodied consciousness which reflects on itself. There is no dualism: I am body consciousness, it is through my body that my consciousness exists. My consciousness is my body' (Barnes 1990). It is also to be found in the neighbouring field of phenomenology, as we can see from the following quotation: 'It is through my body that I understand other people, just as it is through my body that I perceive "things" . . . Man taken as a concrete being is not a psyche joined to an organism, but the movement to and fro of existence which at one time allows itself to take corporeal form and at others moves towards personal acts' (Merleau-Ponty 1962: 186, 88). There is a discussion of the whole question of mind and body in Chapter 6 of the book *Existential Thought and Therapeutic Practice* (Cohn

1997), which relates the whole matter to the practice of existential analysis.

The humanistic tradition, of course, also takes body-mind unity for granted as the basis of its work. This includes Gestalt therapy, psychodrama, person-centred therapy, focusing, experiential therapy and so forth. The work of Alvin Mahrer in Canada is perhaps particularly notable in this regard. In a 22-page chapter, he hammers home the point again and again that body and mind are not two separate things. He consistently refuses to accept the language of 'biological foundations' which is still so popular in British psychology:

> From a biological perspective, *physiological needs* are basic in understanding the body; from a totally different perspective of humanistic theory, *potentials for experiencing* are basic in understanding the human body. Physiological and humanistic constructs bear no hierarchical relationship toward one another; each set enjoys independent integrity.
>
> (Mahrer 1978: 152)

More recently, Eugene Gendlin has been saying some very good things about the body, based on his long experience with focusing. Gendlin is of course a philosopher as well as a psychologist and psychotherapist. One quote from him may suffice:

> This body is not one thing while you are another, a second thing. Your body enacts your situations and constitutes them largely before you can think how. When your attention joins this living, you can pursue many more possibilities and choices then when you merely drive the body as if it were a machine like the car. It lives inherently with others. It is born into interaction and physically implies moves toward and with people. When it first arrives, it implies nursing and being held, and after it absorbs all the complex human circumstances, it can imply an intricate new move in an unheard-of predicament.
>
> (Gendlin 1996: 304)

Perhaps enough has been said to indicate that Level 2 is important and widespread in the world today.

Level 3

Still following Wilber's schema, we leave the centaur level and move on to the psychic and the subtle. Wilber has on occasion called these the lower subtle and the higher subtle. In my own work, I merge these two together and call them both the subtle. Here we move into the transpersonal realm proper, and instead of staying on the level of the personal we move into a realm where soul and spirit have to be taken into account. At Level 2, people often speak of the whole person, as a necessary and desirable way of talking. At Level 3, we still speak of the whole person, but the person now includes a spiritual aspect which is given much more importance.

What is the relationship between the spiritual and the body? In transpersonal therapy we are very clear about this. The body is not opposed to or inferior to the intellect or the mind. Again it is the question of boundaries. We have the power to open the boundaries or to close them. If we want to enter into our bodies and become them, we can do that. If we want to visualize parts of our bodies or conflicts within them, we can do that. There is a magical relationship between ourselves and our bodies, such that all these things are possible.

Nathan Field has made an interesting contribution to this way of thinking, by emphasizing the way in which boundaries between therapist and client can be removed by what he calls 'the four-dimensional state': 'I have in mind those moments where two people feel profoundly united with one another yet each retains a singularly enriched sense of themselves. We are not lost in the other, as in fusion, but found' (Field 1996: 71). I have written about this sort of thing at greater length elsewhere (Rowan 1998c).

One of the most important bodily activities is breathing. And it is interesting that the word for breath, and the word for spirit, is the same in many different languages: *pneuma*, *ruach*, *anima*, *animus*, *prana*, *ch'i*, *ki* – all these are words for breath, which are also words for spirit.

It is very worthwhile paying attention to breathing because it works on four levels: (1) physical – exchange of gases with the environment; (2) emotional – we cannot change our emotions without changing our breathing; (3) intellectual – when we start thinking we stop breathing; (4) spiritual. So it connects up all the levels of our being, and in yoga it is possible to extend this quite consciously so as to link all the chakras in line from the base to the crown:

The most important result of the practice of 'mindfulness with regard to breathing' is the realization that the process of breathing is the connecting link between conscious and subconscious, gross-material and fine-material, volitional and non-volitional functions, and therefore the most perfect expression of the nature of all life.

(Kapleau 1967: 12)

In therapy there are many different kinds of breathing: the deep fast breathing used in regression work; the belly breathing used in relaxation and yoga meditation; the connected breathing used in Leonard Orr rebirthing; the lion breathing used in some Sufi work; the provocative breathing used in some neo-Reichian work and so on. There is a definite relationship between yoga as a schema of psychospiritual development and the kind of work we do in psychotherapy:

The royal, or raja yoga outlined by Patanjali entails ashtanga: eight key practices or limbs. The first two, yama and niyama, are moral training for purity. The next two are asana, the development through physical exercises of a firm and erect posture, or 'seat', and pranayama, exercises for controlling and stilling the breath.

(Goleman 1977: 76)

Stanislav Grof from Czechoslovakia has made a special study of breathing, and uses it very carefully in his work, which he calls holotropic therapy. He points out that specific techniques involving intense breathing or withholding of breath are a part of various exercises in Kundalini yoga, Siddha yoga, the Tibetan vajrayana, Sufi practice, Burmese Buddhist and Taoist meditation, and many others. More subtle techniques which emphasize special awareness in regard to breathing rather than changes of the respiratory dynamics have a prominent place in Soto Zen Buddhism, and in certain Taoist and Christian practices. Indirectly, the breathing rhythm will be profoundly influenced by such ritual performances as the Balinese monkey chant or Ketjak, the Inuit Eskimo throat music and singing of *kirtans*, *bhajans* or Sufi chants. Grof also has some interesting remarks to make about hyperventilation or overbreathing, where we breathe faster and deeper than usual for a period of time:

In some instances, continued hyperventilation leads to increasing relaxation, sense of expansion and wellbeing, and visions of light. The individual can be flooded with feelings of love and mystical connection to other people, nature, the entire cosmos, and God. Experiences of this kind are extremely healing, and the individual should be encouraged to allow them to develop; this should be discussed during the preparation period.

(1988: 171)

Grof also tells us that in Siddha yoga and Kundalini yoga, intentional hyperventilation (*bastrika*) is used as one of the meditation techniques, and episodes of rapid breathing often occur spontaneously as one of the manifestations of Shakti (or activated Kundalini energy) referred to as *kriyas*.

It seems clear from all this that breathing is a bodily phenomenon which is symbolic of the body generally in its breadth of inclusion of so many psychospiritual elements. One of the people who has made a special study of this is Magda Proskauer, who emphasizes that the breath forms a bridge between the conscious and unconscious systems. She tells us that:

The diaphragm dividing the body into an upper and a lower cage can be seen as the organ which divides our two worlds. The lower animal or instinctual world is represented by the abdominal organs, the vegetative life of the earth; and the upper, more conscious world is represented by the lungs, a symbol of the spiritual life. [Lowen (1976) says much the same thing.] Embedded between them is the heart, the seat of our feelings. In order to feel whole we need to bring these two worlds together. In Greek semantics the word schizophrenia means to be split (schizo) in the diaphragm. The word for diaphragm being phren, also mind.

(Proskauer 1977: 60)

These are fascinating ideas, and it is quite possible to get carried away with them. Sometimes, however, the danger is that we lose the distinction between the transpersonal and the extrapersonal. The test is whether we are in touch with the divine somehow, or whether we are slipping into a kind of spiritual materialism. Goodison (1990) has a long and interesting chapter on what she calls 'the luminous body', but much of it seems to me a kind of reduction of the transpersonal to the extrapersonal: 'I have come to feel that in the working of such laws the "divine" is no more – and no less – present than in the workings of gravity, light, heat and the seed that grows into a plant' (Goodison 1990: 373). To say this is to expose one to the danger of simply using all sorts of discoveries about the luminous body to feed the mental ego. We have seen in all our work so far that the transpersonal essentially goes beyond the mental ego, first of all into the real self, and then into the subtle self, the transpersonal self, and from there perhaps even into the causal self. The danger of reducing the luminous body to a series of exercises is that we plunge into the dangers outlined by Chogyam Trungpa:

> Walking the spiritual path properly is a very subtle process; it is not something to jump into naively. There are numerous side-tracks which lead to a distorted, ego-centred version of spirituality; we can deceive ourselves into thinking we are developing spiritually when instead we are strengthening our egocentricity through spiritual techniques. This fundamental distortion may be referred to as spiritual materialism.
>
> (1973: 3)

But perhaps the person who has had most to say about the connection between the body and the transpersonal realms is David Boadella. It is very interesting to see the way in which he has developed from a basic Reichian into the much more well-rounded therapist that he has become today. He says:

> We can see it whenever someone succeeds in making the transition from hysterical acting out and over-emotionalising, to the being filled with the depth of oneself that transforms the breathing. When this happens the breathing loses all panic, all contractedness, all pressurisation and self-torture. I can hear the ocean in it. It moves through the body like tides . . . The task of all true therapies and the aim of the core teaching in all true religions is to re-connect us with the depth of ourselves . . . Religion has used the word 'God' for the inexhaustible depth and ground of being . . . We need to help the person to find his inner ground, his essence, the source from which his own healing energy wells up with the power to integrate him anew in spite of whatever he learned about how not to feel alive.
>
> (Boadella 1987: 169–72)

In spite of the sexist pronouns, it seems hard to put it better than that. More recent writers on the transpersonal all have interesting things to say about the body. James and Melissa Griffith (2002) are continually bringing the body into their spiritual work and finding it of huge relevance, and their previous book (Griffith & Griffith 1994) is entirely devoted to this. Jenny Wade (2000) speaks eloquently of the connection between sexual and spiritual experience. Brant Cortright (1997) reminds us that breathing and breath awareness are very important in a number of spiritual traditions.

To sum up, then, it seems that we can theorize and experience the body in at least these three different ways. Which one we adopt will depend on the needs of the client as well as on our own personal development.

Level 1, with all its dualistic drawbacks, will continue to be the most common way of seeing and experiencing the body for the foreseeable future. We cannot avoid it, because it is the classic western consciousness which pervades our whole civilization.

Level 2 seems to be gaining in importance in the field of psychotherapy and the like, because it offers a much deeper and more effective set of interventions. It is still not as well understood or as widespread as it really needs to be if the needs of patients and clients are to be met. It has to be said that the humanistic approaches, which include what is called experiential therapy (Greenberg *et al.* 1998), are the most at home with this kind of thinking, and represent its leading edge.

Level 3, at least in my own view, represents the wave of the future. It offers much more scope, particularly in the field of cross-cultural therapy, than any other version. It gives much greater access to different belief systems, and therefore enables the practitioner to work over a much great range of problems. The transpersonal field, which I have written about at greater length elsewhere (Rowan 1993), is rich and potentially valuable, and is becoming popular in a number of countries at the present time.

Implications for training

It seems that we have to be much clearer about the threefold division between instrumental, authentic and transpersonal approaches to the self.

Any training which focuses mainly upon the instrumental self will have little in the way of deep theory, but plenty of practice in assessment and the development of treatment plans. There will be plenty of skills exercises, including micro-skills, and a great deal of specific and focused feedback on performance under various conditions. The aim is to produce a therapist who is highly skilled at assessment and the prescription of treatment, and has the ability to handle a variety of clients at face value. The goals of the client will become the goals of the therapist as directly as possible.

Any training which focuses mainly upon the authentic self will have sufficient theory to enable the practitioner to pick up clues and cues about the fundamental dynamics of the client. But the emphasis will be on the achievement of sufficient depth within the psyche of the trainee to enable him or her to relate to the client in an authentic way, and at relational depth.

Any training which focuses mainly upon the transpersonal self will emphasize even more the state of mind – the being – of the therapist. And if we recognize that this is to include, rather than to exclude, the body, we have a truly inclusive therapy. And of course any training which ignores all this will hardly be adequate to meet the challenges of the future.

Appendix: The spectrum of interventions

First octave: listening
Silence
Bridging
Restating
Summarizing
Encouraging talking
Reflecting the obvious
Inviting expansion
Repetition

Second octave: experimenting
Repetition/contradiction
Direct talking
Regression/recession
Imaging
Artwork
Subpersonality work
Interpreting
Touching

Third octave: bodywork
Touching
Focusing
Accentuating
Soft massage
Massage
Hard massage
Exercises
Confronting

Fourth octave: existence
Confronting
Expressing the here and now
Exposing transference
Exposing countertransference
Mirroring
Exposing contradictions
Being real
Open questions

Fifth octave: guiding
Open questions
Selecting a part
Factual informing
Immediate structuring
Unweighted alternatives
General structuring
Suggesting topics
Moderately focused questions

Sixth octave: instructing
Moderate questions
Rational advising
Supporting
Reassuring
Teaching
Weighted alternatives
Limited directing
Narrow questions

Seventh octave: requiring
Narrow questions
Urging
Approving
Challenging
Reinforcing or disapproving
Superseding
Commanding
Rejecting

Based on Rowan (1998b)

References

Aitken, Gill (1996) The covert disallowing and discrediting of qualitative research, *Changes*, 14(3): 192–8.

Albery, Nicholas (1983) *How to Save the Body*. London: Revelaction Press.

Albery, Nicholas (1985) *How to Feel Reborn?* London: Revelaction Press.

Almaas, A. H. (1988) *The Pearl Beyond Price: Integration of Personality into Being: An Object Relations Approach*. Berkeley, CA: Diamond Books.

Anderson, Rosemarie & Braud, William (1998) Additional suggestions, ethical considerations and future challenges, in W. Braud & R. Anderson (eds) *Transpersonal Methods for the Social Sciences*. Thousand Oaks, CA: Sage.

Assagioli, Roberto (1975) *Psychosynthesis*. London: Turnstone Books.

BACP (2002) *Ethical Framework for Good Practice in Counselling and Psychotherapy* (revised edn). Rugby: BACP.

Balint, Michael (1968) *The Basic Fault*. London: Tavistock Publications.

Bandler, Richard (1985) *Using Your Brain – For a Change*. Moab: Real People Press.

Bandler, R. & Grinder, J. (1975) *The Structure of Magic*, vol. 1. Palo Alto: Science and Behaviour Books.

Barnes, Hazel (1990) Sartre's concept of the self, in *Sartre and psychology: Review of existential psychology and psychiatry*. Seattle, WA.

Beebe, John (1995) Sustaining the potential analyst's morale, in P. Kugler (ed.) *Jungian Perspectives on Clinical Supervision*. Einsiedeln: Daimon.

Beier, Ernst G. & Young, David M. (1980) Supervision in communications analytic therapy, in A. K. Hess (ed.) *Psychotherapy Supervision: Theory, Research and Practice*. New York: John Wiley.

Beisser, A (1972) The paradoxical theory of change, in J. Fagan & I. L. Shepherd (eds) *Gestalt Therapy Now*. New York: Harper & Row.

Belenky, Mary S., Clinchy, Blythe McV., Goldberger, Nancy R. & Tarule, Jill M. (1986) *Women's Ways of Knowing: The Development of Self, Voice and Mind*. New York: Basic Books.

Bentz, Valerie Malhotra & Shapiro, Jeremy J. (1998) *Mindful Inquiry in Social Research*. Thousand Oaks, CA: Sage.

Berg, David N. & Smith, Kenwyn K. (1988) The clinical demands of research methods, in D. N. Berg & K. K. Smith (eds) *The Self in Social Inquiry*. Newbury Park, CA: Sage.

Berman, J. S. & Norton, N. C. (1985) Does professional training make a therapist more effective? *Psychological Bulletin*, 98: 401–7.

Bingham, Lord (2003) Confidentiality: an interdisciplinary issue, *British Journal of Psychotherapy*, 19(4): 467–81.

Binswanger, Ludwig (1963) *Being in the World: Selected Papers* (ed. J. Needleman). New York: Basic Books.

Blatt, S. J. & Ehrlich, H. S. (1982) Levels of resistance in the psychotherapeutic process, in P. L. Wachtel (ed.) *Resistance: Psychodynamic and Behavioural Approaches*. New York: Plenum.

Blomberg, Johan, Lazar, Anna and Sandell, Rolf (2001) Long-term outcome of psychoanalytically-oriented therapies: first findings of the Stockholm outcome of psychotherapy and psychoanalysis study, *Psychotherapy Research*, 11(4): 361–82.

Boadella, David (1985) *Wilhelm Reich: The Evolution of his Work*. London: Arkana.

Boadella, David (1987) *Lifestreams: An Introduction to Biosynthesis*. London: Routledge.

Boadella, David (1988) Biosynthesis, in J. Rowan & W. Dryden (eds) *Innovative Therapy in Britain*. Buckingham: Open University Press.

Boadella, David (1997a) Embodiment in the therapeutic relationship, *International Journal of Psychotherapy*, 2(1): 31–44.

Boadella, David (1997b) Psychotherapy, science and levels of discourse, *Energy & Character*, 28(1): 13–20.

Bohart, Arthur C. (1993) Experiencing: the basis of psychotherapy, *Journal of Psychotherapy Integration*, 3(1): 51–67.

Bohart, Arthur C. & Tallman, Karen (1996) The active client: therapy as self-help, *Journal of Humanistic Psychology*, 36(3): 7–30.

Bomford, Rodney (2002) God and the unconscious, *British Journal of Psychotherapy*, 18(3): 339–48.

Bond, Tim (1993) *Standards and Ethics for Counselling in Action*. London: Sage.

Boorstein, Seymour (1996) Introduction, in S. Boorstein (ed.) *Transpersonal Psychotherapy*, 2nd edn. Albany, NY: SUNY Press.

Bor, Robert & Watts, Mary (1999) *The Trainee Handbook: A Guide for Counselling and Psychotherapy Trainees*. London: Sage.

Boydell, Tom & Pedler, Mike (eds) (1981) *Management Self-development*. Farnborough: Gower.

Bragdon, Emma (1988) *A Sourcebook for Helping People in Spiritual Emergency*. Los Altos: Lightening Up Press.

Bragdon, Emma (1990) *The Call of Spiritual Emergency*. New York: Harper & Row.

Brammer, Lawrence M., Abrego, Philip J. & Shostrom, Everett L. (1993) *Therapeutic Counseling and Psychotherapy*, 6th edn. Upper Saddle River, NJ: Prentice Hall.

Braud, William & Anderson, Rosemarie (eds) (1998) *Transpersonal Methods for the Social Sciences*. Thousand Oaks, CA: Sage.

Brazier, David (1995) *Zen Therapy* London: Constable.

Brookes, Crittenden E. (1995) On supervision in Jungian continuous case seminars, in P. Kugler (ed.) *Jungian Perspectives on Clinical Supervision*. Einsiedeln: Daimon.

Brown, Laura S. (1997) *Ethics in psychology: Cui Bono?*, in D. Fox & I. Prilleltensky (eds) *Critical Psychology: An Introduction*. London: Sage.

Buber, Martin ([1923] 1970) *I and Thou*. Edinburgh: Clark.

Buber, Martin (1975) *Tales of the Hasidim*. New York: Schocken.

Budgell, Rosemary (1995) *Being Touched Through Space*, dissertation, School of Psychotherapy & Counselling, Regent's College, London.

Bugental, James F. T. (1981) *The Search for Authenticity* (enlarged edn). New York: Irvington.

Bugental, James (1987) *The Art of the Psychotherapist*. New York: W. W. Norton

Burman, Erica (ed.) (1990) *Feminists and Psychological Practice*. London: Sage.

Burns, Jan (1990) Women organizing within psychology: 2, in E. Burman (ed.) *Feminists and Psychological Practice*. London: Sage.

Campbell, Joseph (1988) *Historical Atlas of World Mythology: Vol.1 – The Way of the Animal Powers, Part 2: Mythologies of the Great Hunt*. New York: Harper & Row.

Carkhuff, R. R. (1969) *Helping and Human Relations: Vol.1 – Selection and Training*. New York: Holt, Rinehart & Winston.

Carroll, Michael (1996) *Counselling Supervision: Theory, Skills and Practice*. London: Cassell.

Caudill, Brandt (1999) Malpractice and licensing pitfalls for therapists: a defence attorney's list, in L. Vandecreek & T. L. Jackson (eds) *Innovations in Clinical Practice: A Source Book*. Sarasota, FL: Professional Resource Press.

Chamberlain, David (1998) *The Mind of your Newborn Baby*. Berkeley, CA: North Atlantic Books.

Chaplin, Jocelyn (1988) *Feminist Counselling in Action*. London: Sage.

Cheng, Ellen M. (1989) *The Tao Te Ching: A New Translation With Commentary*. New York: Paragon House.

Cinnirella, Marco & Loewenthal, Kate Miriam (1999) Religious and ethnic group influences on beliefs about mental illness: a qualitative interview study, *British Journal of Medical Psychology*, 72(4): 505–24.

Clarke, Isabel (2001) Psychosis and spirituality: finding a language, in S. King-Spooner & C. Newnes (eds) *Spirituality and Psychotherapy* Ross-on-Wye: PCCS Books.

Clarke, J. J. (1994) *Jung and Eastern Thought*. London: Routledge.

Clarke, J. J. (ed) (1995) *Jung on the East*. London: Routledge.

Clarkson, Petruska (1998) Supervised supervision: including the archetopoi of supervision, in P. Clarkson (ed.) *Supervision: Psychoanalytic and Jungian Perspectives*. London: Whurr.

Clarkson, Petruska (2003) *The Therapeutic Relationship*, (2nd edn). London: Whurr.

Clarkson, Petruska & Mackewn, Jennifer (1993) *Fritz Perls*. London: Sage.

Cobb, Noel (1997) On the sublime: Eva Loewe and the practice of psychotherapy, or Aphrodite in the consulting room, in P. Clarkson (ed.) *On the Sublime in Psychoanalysis, Archetypal Psychology and Psychotherapy*. London: Whurr.

Cohn, Hans W. (1997) *Existential Thought and Therapeutic Practice*. London: Sage.

Collen, Arne (1998) Human science research: an important focus for the next century, paper delivered at the international conference, Humanistic Psychology Towards the XXI Century, Lithuanian Association for Humanistic Psychology, Vilnius.

Connell, R. W. (1995) *Masculinities*. Berkeley, CA: University of California Press.

Cooper, Cassie (1990) Psychodynamic therapy: the Kleinian approach, in W. Dryden (ed.) *Individual Therapy: A Handbook*. Milton Keynes: Open University Press.

Cooper, Mick (1999) If you can't be Jekyll be Hyde: an existential-phenomenological exploration of lived-plurality, in J. Rowan & M. Cooper (eds) *The Plural Self: Multiplicity in Everyday Life*. London: Sage.

Cooper, Mick (2003) *Existential Therapies*. London: Sage.

Cooper, Mick & Cruthers, Helen (1999) Facilitating the expression of subpersonalities: a review and analysis of techniques, in J. Rowan & M. Cooper (eds) *The Plural Self: Multiplicity in Everyday Life*. London: Sage.

Corbett, Lionel (1995) Supervision and the mentor archetype, in P. Kugler (ed.) *Jungian Perspectives on Clinical Supervision*. Einsiedeln: Daimon.

Corbin, H. (1969) *Creative Imagination in the Sufism of Ibn 'Arabi*. Princeton, NJ: Princeton University Press.

Cortright, Brant (1997) *Psychotherapy and Spirit: Theory and Practice in Transpersonal Psychotherapy*. Albany, NY: Suny Press.

Craig, Grace J. (1992) *Human Development*, 6th edn. Englewood Cliffs, NJ: Prentice-Hall.

Crampton, Martha (1969) *The Use of Mental Imagery in Psychosynthesis*. New York: Psychosynthesis Research Foundation.

Cunningham, J. M. (1999) Primal therapies – stillborn theories, in C. Feltham (ed.) *Controversies in Psychotherapy and Counselling*. London: Sage.

Daniels, Thomas G., Rigazo-Digilio, Sandra A. & Ivey, Allen E. (1997) Microcounselling: a training and supervision paradigm for the helping professions, in C. E. Watkins (ed.) *Handbook of Psychotherapy Supervision*. New York: John Wiley.

Darongkamas, Jurai, Burton, Mary V. & Cushway, Delia (1994) The use of personal therapy by clinical psychologists working in the NHS in the United Kingdom, *Clinical Psychology and Psychotherapy*, 1(3): 165–73.

Davies, Dominic & Neal, Charles (1996) *Pink Therapy: A Guide for Counsellors and Therapists Working with Lesbian, Gay and Bisexual Clients*. Buckingham: Open University Press.

Denzin, Norman K. & Lincoln, Yvonna S. (2000) The discipline and practice of qualitative research, in N. K. Denzin & Y. S. Lincoln (eds) *Handbook of Qualitative Research*, 2nd edn. Thousand Oaks, CA: Sage.

Dineen, T. (1998) *Manufacturing Victims: What the Psychology Industry is doing to People*, 3rd edn. Robert Davis Publishing.

Dinnage, R. (ed.)(1988) *One to One: Experiences of Psychotherapy*. London: Penguin.

Douglas, Anne (1989) The limits of cognitive-behaviour therapy: can it be integrated with psychodynamic therapy? *British Journal of Psychotherapy*, 5(3): 390–401.

Dryden, Windy (1994) Possible future trends in counselling and counselling training: a personal view, *Counselling*, 5(3): 194–7.

Dryden, Windy & Feltham, Colin (eds) (1992) *Psychotherapy and its Discontents*. Buckingham: Open University Press.

Dryden, Windy & Neenan, Michael (eds) (2002) *Rational Emotive Behaviour Group Therapy*. London: Whurr.

Dryden, W. & Norcross, J. C. (1990) *Eclecticism and Integration in Counselling and Psychotherapy*. Loughton: Gale Centre Publications.

Duncan, B. L. & Moynihan, D. W. (1994) Applying outcome research: intentional utilization of the client's frame of reference, *Psychotherapy*, 31: 294–301.

Egan, Gerard (1976) Confrontation, *Group & Organization Studies*, 1(2): 223–43.

Ekstein, R. & Wallerstein, R. S. (1972) *The Teaching and Learning of Psychotherapy*, 2nd edn. New York: Basic Books.

Ellenberger, H. F. (1970) *The Discovery of the Unconscious*. New York: Basic Books.

Elliott R. Hill, C. E., Stiles, W. B., Friedlander, M. L., Mahrer, A. R. & Margison, F. R. (1987) Primary therapist response modes: comparison of six rating systems, *Journal of Consulting and Clinical Psychology*, 55: 218–23.

Ellis, A. (1980) Treatment of erectile dysfunction, in S. R. Leiblum & L. A. Pervin (eds) *Principles and Practice of Sex Therapy*. London: Tavistock.

Ellis, A. (1983) Failures in rational-emotive therapy, in E. B. Foa & P. M. G. Emmelkamp (eds) *Failures in Behaviour Therapy*. New York: John Wiley.

Ellis, Carolyn & Bochner, Arthur P. (2000) Authoethnography, personal narrative, reflexivity, in N. K. Denzin & Y. S. Lincoln (eds) *Handbook of Qualitative Research*, 2nd edn. Thousand Oaks, CA: Sage.

Emerson, William & Schorr-Kon, Stephan (1994) Somatotropic therapy, in D. Jones (ed.) *Innovative Therapy: A Handbook*. Buckingham: Open University Press.

Emmons, M. L. (1978) *The Inner Source*. San Luis Obispo: Impact.

Epstein, Mark (1996) *Thoughts Without a Thinker*. London: Duckworth.

Epstein, Mark (1998) *Going to Pieces Without Falling Apart: A Buddhist Perspective on Wholeness*. London: Thorsons.

Erickson, Milton (1980) Deep hypnosis and its induction, in E. L. Rossi (ed.) *The Nature of Hypnosis and Suggestion: The Collected Papers of Milton H. Erikson on Hypnosis*, vol. 1. New York: Irvington Publishers.

Erikson, Eric H. (1965) *Childhood and Society*. London: Penguin.

Ernst, Sheila & Goodison, Lucy (1981) *In Our Own Hands: A Handbook of Self-help Therapy*. London: The Women's Press.

Erskine, Richard G. & Moursund, Janet P. (1988) *Integrative Psychotherapy in Action*. Newbury Park, CA: Sage.

Estes, Clarissa Pinkola (1992) *Women Who Run With The Wolves*. London: Rider.

Evison, Rose & Horobin, Richard (1988) Co-counselling, in J. Rowan & W. Dryden (eds) *Innovative Therapy in Britain*. Milton Keynes: Open University Press.

Farrant, Graham (1986) Cellular consciousness, keynote address at 14th IPA Convention, 30 August.

Farrell, W. (1990) *Why Men Are the Way They Are*. London: Bantam.

Feinberg, Todd E. (2002) *Altered Egos*. New York: Oxford University Press.

Feltham, Colin & Dryden, Windy (eds) (1993) *Dictionary of Psychotherapy*. London: Whurr.

Ferrucci, Piero (1982) *What We May Be*. Wellingborough: Turnstone Press.

Field, Nathan (1996) *Breakdown and Breakthrough: Psychotherapy in a new Dimension*. London: Routledge.

Finch, Janet (1981) It's great to have someone to talk to: the ethics and politics of interviewing women, in H. Roberts (ed.) *Doing Feminist Research*. London: Routledge.

Fine, Michelle (1994) Working the hyphens: reinventing self and other in qualitative research, in N. K. Denzin & Y. S. Lincoln (eds) *Handbook of Qualitative Research*. Thousand Oaks, CA: Sage.

Finlay, L. (1998) Reflexivity: an essential component for all research? *British Journal of Occupational Psychology*, 61(10): 453–6.

Firman, John & Gila, Ann (1997) *The Primal Wound: A Transpersonal View of Trauma, Addiction and Growth*. Albany, NY: State University of New York Press.

Fletcher, J., Fahey, T. & McWilliams, J. (1995) Relationship between provision of counselling and the prescribing of antidepressants, hypnotics and anxiolytics in general practice, *British Journal of General Practice*, 45: 467–9.

Fonagy, Peter (1989) On the integration of cognitive-behaviour therapy with psychoanalysis, *British Journal of Psychotherapy*, 5(4): 557–63.

Fordham, Michael (1979) Analytical psychology and countertransference, in L. Epstein & A. Finer (eds) *Countertransference*. New York: Jason Aronson.

Forsyth, Douglas R. & Ivey, Allen E. (1980) Microtraining: an approach to differential supervision, in Allen K. Hess (ed.) *Psychotherapy Supervision: Theory, Research and Practice*. New York: John Wiley.

Fox, Warwick (1995) *Toward a Transpersonal Ecology*. Foxhole, Devon: Green Books Ltd.

Freedman, Jill & Combs, Gene (1996) *Narrative Therapy: The Social Constructiuon of Preferred Realities*. New York: W. W. Norton.

Freeman, A. & Reinecke, M. A. (1995) Cognitive therapy, in A. S. Gurman & S. B. Messer (eds) *Essential Psychotherapies: Theory and Practice*. New York: Guilford Press.

Friedman, Maurice (1964) Problematic rebel: an image of modern man, in M. Friedman (ed.) *The Worlds of Existentialism: A Critical Reader*. Chicago: University of Chicago Press.

Fukuyama, Mary A. & Sevig, Todd D. (1999) *Integrating Spirituality into Multicultural Counselling*. Thousand Oaks, CA: Sage.

Gee, Hugh (1998) Developing insight through supervision: relating, then defining, in P. Clarkson (ed.) *Supervision: Psychoanalytic and Jungian Perspectives*. London: Whurr.

Geertz, Clifford (1973) *The Interpretation of Cultures: Selected Essays*. New York: Basic Books.

Geertz, Clifford (1983) *Local Knowledge: Further Essays in Interpretive Anthropology*. New York: Basic Books.

Geertz, Clifford (1988) *Works and Lives: The Anthropologist as Author*. Stanford, CA: Stanford University Press.

Gendlin, Eugene T. (1996) *Focusing-oriented Psychotherapy: A Manual of the Experiential Method*. New York: Guilford Press.

Gibson, Terrill L. (2000) Wholeness and transcendence in the practice of pastoral psychotherapy from a Judaeo-Christian perspective, in P. Young-Eisendrath & M. E. Miller (eds) *The Psychology of Mature Spirituality*. London: Routledge.

Gilligan, Carol (1982) *In a Different Voice: Psychological Theory and Women's Development*. London: Harvard University Press.

Glouberman, Dina (1995) *Life Choices, Life Changes*, 3rd edn. London: Thorsons.

Gold, Jerold R. (1994) When the patient does the integrating: lessons for theory and practice, *Journal of Psychotherapy Integration*, 4: 133–58.

Goldberg, C. (2001) Influence and moral agency in psychotherapy, *International Journal of Psychotherapy*, 6(2) 107–14.

Goldstein, Kurt ([1934] 1995) *The Organism*. New York: Zone Books.

Goleman, Daniel (1977) *The Varieties of the Meditative Experience*. London: Rider.

Gomes, Mary E. & Kanner, Allen D. (1995) The rape of the well-maidens, in T. Roszak, M. E. Gomes & A. D. Kanner (eds) *Ecopsychology*. San Francisco: Sierra Club.

Gomez, L. (1997) *An Introduction to Object Relations*. London: Free Association Books.

Goodison, Lucy (1990) *Moving Heaven and Earth: Sexuality, Spirituality and Social Change*. London: The Women's Press.

Gordon-Brown, Ian & Somers, Barbara (1988) Transpersonal psychotherapy, in J. Rowan & W. Dryden (eds) *Innovative Therapy in Britain*. Milton Keynes: Open University Press.

Gottsegen, G. & Gottsegen, M. (1979) Countertransference – the professional identity defence, *Psychotherapy: Theory, Research & Practice*, 16.

Greenberg, Leslie S., Watson, Jeanne C. & Lietaer, Germain (eds) (1998) *Handbook of Experiential Psychotherapy*. New York: Guilford Press.

Grieger, R. (1989) A client's guide to rational-emotive therapy (RET), in W. Dryden & F. Trower (eds) *Cognitive Psychotherapy: Stasis and Change*. London: Cassell.

Griffin, D. R. (1998) *Unsnarling the World-knot: Consciousness, Freedom and the Mind-body Problem*. Berkeley, CA: University of California Press.

Griffin, J. & Tyrrell, I. (1999) *Breaking the Cycle of Depression: Organising Ideas*. Monograph, ETSI.

Griffith, James L. & Griffith, Melissa E. (1994) *The Body Speaks: Therapeutic Dialogues for Mind/body Problems*. New York: Basic Books.

Griffith, James L. & Griffith, Melissa E. (2002) *Encountering the Sacred in Psychotherapy: How to Talk with People About their Spiritual Lives*. New York: Guilford Press.

Grof, Stanislav (1979) *Realms of the Human Unconscious: Observations from LSD Research*. London: Souvenir Press.

Grof, Stanislav (1980) *LSD Psychotherapy*. Pomona: Hunter House.

Grof, Stanislav (1985) *Beyond the Brain*. Albany, NY: State University of New York Press.

Grof, Stanislav (1988) *The Adventure of Self-discovery*. Albany, NY: SUNY Press.

Grof, Stanislav (1992) *The Holotropic Mind: The Three Levels of Human Consciousness and How they Shape our Lives*. New York: Harper & Row.

Grof, Stanislav & Grof, Christina (1989) *Spiritual Emergency*. Los Angeles: Tarcher.

Grof, Christina & Grof, Stanislav (1990) *The Stormy Search for the Self*. Los Angeles: Tarcher.

Grove, David & Panzer, B. I. (1989) *Resolving Traumatic Memories: Metaphors and Symbols in Psychotherapy*. New York: Irvington Publishers.

Guy, J., Stark, M. J. & Poelstra, P. L. (1988) Personal therapy for psychotherapists before and after entering professional practice, *Professional Psychology: Research and Practice*, 19: 474–6.

Hanna, Fred J. (1996) Precursors of change: pivotal points of involvement and resistance in psychotherapy, *Journal of Psychotherapy Integration*, 6(3): 227–64.

Hanna, Fred J. & Ottens, Allen J. (1995) The role of wisdom in psychotherapy, *Journal of Psychotherapy Integration*, 5(3): 195–219.

Hardy, Jean (1987) *A Psychology with a Soul: Psychosynthesis in Evolutionary Context*. London: Routledge.

Harrison, Roger (1984) Leadership and strategy for a new age, in J. D. Adams (ed.) *Transforming Work*. Alexandria, VA: Miles River Press.

Hattie, J. A., Sharpley, C. F. & Rogers, H. J. (1984) Comparative effectiveness of professional and paraprofessional helpers, *Psychological Bulletin*, 95: 534–41.

Haugh, Sheila & Merry, Tony (2001) *Empathy* (*Rogers' Therapeutic Conditions*, vol. 2). Ross-on-Wye: PCCS Books.

Hawkins, Peter & Shohet, Robin (2000) *Supervision in the Helping Professions*, 2nd edn. Buckingham: Open University Press.

Heidegger, Martin (1962) *Being and Time*. New York: Harper & Row.

Heimann, Paula (1950) On countertransference, *International Journal of Psycho-Analysis*, 31: 81–4.

Heinl, Peter (2001) *Splintered Innocence: An Intuitive Approach to Treating War Trauma*. Hove: Brunner-Routledge.

Henderson, David (1998) Solitude and solidarity: a philosophy of supervision, in P. Clarkson (ed.) *Supervision: Psychoanalytic and Jungian Perspectives*. London: Whurr.

Henderson, Joseph L. (1995) Assessing progress in supervision, in P. Kugler (ed.) *Jungian Perspectives on Clinical Supervision*. Einsiedeln: Daimon.

Heron, John (1988) Impressions of the other reality: a co-operative inquiry into altered states of consciousness, in P. Reason (ed.) *Human Inquiry in Action*. London: Sage.

Hill, Clara E. (1985) *Manual for the Hill Counsellor and Client Verbal Response Modes Category System* (rev. edn). Unpublished manuscript, University of Maryland.

Hillman, James (1975) *Re-visioning Psychology*. New York: Harper & Row.

Hillman, James (1981) Psychology: monotheistic or polytheistic?, in D. L. Miller (ed.) *The New Polytheism: Rebirth of the Gods and Goddesses*. Dallas, TX: Spring.

Hillman, James (1990) *The Essential James Hillman: A Blue Fire* (introduced and edited by Thomas Moore). London: Routledge.

Hinshelwood, R. D. (1989) *A Dictionary of Kleinian Thought*. London: Free Association Books.

Holland, R. (1999) Reflexivity, *Human Relations*, 52(4) 463–84.

Holloway, Elizabeth (1995) *Clinical Supervision: A Systems Approach*. Thousand Oaks, CA: Sage.

Hopkins, J. (1974) *Deity Yoga*. London: Wisdom Publications.

House, Richard & Totton, Nick (1997) *Implausible Professions: Arguments for Pluralism and Autonomy in Psychotherapy and Counselling*. Ross-on-Wye: PCCS Books.

Houston, Gaie (1995) *Supervision and Counselling (new revised edition)*. London: Rochester Foundation.

Houston, Jean (1982) *The Possible Human*. Los Angeles: Tarcher.

Houston, Jean (1987) *Search for the Beloved: Journeys in Sacred Psychology*. Los Angeles: Tarcher.

Howard, Alex (1996) *Challenges to Counselling and Psychotherapy*. Basingstoke: Macmillan.

Hycner, Richard (1993) *Between Person and Person*. Highland, NY: Gestalt Journal Press.

Irving, Judi & Williams, David (1996) The role of groupwork in counselling training, *Counselling*, 7(2) 137–9.

Jaffe, Dennis T. & Scott, Cynthia D. (1993) Building a committed workplace: an empowered organization as a competitive advantage, in M. Ray & A. Rinzler (eds) *The New Paradigm in Business*. Los Angeles: Tarcher.

James, Muriel (1995) Transactional analysis, in A. S. Gurman & S. B. Messer (eds) *Essential Therapies: Theory and Practice*. New York: Guilford Press.

Janov, Arthur (1983) *Imprints: The Lifelong Effects of the Birth Experience*. New York: Coward-McCann.

Jefferies, Jinnie (1998) The processing, in M. Karp, P. Holmes & K. B. Tauvon (eds) *The Handbook of Psychodrama*. London: Routledge.

Joba, Cynthia, Maynard, Herman Bryant & Ray, Michael (1993) Competition, cooperation and co-creation: insights from the World Business Academy, in M. Ray & A. Rinzler (eds) *The New Paradigm in Business*. Los Angeles: Tarcher.

Jones, E. E. (1993) Single-case research in psychotherapy, *Journal of Consulting and Clinical Psychology*, 61: 371–430.

Jukes, Adam (1993) *Why Men Hate Women*. London: Free Association Books.

Jung, Carl Gustav (1966) Psychotherapy and a philosophy of life, in *Collected Works*, vol.16, para. 179. London: Routledge.

Kapleau, Philip (1967) *The Three Pillars of Zen*. Boston, MA: Beacon.

Karp, Marcia, Holmes, Paul & Tauvon, Kate Bradshaw (1998) *The Handbook of Psychodrama*. London: Routledge.

Keleman, Stanley (1985) *Emotional Anatomy*. Berkeley, CA: Center Press.

Kennard, D., Roberts, J. & Winter, D. (1993) *A Work Book of Group-analytic Interventions*. London: Routledge.

Kidder, Louise H. and Fine, Michelle (1987) Qualitative and quantitative methods: when stories converge, in M. M. Mark & L. Shotland (eds) *New Directions in Program Evaluation*. San Francisco: Jossey-Bass.

Kidder, Louise H. & Fine, Michelle (1997) Qualitative inquiry in psychology: a radical tradition, in D. Fox & I. Prilleltensky (eds) *Critical Psychology: An Introduction*. Thousand Oaks, CA: Sage.

Kirschenbaum, Howard & Henderson, Valerie L. (1990) *The Carl Rogers Reader*. London: Constable.

Klimo, John (1988) *Channelling Aquarius*. Wellingborough: Aquarius.

Kogan, G. (1980) *Your Bodyworks: A Guide to Health, Energy and Balance*. Berkeley, CA: Transformation Press.

Kohlberg, Lawrence (1981) *The Philosophy of Moral Development*. New York: Harper & Row.

Kramer, Charles H. (2000) Revealing our selves, in M. Baldwin (ed.) *The use of self in therapy*, 2nd edn. Binghamton: Haworth Press.

Kurtz, Ron & Prestera, Hector (1977) *The Body Reveals*. New York: Bantam.

Lacey, Tim (2004) Group therapy and CBT, *Counselling and Psychotherapy Journal*, 15(2) 34–5.

Lago, Colin & Smith, Barbara (2003) *Anti-discriminatory Counselling Practice*. London: Sage.

Lago, Colin & Thompson, Joyce (1996) *Race, Culture and Counselling*. Buckingham: Open University Press.

Laing, R. D. (1983) *The Voice of Experience*. Harmondsworth: Penguin.

Lake, Frank (1980) *Constricted Confusion*. Oxford: Clinical Theology Association.

Lambert, M. J. (1986) Some implications of psychotherapy outcome research for eclectic psychotherapy, *International Journal of Eclectic Psychotherapy*, 5: 16–46.

Lambert, M. J. & Bergin, A. E. (1983) Therapist characteristics and their contribution to therapeutic outcome, in C. E. Walker (ed.) *The Handbook of Clinical Psychology: Theory, Research and Practice*. Homewood: Dow, Jones-Irwin.

Lambert, M. J., Shapiro, D. A. & Bergin, A. E. (1986) The effectiveness of psychotherapy, in S. L. Garfield & A. E. Bergin (eds) *Psychotherapy and Behaviour Change* (3rd edn). New York: John Wiley.

Lamm, Zvi (1984) Ideologies in a hierarchical order: a neglected theory, *Science and Public Policy*, February: 40–6.

Langs, Robert J. (1980) Supervision and the bipersonal field, in Allen K. Hess (ed.) *Psychotherapy Supervision: Theory, Research and Practice.* New York: John Wiley.

Lather, Patti (1991) *Getting Smart: Feminist Research and Pedagogy With/in the Postmodern.* London: Routledge.

Laungani, Pittu (1999) Culture and identity: implications for counselling, in S. Palmer & P. Laungani (eds) *Counselling in a Multicultural Society.* London: Sage.

Lazarus, Arnold A. (1989) *The Practice of Multimodal Therapy.* Baltimore: Johns Hopkins University Press.

Lazarus, Arnold A. & Zur, Ofer (2002) *Dual Relationships and Psychotherapy*: New York: Springer.

Leiman, M. & Stiles, W. B. (2001) Dialogical sequence analysis and the zone of proximal developments as conceptual enhancements to the assimilation model: the case of Jan revisited, *Psychotherapy Research,* 11(3): 311–330.

Leuner, Hanscarl (1984) *Guided Affective Imagery.* New York: Thieme-Stratton.

Levant, R. F. & Pollack, W. S. (eds) (1995) *A New Psychology of Men.* New York: Basic Books.

Levin, David M. (1981) Approaches to psychotherapy: Freud, Jung and Tibetan Buddhism, in R. S. Valle & R. von Eckartsberg (eds) *The Metaphors of Consciousness.* New York: Plenum.

Lidmila, Alan (1997) Shame, knowledge and modes of enquiry in supervision, in G. Shipton (ed.) *Supervision of Psychotherapy and Counselling.* Buckingham: Open University Press.

Lieberman, M. A., Yalom, I. D. & Miles, M. B. (1973) *Encounter Groups: First Facts.* New York: Basic Books.

Linehan, Marsha M. (1980) Supervision of behaviour therapy, in Allen K. Hess (ed.) *Psychotherapy Supervision: Theory, Research and Practice.* New York: John Wiley.

Loevinger, Jane (1976) *Ego Development.* San Francisco: Jossy-Bass.

Lovinger, R. J. (1992) Theoretical affiliations in psychotherapy, *Psychotherapy,* 29: 586–90.

Lowen, Alexander (1976) *Bioenergetics.* London: Coventure.

Lowen, A. & Lowen, L. (1977) *The Way to Vibrant Health.* New York: Harper & Row.

Lukoff, David (1985) The diagnosis of mystical experiences with psychotic features, *Journal of Transpersonal Psychology,* 17(2): 155–81. www.blackboard.com/bin/catalog.

Lyons, Amelia (1997) The role of groupwork in counselling training, *Counselling,* 8(3): 211–5.

Macaskill, N. D. (1988) Personal therapy in the training of the psychotherapist: is it effective? *British Journal of Psychotherapy,* 42: 219–26.

Maclagan, David (1997) Fantasy, play and the image in supervision, in G. Shipton (ed.) *Supervision of Psychotherapy and Counselling*. Buckingham: Open University Press.

Macran, Susan & Shapiro, David A. (1998) The role of personal therapy for therapists: a review, *British Journal of Medical Psychology*, 71(1): 13–25.

McClelland, Sheila (1993) The art of science with clients, in H. Payne (ed.) *Handbook of Inquiry in the Arts Therapies*. London: Jessica Kingsley.

McLellan, B. (1995) *Beyond Psychoppression: A Feminist Alternative Therapy*. North Melbourne: Spinifex Press.

McLeod, John (1997) *Narrative and Psychotherapy*. London: Sage.

Maddi, Salvatore R. (1996) *Personality Theories: A Comparative Analysis*, 6th edn. Pacific Grove, CA: Brooks/Cole.

Mahrer, Alvin R. (1978) *Experiencing: A Humanistic Theory of Psychology and Psychiatry*. New York: Brunner/Mazel.

Mahrer, Alvin R. (1985) *Psychotherapeutic Change*. New York: W. W. Norton.

Mahrer, Alvin R. (1989a) *The Integration of Psychotherapies*. New York: Human Sciences Press.

Mahrer, Alvin R. (1989b) *Dreamwork in Psychotherapy and Self-change*. New York: W. W. Norton.

Mahrer, Alvin R. (1996) *The Complete Guide to Experiential Psychotherapy*. New York: John Wiley.

Mahrer, Alvin R. (1998) Embarrassing problems for the field of psychotherapy, *BPS Psychotherapy Section Newsletter*, 23: 19–29.

Malan, David H. (1979) *Individual Psychotherapy and the Science of Psychodynamics*. London: Butterworth.

Marton, F., Fensham, P. & Chaiklin, P. (1994) A Nobel's eye view of scientific intuition: discussions with Nobel prize-winners in physics, chemistry and medicine (1970–86), *International Journal of Scientific Education*, 16(4): 457–73.

Maslow, Abraham H. (1969) *The Psychology of Science: A Reconnaissance*. Chicago: Henry Regnery.

Maslow, Abraham H. (1987) *Motivation and Personality*, 3rd edn. New York: Harper & Row.

Masson, Jeffrey (1988) *Against Therapy*. London: Fontana.

Masters, Robert E. L. & Houston, Jean (1966) *The Varieties of Psychedelic Experience*. London: Turnstone.

Matarazzo, R.G. (1978) Research on the teaching and learning of psychotherapeutic skills, in S. L. Garfield and A. E. Bergin (eds) *Handbook of Psychotherapy and Behaviour Change*, 2nd edn. New York: John Wiley.

May, Robert M. (1991) *Cosmic Consciousness Revisited: The Modern Origins and Development of a Western Spiritual Psychology*. Shaftesbury: Element.

May, Rollo (1980) *Psychology and the Human Dilemma*. New York: W. W. Norton.

May, Rollo (1983) *The Discovery of Being*. New York: W. W. Norton.

Meade, Michael (1993) *Men and the Water of Life: Initiation and the Tempering of Men.* New York: Harper & Row.

Mearns, Dave (1997) Achieving the personal development dimension in professional counsellor training, *Counselling*, 8(2): 113–20.

Mearns, Dave & Dryden, Windy (eds) (1990) *Experiences of Counselling in Action.* London: Sage.

Mearns, Dave & Thorne, B. (2000) *Person-centred Therapy Today: New Frontiers in Theory and Practice.* London: Sage.

Meier, A. & Boivin, M. (2000) The achievement of greater selfhood: the application of theme analysis to a case study, *Psychotherapy Research*, 10(1): 57–77.

Merleau-Ponty, Maurice (1962) *The Phenomenology of Perception.* London: Routledge.

Mertens, Donna M. (1998) *Research Methods in Education and Psychology.* Thousand Oaks, CA: Sage.

Mies, Maria (1983) Towards a methodology for feminist research, in G. Bowles & R. D. Klein (eds) *Theories of Women's Studies.* London: Routledge.

Miller, Alice (1985) *Thou Shalt Not Be Aware.* London: Pluto Press.

Miller, Scott D., Hubble, Mark A. & Duncan, Barry L. (1995) No more bells and whistles, *Family Therapy Networker*, 19: 52–63.

Miller, Scott D., Duncan, Barry L. & Hubble, Mark A. (1997) *Escape from Babel: Toward a Unifying Language for Psychotherapy Practice.* New York: W. W. Norton.

Mindell, Amy (1995) *Metaskills.* Tempe, AZ: New Falcon Publications.

Mindell, Arnold (1985) *Working with the Dreaming Body.* London: Routledge.

Mindell, Arnold & Mindell, Amy (2002) *Riding the Horse Backwards: Process Work in Theory and Practice*, 2nd edn. Portland: Lao Tse Press.

Mitroff, Ian I. (1974) *The Subjective Side of Science.* Amsterdam: Elsevier.

Mitroff, Ian I. & Kilmann, Ralph H. (1978) *Methodological Approaches to Social Science.* San Francisco: Jossey-Bass.

Mittelman, Willard (1991) Maslow's study of self-actualization: a reinterpretation, *Journal of Humanistic Psychology*, 31(1): 114–35.

Mollon, Phil (1997) Supervision as a space for thinking, in G. Shipton (ed.) *Supervision of Psychotherapy and Counselling.* Buckingham: Open University Press.

Money-Kyrle, Roger (1956) Normal countertransference and some of its deviations, in *The Collected Papers of Roger Money-Kyrle.* Perth: Clunie.

Moore, Thomas (1992) *Care of the Soul.* London: Piatkus.

Morgan-Jones, Richard & Abram, Jan (2001) *Psycho-analytic Psychotherapy Trainings: A Guide.* London: Free Association Books.

Moss, Donald M. (1981) Transformation of self and world in Johannes Tauler's mysticism, in R. S. Valle & R. von Eckartsberg (eds) *The Metaphors of Consciousness.* New York: Plenum Press.

Nelson, John E. (1996) Madness or transcendence? Looking to the ancient east for a modern transpersonal diagnostic system, in S. Boorstein (ed.) *Transpersonal Psychotherapy*, 2nd edn. Albany, NY: SUNY Press.

Nichols, Michael P. & Zax, Melvin (1977) *Catharsis in Psychotherapy*. New York: Gardner Press.

Nietzsche, Friedrich ([1901] 1967) *The Will to Power*. New York: Random House.

Nightingale, David & Neilands, Tor (1997) Understanding and practising critical psychology, in D. Fox & I. Prilleltensky (eds) *Critical Psychology: An Introduction*. London: Sage.

Norcross, J. C. & Goldfried, M. R. (eds) (1992) *Handbook of Psychotherapy Integration*. New York: Basic Books.

Norcross, J. C. & Prochaska, J. O. (1983) Clinicians' theoretical orientations: selection, utilization and efficacy, *Professional Psychology*, 14: 197–208.

O'Hara, Maureen (1986) Heuristic inquiry as psychotherapy: the client-centred approach, *Person-Centred Review*, 1: 172–84.

Oakley, Ann (1981) Interviewing women: a contradiction in terms, in Helen Roberts (ed.) *Doing Feminist Research*. London: Routledge.

Page, Steve & Wosket, Val (1994) *Supervising the Counsellor: A Cyclical Model*. London: Routledge.

Painter, Jack (1986) *Deep Bodywork and Personal Development*. Mill Valley, CA: Bodymind Books.

Palmer, S. & Laungani, P. (1999) *Counselling in a Multicultural Society*. London: Sage.

Papadopoulos, Linda, Cross, Malcolm C. & Bor, Robert (2003) *Reporting in Counselling and Psychotherapy: A Trainee's Guide to Preparing Case Studies and Reports*. London: Brunner-Routledge.

Peters, Larry G. (1989) Shamanism: phenomenology of a spiritual discipline, *The Journal of Transpersonal Psychology*, 21(2): 115–37.

Phoenix, Ann (1990) Social research in the context of feminist psychology, in Erica Burman (ed.) *Feminists and Psychological Practice*. London: Sage.

Piaget, Jean (1977) *The Essential Piaget* (ed. H. Gruber & J. Voneche). New York: Basic Books.

Piontelli, Allessandra (2002) *Twins: From Foetus to Child*. London: Routledge.

Plasil, E. (1985) *Therapist*. New York: St Martins Press.

Plaut, Fred (1993) *Analysis Analysed*. London: Routledge.

Progoff, Ira (1975) *At a Journal Workshop*. New York: Dialogue House.

Proskauer, Magda (1977) The therapeutic value of certain breathing techniques, in C. A. Garfield (ed.) *Rediscovery of the Body*. New York: Dell.

Punch, Maurice (1994) Politics and ethics in qualitative research, in N. K. Denzin & Y. S. Lincoln (eds) *Handbook of Qualitative Research*. Thousand Oaks, CA: Sage.

Rabin, Bonnie & Walker, Robert (undated) A contemplative approach to clinical supervision, Boulder, CO: Naropa Institute.

Racker, Heinrich (1968) *Transference and Countertransference*. London: Hogarth Press.

Rawson, Philip (1973) *The Art of Tantra*. New York: Graphic Society.

Reason, Peter & Bradbury, Hilary (2001) Introduction: inquiry and participation in search of a world worthy of human aspiration, in P. Reason & H. Bradbury (eds) *Handbook of Action Research: Participative Inquiry and Practice*. London: Sage.

Reason, Peter & Hawkins, Peter (1988) Storytelling as inquiry, in P. Reason (ed.) *Human Inquiry in Action*. London: Sage.

Reason, Peter & Rowan, John (eds) (1981) *Human Inquiry: A Sourcebook of New Paradigm Research*. Chichester: John Wiley.

Rice, Laura N. (1980) A client-centred approach to the supervision of psychotherapy, in Allen K. Hess (ed.) *Psychotherapy Supervision: Theory, Research and Practice*. New York: John Wiley.

Riegel, K. F. (1984) in M. L. Commons, F. A. Richards and C. Armon (eds) *Beyond Formal Operations: Late Adolescence and Adult Cognitive Development*. New York: Praeger.

Rioch, Margaret J., Coulter, Winifred R. & Weinberger, David M. (1976) *Dialogues for Therapists*. San Francisco: Jossey-Bass.

Robertson, Malcolm (1986) Training eclectic psychotherapists, in J. C. Norcross (ed.) *Handbook of Eclectic Psychotherapy*. New York: Brunner/Mazel.

Robertson, Malcolm (1995) *Psychotherapy Education and Training: An Integrative Perspective*. Madison: International Universities Press.

Rogers, Carl R. (1961) *On Becoming a Person*. London: Constable.

Rogers, Carl R. (1980) *A Way of Being*. Boston, MA: Houghton Mifflin.

Rogers, Penny (1993) Research in music therapy with sexually abused clients, in H. Payne (ed.) *Handbook of Inquiry in the Arts Therapies*. London: Jessica Kingsley.

Roose, Kris *et al.* (1991) An integrative model in psychotherapy training, paper presented at the SEPI congress, London, July.

Rosenbaum, Robert (1998) *Zen and the Heart of Psychotherapy*. Philadelphia: Brunner/Mazel.

Rothschild, Babette (2000) *The Body Remembers: The Psychophysiology of Trauma and Trauma Treatment* New York: W. W. Norton.

Rowan, John (1988) Primal integration therapy, in J. Rowan & W. Dryden (eds) *Innovative Therapy in Britain*. Milton Keynes: Open University Press.

Rowan, John (1990) *Subpersonalities: The People Inside Us*. London: Routledge.

Rowan, John (1993) *The Transpersonal: Psychotherapy and Counselling*. London: Routledge.

Rowan, John (1994) Do therapists ever cure clients? *Self & Society*, 22(5): 4–5.

Rowan, John (1997) *Healing the Male Psyche: Therapy as Initiation*. London: Routledge.

Rowan, John (1998a) *The Reality Game: A Guide to Humanistic Counselling and Psychotherapy*, 2nd edn. London: Routledge.

Rowan, John (1998b) Therapeutic interventions, *Journal of Psychotherapy Integration*, 8(4): 231–48.

Rowan, John (1998c) Linking: its place in therapy, *International Journal of Psychotherapy*, 3(3): 245–54.

Rowan, John (1999) The trauma of birth, in C. Feltham (ed.) *Controversies in Psychotherapy and Counselling*. London: Sage.

Rowan, John (2001a) *Ordinary Ecstasy: The Dialectics of Humanistic Psychology*, 3rd edn. Hove: Brunner-Routledge.

Rowan, John (2001b) The humanistic approach to action research, in P. Reason & H. Bradbury (eds) *Handbook of Action Research*. London: Sage.

Rowan, John (2001c) Therapy as an alchemical process, *International Journal of Psychotherapy*, 6(3): 315–30.

Rowan, John (2002) *The Transpersonal: Psychotherapy and Counselling* (reprint with Afterword). Hove: Brunner-Routledge.

Rowan, John (2003) Being, doing and knowing in transpersonal therapy, *Transpersonal Psychology Review*, 7(1): 56–71.

Rowan, John & Jacobs, M. (2002) *The Therapist's Use of Self*. Buckingham: Open University Press.

Rush, A. K. (1973) *Getting Clear: Bodywork for Women*. New York: Random House.

Russell, Roberta (1981) *Report on Effective Psychotherapy: Legislative Testimony*. New York: R. R. Latin Associates.

Russell, Roberta (1993) *Report on Effective Psychotherapy*. Lake Placid: Hilgarth Press.

Rutherford, Leo (1996) *Shamanism*. London: Thorsons.

Ryle, Anthony (1990) *Cognitive-Analytic Therapy: Active Participation in Change*. Chichester: John Wiley.

Salter, A. (1949) *Conditioned Reflex Therapy*. New York: Farrar Strauss.

Sampson, Edward E. (1993) *Celebrating the Other: A Dialogic Account of Human Nature*. Boulder, CO: Westview.

Samuels, Andrew (1989) *The Plural Psyche*. London: Routledge.

Samuels, Andrew (1993) *The Political Psyche*. London: Routledge.

Samuels, Andrew (1997) Countertransference, the imaginal world and the politics of the sublime, in P. Clarkson (ed.) *On the Sublime: In Psychoanalysis, Archetypal Psychology and Psychotherapy*. London: Whurr.

Samuels, Andrew, Shorter, Bani & Plaut, Fred (1986) *A Critical Dictionary of Jungian Analysis*. London: Routledge & Kegan Paul.

Sands, A. (2000) *Falling for Therapy: Psychotherapy from a Client's Point of View*. London: Palgrave.

Sanella, Lee (1987) *The Kundalini Experience*. Lower Lake, CA: Integral Publishing.

Sapriel, Lolita (1998) Can Gestalt therapy, self-psychology and intersubjectivity theory be integrated? *British Gestalt Journal*, 7(1): 33–44.

Sartre, Jean-Paul (1948) *Existentialism and Humanism*. London: Methuen.

Schneider, Kirk & May, Rollo (1995) *The Psychology of Existence: An Integrative, Clinical Perspective*. New York: McGraw-Hill.

Schutz, Will C. (1984) *The Truth Option*. Berkeley, CA: Ten Speed Press.

Schwartz, Robert M. (1993) The idea of balance and integrative psychotherapy, *Journal of Psychotherapy Integration*, 3(2): 159–81.

Schwartz-Salant, N. (1984) in N. Schwartz-Salant and M. Stein (eds) *Transference, Countertransference*. Wilmette, IL: Chiron.

Schwartz-Salant, N. (1991) in N. Schwartz-Salant and M. Stein (eds) *Liminality and Transitional Phenomena*. Wilmette, IL: Chiron.

Scott, Michael J. & Stradling, Stephen G. (1988) *Brief Group Counselling: Integrating Individual and Group Cognitive-behavioural Approaches*. Chichester: John Wiley.

Searles, H. F. (1979) *Countertransference and Related Subjects*. New York: International Universities Press.

Seiser, Lynn & Wastell, Colin (2002) *Interventions and Techniques*. Buckingham: Open University Press.

Shadley, Meri L. (2000) Are all therapists alike? Revisiting research about the use of self in therapy, in M. Baldwin (ed.) *The Use of Self in Therapy*. Binghamton: Haworth Press.

Shaffer, John & Galinsky, David (1989) *Models of Group Therapy*, 2nd edn. Englewood Cliffs, NJ: Prentice Hall.

Shamdasani, Sonu (1998) *Cult Fictions: C. G. Jung and the Founding of Analytical Psychology*. London: Routledge.

Sharaf, Myron (1983) *Fury on Earth*. London: Andre Deutsch.

Shipton, Geraldine (ed.) (1997) *Supervision of Psychotherapy and Counselling: Making a Place to Think*. Buckingham: Open University Press.

Shore, Jeff (2000) A Buddhist model of the human self, in P. Young-Eisendrath and S. Muramoto (eds) *Awakening and Insight: Zen Buddhism and Psychotherapy*. Hove: Brunner-Routledge.

Sibbald, B., Addington-Hall, J., Brennemon, D. & Freeling, P. (1996) Investigation of whether on site general practice counsellors have an impact on psychotropic prescribing rates and costs, *British Journal of General Practice*, 65: 63–7.

Siegel, Allen M. (1996) *Heinz Kohut and the Psychology of the Self*. London: Routledge.

Singer, June (1972) *Boundaries of the Soul: The Practice of Jung's Psychology*. New York: Anchor Doubleday.

Smith, M. L., Glass, G. V. & Miller, T. I. (1980) *The Benefits of Psychotherapy*. Baltimore, MD: John Hopkins University Press.

Smith, Peter B. (1973) *Groups Within Organizations* London: Harper & Row.

Southwell, Clover (1988) The Gerda Boyesen method: biodynamic therapy, in J. Rowan & W. Dryden (eds) *Innovative Therapy in Britain*. Milton Keynes: Open University Press.

Spear, Harold S. (1968) Notes on Carl Rogers' concept of congruence and his general law of interpersonal relationships, in A. G. Athos & R. E. Coffey (eds) *Behaviour in Organizations: A Multidimensional View*. Englewood Cliffs, NJ: Prentice-Hall.

Spinelli, Ernesto (1989) *The Interpreted World: An Introduction to Phenomenological Psychology*. London: Sage.

Spinelli, Ernesto (2001) *The Mirror and the Hammer: Challenges to Therapeutic Orthodoxy*. London: Continuum.

Starhawk (1982) *Dreaming the Dark*. New York: Harper & Row.

Starhawk (1987) *Truth or Dare: Encounters with Power, Authority and Mystery*. New York: Harper & Row.

Stein, Karen Farchaus & Markus, Hazel Rose (1994) The organization of the self: an alternative focus for psychopathology and behavior change, *Journal of Psychotherapy Integration*, 4(4): 317–53.

Stenner, P. & Eccleston, C. (1994) On the textuality of being, *Theory & Psychology*, 4(1): 85–103.

Stiles, William B. (1986) Development of a taxonomy of verbal response modes, in L. S. Greenberg & W. M. Pinsof (eds) *The Psychotherapeutic Process*. New York: Guilford Press.

Stiles, William B., Morrison, L. A., Haw, S. K., Harper, H., Shapiro, D. A. & Firth-Cozens, J. (1991) Longitudinal study of assimilation in exploratory psychotherapy, *Psychotherapy*, 28: 195–206.

Stiles, William B., Meshot, C. M., Anderson, T. M. & Sloan, W. W. Jr (1992) Assimilation of problematic experiences: The case of John Jones, *Psychotherapy Research*, 2: 81–101.

Stolorow, Robert D. & Atwood, George E. (1992) *Contexts of Being: The Intersubjective Foundations of Psychological Life*. London: Analytic Press.

Stolorow, Robert D., Brandschaft, B. & Atwood, George E. (1987) *Psychoanalytic Treatment: An Intersubjective Approach*. London: Analytic Press.

Striano, J. (1988) *Can Psychotherapists Hurt You?* Santa Barbara: Professional Press.

Stricker, G. & Gold, J. R. (eds) (1993) *Comprehensive Handbook of Psychotherapy Integration*. New York: Plenum Press.

Strupp, H. H. (1982) Some observations on clinical psychology, *Clinical Psychology*, 36: 6–7.

Strupp, H. H. (1989) Psychotherapy: can the practitioner learn from the researcher? *American Psychologist*, 44: 717–24.

Suzuki, Shunru (1970) *Zen Mind, Beginner's Mind: Informal Talks on Zen Meditation and Practice*. New York: Weatherhill.

Svartberg, M. & Stiles, T. C. (1994) Therapeutic alliance, therapeutic competence, and client change in short-term anxiety-provoking psychotherapy, *Psychotherapy Research*, 4: 20–33.

Szasz, Thomas S. (1961) *The Myth of Mental Illness: Foundations of a Theory of Personal Conduct*. New York: Dell.

Tart, Charles T. (1990) *Altered States of Consciousness*, 3rd edn. San Francisco: Harper.

Tedlock, Barbara (2000) Ethnography and ethnographic representation, in N. K. Denzin & Y. S. Lincoln (eds) *Handbook of Qualitative Research*, 2nd edn. Thousand Oaks, CA: Sage

Thorne, Brian (1986) Questions of empathy, *Person-Centred Review*, 1(2): 129.

Thorne, Brian (1992) *Carl Rogers*. London: Sage.

Tindall, Carol (1994) Issues of evaluation, in P. Banister, E. Burman, I. Parker, M. Taylor & C. Tindall (eds) *Qualitative Methods in Psychology: A Research Guide*. Buckingham: Open University Press.

Tompkins, Penny & Lawley, James (1997) *Principles of Grovian Metaphor Therapy*. London: The Developing Company.

Torbert, William (1989) Leading organizational transformation, in W. Pasmore, & R. Woodman (eds) *Research in Organizational Change and Development* vol. 3. Greenwich, CI: JAI.

Totton, Nick & Edmondson, Em (1988) *Reichian Growth Work*. Bridport: Prism Press.

Traylen, Hilary, (1994) Confronting hidden agendas: co-operative inquiry with health visitors, in P. Reason (ed.) *Participation in Human Inquiry*. London: Sage.

Trungpa, Chogyam (1973) *Cutting Through Spiritual Materialism*. Boulder, CO: Shambhala.

Valle, Ron (ed.) (1998) *Phenomenological Inquiry in Psychology: Existential and Transpersonal Dimensions*. New York: Plenum Press.

van Deurzen, Emmy (2002) *Existential Counselling and Psychotherapy in Practice*. London: Sage.

van Deurzen-Smith, Emmy (1997) *Everyday Mysteries: Existential Dimensions of Psychotherapy*. London: Routledge.

Vaughan, Frances (1985) *The Inward Arc*. Boston, MA: New Science Library.

Vick, Philippa (2002) Psycho-spiritual body psychotherapy, in T. Staunton (ed.) *Body Psychotherapy*. Hove: Brunner-Routledge.

von Eckartsberg, Rolf (1998) Introducing existential-phenomenological psychology, in R. Valle (ed.) *Phenomenological Inquiry in Psychology: Existential and Transpersonal Dimensions*. New York: Plenum Press.

Wachtel, P. L. (1977) *Psychoanalysis and Behaviour Therapy: Toward an Integration*. New York: Basic Books.

Wachtel, P. L. (ed.) (1982) *Resistance: Psychodynamic and Behavioural Approaches*. New York: Plenum Press.

Wade, Jenny (1989) *Validating the Existential Perception of Death.* Unpublished manuscript.

Wade, Jenny (1996) *Changes of Mind: A Holonomic Theory of the Evolution of Consciousness.* Albany, NY: SUNY Press.

Wade, Jenny (2000) The love that dares not speak its name, in T. Hart, P. L. Nelson & K. Puhakka (eds) *Transpersonal Knowing: Exploring the Horizon of Consciousness.* Albany, NY: SUNY Press.

Walker, Barbara (1983) *The Woman's Encyclopedia of Myths and Secrets.* New York: Harper & Row.

Wallis, Roy (1985) Betwixt therapy and salvation: the changing form of the human potential movement, in R. K. Jones (ed.) *Sickness and Sectarianism.* Aldershot: Gower.

Walsh, Roger (1993) The transpersonal movement: a history and state of the art, *Journal of Transpersonal Psychology*, 25(2): 123–39.

Walsh, Russell (2003) The methods of reflexivity, *Humanistic Psychologist*, 31(4) 51–66.

Watkins Mary (1976) *Waking Dreams.* New York: Harper Colophon.

Watson, Jeanne C., Goldman, Rhonda & Vanaerschot, Greet (1998) Empathic: a postmodern way of being?' in L. S. Greenberg, J. C. Watson & G. Lietaer (eds) *Handbook of Experiential Psychotherapy.* New York: Guilford Press.

Wellings, Nigel, & McCormick, Elizabeth W. (2000) *Transpersonal Psychotherapy: Theory and Practice.* London: Continuum.

Wessler, Richard L. & Ellis, Albert (1980) Supervision in rational-emotive therapy, in A. K. Hess (ed.) *Psychotherapy Supervision: Theory, Research and Practice.* New York: John Wiley.

West, Willliam (1994) Post-Reichian therapy, in D. Jones (ed.) *Innovative Therapy: A Handbook.* Buckingham: Open University Press.

West, William (2000) Supervision difficulties and dilemmas for counsellors around healing and spirituality, in B. Lawton & C. Feltham (eds) *Taking Supervision Forward: Dilemmas, Insights and Trends.* London: Sage.

Whiteman, J. H. M. (1986) The mystical way and habitualization of mystical states, in B. J. Wolman & M. Ullman (eds) *Handbook of States of Consciousness.* New York: Van Nostrand Reinhold.

Whitfield, Geoffrey (1988) Bioenergetics, in J. Rowan & W. Dryden (eds) *Innovative Therapy in Britain.* Milton Keynes: Open University Press.

Whitmore, Diana (1991) *Psychosynthesis Counselling in Action.* London: Sage.

Whitmore, Diana (1999) Supervision from a transpersonal context. Handout from course workshop on supervision (Psychosynthesis and Education Trust).

Whitton, Eric (ed.) (2003) *Humanistic Approaches to Psychotherapy.* London: Whurr.

Wilber, Ken (1979) *No Boundary*. London: Routledge.

Wilber, Ken (1981) *No Boundary*, 2nd edn. Boston, MA Shambhala.

Wilber, Ken (1986) The spectrum of development and The spectrum of psychopathology, in K. Wilber *et al.* (eds) *Transformations of Consciousness*. Boston, MA: Shambhala.

Wilber, Ken (1995) *Sex, Ecology, Spirituality*. Boston, MA: Shambhala.

Wilber, Ken (1996) *The Atman Project*, 2nd edn, Wheaton IL: Quest Books.

Wilber, Ken (1997) *The Eye of Spirit*. Boston MA: Shambhala.

Wilber, Ken (1998) *The Marriage of Sense and Soul: Integrating Science and Religion*. New York: Random House.

Wilber, Ken (1999) *Collected Works*, vol. 1. Boston, MA: Shambhala.

Wilber, Ken (2000a) *Integral Psychology*. Boston MA: Shambhala.

Wilber, Ken (2000b) *Collected Works*, vol. 6. Boston, MA: Shambhala.

Wilber, Ken (2000c) *Collected Works*, vol. 8. Boston, MA: Shambhala.

Wilber, Ken, Engler, Jack & Brown, Daniel P. (1986) *Transformations of Consciousness*. Boston, MA: Shambhala.

Wile, D. B. (1984) Kohut, Kernberg and accusatory interpretations, *Psychotherapy*, 21(3): 353–64.

Wilkinson, S. (ed.)(1986) *Feminist Social Psychology: Developing Theory and Practice*. Milton Keynes: Open University Press.

Wilson, Michael (1994) Spiritual terrain, *Counselling News*, 16 (December): 24–5.

Winnicott, Donald (1971) *Playing and Reality*. London: Routledge.

Winter, D. A. (1997) Everybody has still won but what about the booby prizes? *BPS Psychotherapy Section Newsletter*, 21: 1–15.

Wolf, Alexander & Kutash, Irwin L. (1986) Psychoanalysis in groups, in I. L. Kutash & A. Wolf (eds) *Psychotherapist's Notebook*. San Francisco: Jossey-Bass.

Wolitzky, D. A. (1995) The theory and practice of traditional psychoanalytic psychotherapy, in A. S. Gurman & S. B. Messer (eds) *Essential Psychotherapies: Theory and Practice*. New York: Guilford Press.

Woolger, R. J. (1990) *Other Lives, Other Selves: A Jungian Psychotherapist Discovers Past Lives*. Wellingborough: Crucible.

Wright, David L. (1973) Images of human nature underlying sociological theory: a review and synthesis. Paper presented at the annual meeting of the American Sociological Association.

Yontef, Gary (1993) *Awareness, Dialogue and Process*. Highland: Gestalt Journal Press.

Zimring, Fred (2001) Empathic understanding grows the person, in S. Haugh & T. Merry (eds) *Empathy* (*Rogers'Therapeutic Conditions*), vol. 2. Ross-on-Wye: PCCS.

Subject index

AHPP 24
alchemical sequence 27–29
alliance 26
archetypes 14, 36, 47, 87, 88,
  106, 117, 128, 178
assumptions, letting go of 35, 36,
  39, 107, 146, 147, 104, 107,
  109, 123
authenticity ix, 4, 5, 9, 13, 20, 40,
  53, 59, 81, 102, 116, 123,
  126, 127, 133, 146, 195;
  and research 168, 170–174;
  authentic consciousness 6, 12,
  35–36, 105, 215;
  authentic level of work 44, 45,
  71, 72, 85, 135–6, 143, 149,
  169, 188;
  authentic therapist 35, 50,
  104, 131, 132, 144, 190;
  as suspect 80

BACP 21, 24
birth, *see* pre and perinatal
bodywork 23, 66, 95, 203–8

causal 6, 15, 18, 19, 48, 105,
  106–14
centaur 6, 13, 14, 15, 17, 19, 43,
  45, 203

communication 31–35, 125,
  152–4, 164, 165, 167
compassion 110, 113
confidentiality 84
conjunctio 16
countertransference 4, 41, 50,
  53, 65, 86, 101, 103, 145,
  187–8, 196; and
  authenticity 72–3, 87, 127
contractions 44, 48
creativity 19, 36, 120;
  in supervision 85;
  co-creation 181

diagnosis 33
dialectics ix, 36, 39, 40, 182
dialogue 33
dialogic 39

ecstasy 47, 49, 148
ego development 8, 12
empathy 75, 101, 125, 149–57,
  184, 193;
  and research 145
ethics 84, 134, 205;
  and errors 85
existential 13, 45, 46, 71, 81, 138,
  149;
  existential-humanistic 26, 72

feelings 75, 137, 193–4, 207

I–It 3, 35
imaginal world 36, 89, 106, 184
initiation 45, 89, 175
instrumental ix, 3, 5, 8, 20,
        29–31, 40, 53, 99, 114, 131,
        133, 135, 159, 160, 188–90,
        191, 202, 214;
    and ethics 141–3;
    and skills 57–71;
    and supervision 82–5;
    and research 167–8
integration 20, 43, 49, 51, 52, 71,
        96, 106, 200–1
internet 3
interventions 58–61, 65–71,
        216–7
intuition 20, 36, 73–4, 89, 106,
        148, 180–1, 200
    problems with 78
I–Thou 3, 35

joy 13

liberation 44
listening 74–8
love 110–13

meditation 18, 19, 89–90, 106,
        211–2
memory 55
mental ego 6, 8, 42, 45, 203
moral development 8, 12
multicultural, see transcultural,
mysticism 14, 16, 45, 47, 48, 74,
        113–14, 212;
    and psychosis 197

narcissism of therapist 187–8,
        190, 196

narrative 37
NHS 2
non–defensive 35, 153–4

objectivity 103

personal development 8, 44
polytheistic psychology 14
prenatal and perinatal
        experience 41, 54,186,
        197–9
psychiatry 2
psychoanalysis 14, 18, 21, 22, 41,
        42, 43, 50, 53, 62, 72, 95,
        199
psychoanalysts 23, 30–1, 33, 63,
        65, 190, 191

randomised trials 2
rebirth 45
reflexivity 143, 144, 147, 169–70
reification 159–60
research 49, 64, 65, 70, 103, 122,
        131, 141, 145, 151, 158–83,
        193, 197–8;
    on training 25–9, 98;
    problems with categories
        64–5;
    on therapists 99–101, 190,
        194;
resistance 44, 65, 102, 203;
    by therapist 186–97

schools ix, 41
self–actualization 8;
    characteristics of 9–12
silence 18
skills ix, 29
social field 37, 40
soul 14, 15, 16, 17, 46, 80, 148,
        179

spirit 48, 80,111, 148, 179
subpersonalities 45, 60, 128;
    and the unconscious 72
subtle body 15, 48, 55
subtle consciousness 6, 14, 15,
    16, 17, 19, 20, 46, 93, 105,
    107, 110, 113, 210
superconscious 16, 17, 36, 65, 89

tantra 48
transactional analysis 34
transcultural work 78, 137–9;
    and prejudice 79
    transpersonal ix, 5, 17, 20, 36,
        40, 41, 61, 65, 68, 81, 89,
        104, 127, 132, 133, 164, 200,
        210, 213, 214;

research 174–7, 179–82;
    as suspect 80, 199;
    level of work 47, 48, 73, 87,
        136, 147–9, 188, 196, 215;
    therapist 93, 197
transpersonal 1, 5, 6, 14, 16, 46
transpersonal 2, 5, 16, 18, 48

UKCP 1, 21, 31, 206
unconscious 3, 4, 16, 17, 49, 53,
    54, 65, 72, 79, 83, 112, 147,
    199, 202, 212;
    and experimental evidence 80
universities 2

yoga 47

Author index

Abram, J. 30
Aitken, G. 174
Albery, N. 187, 205
Alderfer, C. 118
al–Ghazali 7
Almaas, A.H. 7, 19, 48, 106, 110
Althusser, L.P. 163
Anderson, R. 147, 164, 172
Aristotle 202
Assagioli, R. 6, 7, 16, 17, 36, 45, 106, 127, 128, 130
Atwood, G.E. 39, 52
Avabhasa, A. 6

Bandler, R. 29, 75
Balint, M. 42, 198
Barnes, H. 208
Barthes, R. 163
Beck, A. 7, 189
Beebe, J. 88
Beier, E. 85
Beisser, A. 11, 121
Bentz, V.M. 145, 148, 164, 172
Berg, D. 145
Berger, M.M. 122
Bergin, A.E. 73
Belenky, M.S. 8, 13, 135
Berman, J.S. 25

Bingham, Lord 84
Binswanger, L. 13
Bion, W. 4
Blatt, S.J. 189
Blomberg, J. 27
Boadella, D. 70, 204, 206, 213
Bochner, A. 169
Bohart, A.C. 7, 26, 68
Boivin, M. 27
Bolen, J.S. 7
Bomford, R. 17
Bond, T. 143, 149
Bor, R. 135
Boydell, T. 45
Boorstein, S. 7, 77
Bor, R. 3
Boyesen, G. 205
Bozarth, J. 7
Bradbury, H. 169
Bragdon, E. 50, 90, 91
Brammer, L. 65, 126
Braud, W. 147, 164, 172
Brazier, D. 7, 18, 48, 107, 110
Breyer, D. 206
Brookes, C. 88
Brown, L. 146
Buber, M. 35, 45, 171
Budgell, R. 5

Bugental, J.F.T. 6, 7, 13, 34, 65, 126
Burman, E. 173
Burns, J. 173

Campbell, J. 48
Carkhuff, R.R. 151–2
Carroll, M. 82
Casement, R. 4
Castaneda, C. 163
Caudill, B. 85
Chamberlain, D. 197
Chaplin, J. 27
Cheng, E. 179
Cinnirella, M. 93
Clarke, I. 17
Clarke, J.J. 36
Clarkson, P. 4, 5, 17, 34, 50, 68, 73, 88, 120, 143, 169, 200
Cohn, H. 208–9
Cohn, R. 122
Collen, A. 159
Combs, G. 78
Connell, R. 194
Cooper, M. 54, 69, 71–2
Coormaraswamy, V. 48
Corbett, L. 88
Corbin, H. 16, 89
Cortright, B. 107, 214
Craig, G.J. 42
Crampton, M. 128
Cruthers, H. 69
Cunningham, J.M. 53

Daniels, T. 29, 57
Dante, A. 7, 111
Darongkamas, J. 99
Davies, D. 79
Denzin, N. 162–3
Derrida, J. 163
Descartes, R. 202

Desoille, R. 128, 129
Dineen, T. 98
Dinnage, R. 192
Douglas, A. 51
Doyle, K. 115
Dryden, W. 25, 29, 49, 68, 114–15, 193, 194
Duncan, B.L. 26

Eccleston, C. 38
Eckhart, M. 7
Edmondson, E. 207
Egan, G. ix, 7, 33, 125
Ekstein, R. 83, 187
Ellenberger, H.F. 22
Elliot, R. 65
Ellis, A. 6, 7, 83, 115, 122, 169, 189, 202
Emerson, W. 205
Emmons, M.L. 46
Epstein, M. 7, 18, 48, 110, 111
Erickson, M.H. 6, 7, 29, 30
Erikson, E.H. 9
Erlich, H.S. 189
Ernst, S. 116, 122–3, 126
Erskine, R. 49
Estes, C. 195
Evison, R. 123
Eysenck, H.J. 7

Fairbairn, R. 43
Farrant, G. 54–5
Farrell, W. 194
Feinberg, T.E. 52
Feltham, C. 25, 68
Ferenczi, S. 203
Ferrucci, P. 17, 46, 104, 107, 127, 130
Field, N. 7, 15, 210
Finch, J. 173
Fine, M. 145, 162

Finlay, L. 169
Firman, J. 107, 156–7
Fletcher, J. 99
Fonagy, P. 51,
Fordham, M. 65, 87
Forsyth, D. 82
Foulkes, S.H. 122
Fox, G. 6, 7, 182
Francis, Saint 202
Freeman, A. 53
Freedman, J. 78
Freud, A. 12
Freud, S. 7, 44, 69, 102, 107, 159, 194, 198, 202–3
Friedman, M. 39–40
Fromm, E. 42
Fukushima, K. 19
Fukuyama, M. 7, 93

Galinsky, D. 122–3, 126
Garfinkel, S. 163
Gee , H. 191–2
Geertz, C. 162–3
Gendlin, E. 71, 209
Gibson, T. 143
Gila, A. 107, 156–7
Gilligan, C. 8, 12
Gindler, E 206
Glouberman, D. 48, 68
Gold, J. 27, 71
Goldberg, C. 192
Goldfried, MR 71
Goldstein, K. 8
Goleman, D. 211
Gomez, L. 199
Goodison, L. 116, 122–3, 126, 212–3
Gordon-Brown, I. 7, 60, 68
Gottsegen, G. 65
Gottsegen, M. 65
Gomes, M. 174

Greenberg, L. 85, 214
Grieger, R. 189
Griffin, J. 98, 171
Griffith, J. 214
Griffith, M. 214
Grindler, J. 75
Grof, S. 7, 45, 50, 54, 60, 68, 90, 92, 177, 186, 198, 199, 211–2
Grof, C. 90, 92, 177
Grove, D. 69, 207–8
Guntrip, H. 42
Guy, J. 102

Haley, J. 7
Hanna, F. 64–5
Haugh, S. 101
Hardy, J. 65
Hartmann, H. 159
Harrison, R. 180
Hattie, J.A. 25
Hawkins, P. 86, 174, 178–9, 180, 182
Heidegger, M. 13
Heinel, P. 74
Heinmann, P. 127
Henderson, D. 88
Henderson, J. 87–9
Henderson, V.L. 120, 150
Heron, J. 175–7, 180
Hill, C. 64
Hillman, J. 7, 14, 16, 36, 77, 106, 200
Hinshelwood, R.D. 199
Hisamatsu, S. 111
Holland, R. 169
Holloway, E. 82
Hora, T. 122
Horney, K. 42
Horobin, R. 123
House, R. 142
Houston, G. 86

Houston, J. 7, 104, 107
Howard, A. 25
Hycner, R. 7, 35, 104

Irving, J. 126
Ivey, A. 7, 57, 82

Jacobs, M. 20, 59, 72, 101
Jaffe, D. 180
James, M. 34
James, V. 88
Janov, A. 198
Jefferies, J. 71
Joba, C. 181
Johnson, R. 106
Jones, E.E. 168
Jukes, A. 43
Jung, C.G. 7, 16–17, 36, 80, 106, 107, 111, 117, 124, 127, 128

Kanner, A. 174
Kapleau, P. 107, 211
Karp, M. 120
Keleman, S. 206
Kennard, D. 190
Kidder, L.H. 162
Kilmann, R.H. 172, 182
Kirschenbaum, H. 120, 150
Klein, M 199
Kramer, C. 61
Klimo, J. 47, 92
Kogan, G. 206
Kohlberg, L. 8, 12, 116, 118
Kohut, H. 159
Kurtz, R. 205
Kutash, I. 124

Lacey, T. 114
Laing, R.D. 7, 12, 68, 153
Lake, F. 186, 198
Lambert, M.J. 27, 73

Lamm, Z 108
Langs, R. 83
Lago, C. 87, 139
Lao Tzu 7
Lather, P. 144
Laungani, P. 87, 137
Lawley, J. 207
Lazarus, A.A. 7, 43, 141–2
Leiman, M. 27
Leuner, H. 128–30
Levant, R. 194
Levin, D. 107
Levi–Strauss, C. 163
Lidmilla, A. 82
Lieberman, M. 122, 190
Lincoln, Y. 162–3
Linehan, M.M. 7, 83
Loevinger, J. 8, 12, 118
Loewenthal, K. 93
Lomas, P 4, 7
Lovinger, R.J. 30
Lowen, A. 203–6
Lowen, L. 203, 205
Lukoff, D. 197
Lyons, A. 126

McClelland, S. 69, 175
McCormick , E 104
McLeod, J. 39
McLellan, B. 44, 79
Macaskill, N.D. 100
Mackewn, J. 120
Maclaggan, D. 88–9
Macran, S. 100, 102
Maddi, S. 79, 81
Maguire, K. 7
Maharaj, N. 110
Maharshi, R. 7
Mahrer, A.R. 7, 11, 45, 51, 64, 69, 71, 101, 152–3, 172, 200, 209

Mailer, N. 163
Markus, H. 69
Malan, D. 186
Marton, F. 73
Maslow, A.H. 7–10, 12, 80,
    116–8, 120–1, 123, 132, 170–3
Masson, J. 142, 193
Masters, R. 107
Matarazzo, R.G. 103
May, R. 6, 13, 43, 45,
May, R. 107, 174
Mead, G.H. 40
Meade, M. 174, 179
Mearns, D. 72, 122, 126, 155,
    193, 194
Meichenbaum, D. 7, 122
Meier, A. 27
Merleau–Ponty, M. 171, 208
Merry, T. 101, 122
Mertens, D. 64
Middendorf, I. 206
Mies, M. 174
Miller, A. 207
Miller, S.D. 26
Mindell, Amy 7, 19, 104–5, 106,
    11011, 208
Mindell, Arnold 7, 105–6, 200,
    208
Mitroff, I. 161, 172, 183
Mittelman, W. 12
Mollon, P. 84
Money–Kyrle, R. 14
Moore, T. 15
Moreno, J.L. 7, 71, 120, 122
Morgan–Jones, R. 30
Moss, D.M. 47, 206
Moursund, J.P. 49
Moynihan, D.W. 26
Mullan, H. 122

Naropa 6

Neal, C. 79
Neenan, M. 114–16
Neilands, T. 146
Nelson, J. 90
Nichols, M.P. 199, 207
Nietsche, F. 37–8
Nightingale, D. 146
Norcross, J.C. 49, 71
Norton, N.C. 25

O'Hara, M. 27
Oakley, A. 173
Orr, L. 211
Ottens, A. 64

Page, S. 86
Painter, J. 205
Palmer, S. 87
Panzer, B. 69, 207
Papadopolous, L. 135
Pedler, M. 45
Perls, F. S. 7,11, 45–6, 69, 120–2,
    160
Peters, L. 47
Philips, A. 163
Phoenix, A. 174
Piaget, J. 9, 118
Piontelli, A. 198
Plato 202
Plasil, E. 192
Plaut, F. 70
Pollack, W. 194
Prestera, H. 205
Prochaska, J.O. 49
Progoff, I. 130
Proskauer, M. 206, 212
Punch, M. 145

Rabin, B. 89–90
Racker, H. 87
Ram Dass 7, 112

Rawson, P. 48
Reason, P. 145, 169, 173–4, 178–179, 180, 182
Reich, W. 55, 198, 203–6
Reinecke, M. A. 53,
Rice, L. 86
Rioch, M. 86
Robertson, M. 30, 168
Rogers, C. R. ix, 7, 11, 29, 69, 72, 122–3, 150–1, 153, 168
Roose, K. 50
Rosen, J. 142
Rosen, M. 206
Rosenbaum, R. 7, 48, 110
Rothschild, B. 55
Rowan, J. 11, 23, 29, 50, 54, 58–9, 62, 65, 69, 72, 77, 101, 107, 109, 116, 123, 128, 145, 164, 173, 200–10, 214, 217
Rush, A. K. 206
Russell, R. 25–6, 76, 98
Rutherford, L. 91
Ryle, A. 43, 50

Saint Francis 202
Salter, A. 188
Sampson, E. E. 37
Samuels, A. 16, 52, 89, 117, 145
Sands, A. 192
Sanella, L. 90
Sapriel, L. 38
Sartre, J.–P. 13, 165
Satir, V. 7
Schneider, K. 44, 71
Schutz, W. 11, 122
Schwartz, R. M. 43
Schwartz, W. 122, 153
Schwartz–Salant, N. 15–16
Scott, C. 180
Scott, M. 114
Searles, H. 4, 7, 73

Seiser, L. 61
Sevig, T. 93
Shadley, M. 61
Shaffer, J. 122–23, 126
Shamdasani, S. 36
Shankara 6, 7
Shapiro, D. 100, 102
Shapiro, J. J. 145, 148, 164, 172
Sharaf, M. 204
Sheng–Yen 7
Shipton, G 84
Shohet, R. 86
Shore, J. 48, 111
Shorr–Kon, S. 205
Sibbald, B. 99
Siegel, A. M. 159
Skinner, B. F. 7, 32
Smith, B. 139
Smith, K. 145
Smith, P. B. 73, 117
Singer, J. 132
Somers, B. 60, 68
Southwell, C. 205
Spear, H. S. 33
Spinelli, E. 72, 144, 200
Stradling, S. 114
Strupp, H. 73
Starhawk 7, 46, 125
Stein, K. 69
Stenner, P. 38
Stiles, T. C. 26
Stiles, W. B. 27, 64
Striano, J. 191
Stricker, G. 71
Strupp, H 191
Stolorow, R. D. 39, 52
Suzuki, S. 104, 108
Svartberg, M. 26
Swartley, W. 200
Syme, G. 24
Szasz, T. 198

Tallman, K 26
Tart, C. 175
Tedlock, B. 169
Thompson, J. 87
Thorne, B. 72, 122, 151, 155
Tompkins, P. 207
Totton, N. 142, 207
Traylen, H. 180
Truax, C. B. 151
Trungpa, C. 213
Turner, V. 163
Tyrrell, I. 98

Valle, R. 144, 171
van Deurzen, E. 81, 127
Vaughan, F. 46
Vick, P. 5
von Eckartsberg, R. 144, 172
von Frantz, M.–L. 106

Wachtel, P.L. 43, 65
Wade, J. 4, 5, 8, 12, 214
Wallerstein, R. S. 83, 187
Wallis, R. 44
Walker, B. 17, 104
Walker, R. 89–90
Walsby, H. 108
Walsh, R. 47, 169, 170
Wastell, C. 61
Watkins, M 7, 129–30
Watson, J. C. 155–6
Watts, M. 3, 135
Watzlawick, H. 7

Wei, W. W. 108
Wellings, N. 104
Wessler, R. L. 7, 83
West, W. 94, 203–4
Wheelis, A. 6
Whitaker, D. S. 122
Whitehead, A. N. 159
Whiteman, J.H.M. 175
Whitfield, G. 205
Whitmore, D. 7, 36, 89, 128, 130
Whitton, E. 104
Wilber, K. 4, 5, 8, 11, 13, 14, 36,
    41, 42, 45, 51, 52, 65, 77, 82,
    93, 107–11, 118–9, 172, 197,
    199, 201, 203, 210
Wile, D. 191
Wilkinson, S. 174
Williams, D. 126
Wilson, M. 51
Winnicott, R. W. 4, 7, 43, 69, 73,
    127
Winter, D. 188, 190–1
Wolf, A. 122 124
Woolger, R. 55, 91
Wolitzky, D. A. 53,
Wosket, V. 86

Yontef, G. 39, 71
Young, D. 85

Zax, M. 199, 207
Zimring, F. 120–1
Zur, O. 141–2